Alvidia

Yet Another Horizon

Luís Peazê

2018 (English edition)

First edition in Portuguese published in 2000

Publisher′s Cataloging-in-Publication Data

Peazê, Luís, 1958-
    Alvidia, Yet Another Horizon / Peazê, Luís
    392p. 35 x 23cm.
    Includes Index.
    ISBN 978-0-692-08470-0 (pbk)
    1. Life story, endurance 2. USA, Australia,– Brazil 3. Dream, Love
    I. Peazê, Luís, 2018. II. Title

    871.XXX—xx00 P376c
                                           2018

*"I couldn´t stop reading, at times got me nervous,
other times cracked me up."*

Eillen

"You two gave me hope that love does exist."

Nani

"Let´s face that, we are mad."

Sailor couple, Church Point, Sydney, Australia

*"Unique spiral structure of the narrative, which we felt very much
lent itself to the adventure (...) gorgeous."*

Jane Dystel (Literary Agent, New York)

Luís Peazê

Acknowledgments

Here is to all friends cited in this book, with out them
nothing would be possible.

Thanks to Christine Dixon for a dedicated revision,
to Sabrina Hemingway for looking the print proof

and to Helga for standing by me.

"For what is a man profited, if he shall gain the whole world, and lose his
own soul?" Matthew 16:26

Luís Peazê

To my son Lucas

Luís Peazê

Content

Acknowledgments
Preface
The Dream
...What a dream is capable of
...Big world but it can fit through a window open to the sea!
...There is no right time to start to dream
...A dream can be simply love
...There will be mirages
...We knock at the wrong dream´s door, sometimes
...From dreaming so much
...Some times they are nightmares
...False wizards show up
...A dream take us faraway
...For love we flew on flocks
...A dream leads us to madness
The Building
...All we want is to go back
...A dream cannot split the love
...Dream and love
...Love is to dream together
...To sort out what it is from what is not
...To serve a time together, if needed
...To plan the escape together
...Dig it out the love tunnel
...To have fun even at escaping
...Pretend to be blind
The cruise
...February, the first month
...April
...May and June, just remembering gives me shivers
...July, Help! Help! Help!
...Twenty bathrooms
...August, seventh month living aboard
...September and October, what randiness!
...November, no comments
...December
...January
...February again, one year aboard
...March, don´t stress yourself
...April, we left
...May, God bless you always
...June, what a gorgeous sailing day!
...July, salt water in the veins
...August, yet another horizon
Epilogue
The author

Luís Peazê

Preface

It's been 23 years since I made my dream come true, and Alvidia is still inspiring to me; first it was the boat story to inspire writing the book, now it is the book's turn to inspire me to carry on dreaming with boats and to live aboard. Whenever I open a random page of it I feel renewed and encouraged to overcome any eventual challenge, difficulty, odd, to reach my goals. And Helga is an accomplice to that.

The boat was finished in 1995, the book was released in the year of 2000 (Portuguese edition) when the Internet in Brazil and in many parts of the world was not a reality just by then. I´ve received emails from readers who become friends and, although I can't actually have a relationship or closeness with all of them, each friend through Alvidia makes me feel like part of a chain of dreamers. I truly wish that each one feels the same inspiration that I had to make my dream come true.

The same thing with each true character of Alvidia nourished permanently. I think of them often, those are not anymore among us sailing in waters down on the Earth and those still in the places we met, it fills me with joy.

The building of the dream, that is the boat, took one year only, a feverish fire which made me give up things and was contagious to Helga, the feeder of the fire. It's the reason why I show our wedding picture (in the website), to illustrate what happens when you let children play with fire.

To liveaboard of a boat built with your own hands, staying in anchorages that look like paradise itself, meeting extraordinary human beings, to sail more than eight thousand miles in three of the most dangerous seas of the world without prior experience either in boatbuilding nor in sailing, learning the hard way (not recommended to everyone), you know what? The fire remains ardent. All we do today reflects our learning on the Alvidia adventure, much beyond the original dream, yet another horizon.

Luís Peazê

Luís Peazê

The Dream

Luís Peazê

...What a dream is capable of!

"Now it has become everyone´s wish - to travel overseas, return home, and write a book."

This is what I was told – after two round-the-world trips – from a bibliophile friend of mine in his late seventies, who lived surrounded by books of all sorts that he had discovered in old books stores throughout Brazil and abroad.

"Ho no, Mr. Kleber, I´ve made a dream of mine to come true, I´ve built a 30-foot yacht with my own hands from scratch, with the help of nobody but my wife." I tried to capture his attention.

"Eh, eh," he replied, no single word added.

It was my first cold shower. Then I began to make appearances in the press: on interviews for TV shows, in newspapers, in every Brazilian boating magazine, and even for an Australian boatbuilder magazine.

The six hundred pages plus I'd brought under my arm, written partly while in Malaysia and in Argentina, before my arrival back in Brazil, did not attract the interviewers interest at first, nor the interest of friends or even relatives. Our story – mine, my wife´s and Alvidia´s – was not only about our sea adventure, yet everyone's curiosity gravitated toward the size of waves we'd faced, storms we had weathered, the lack of room on our small boat, how it felt to be left alone in the middle of the ocean at night - that sort of thing. They all wished to see pictures; they were thirsty for pictures, although none stared more than a second at each of one we have shown.

To explain: Mr. Kleber, a potential reviewer, was reluctant to advise about my book; the magazines were interested only in the accomplishment (spectacular for them) of two ordinary Brazilians having sailed the Tasman Sea through the Coral Reef Barrier up north to Carpentaria and Timor, around the south and east coast of Australia.

The pictures stole the attention from the facts that made our story remarkable: I did not know how to sail and had learnt all by myself on a boat that I had built with my own hands; we did not know how to build a thing and built our own yacht all by ourselves; we had only 200 dollars in our pockets, ten employees, were in a foreign country with fifty thousand dollars in debit with suppliers; and, within three months, we had completely changed the entire picture – we had the bills paid off, and had decided to give up a profitable business to build our dream.

Relatives and friends were reserved about our desire to speak of revelations we'd had, that we had a spiritual enlightenment, we experienced a transformation making our dream come true, and that from then on we would do nothing else but pursue dreams, encourage dreamers of all kinds, that we started to live in a different dimension.

I realized that among the several dreams I had hoped to accomplish on this adventure, one of those most important to me was the dream to write a book, my first book. In order to publish it, however, I had to cut the six hundred pages in half, and add a few things people asked me to, which meant going back in time to measure the height of the waves, the speed of the wind and to once again experience all the feelings of fear and the ecstasy of overcoming it.

For those whose dreams have turned into reality, after years of cherishing them, know that we simply can not refrain from speaking of the inner strength and richness we acquire, especially if it was necessary to overcome our weaknesses and to learn how to negotiate with our own desires in the process. We enrich ourselves in such way that we start to share our formula. We become so strong that we no longer doubt our own capacity of self-fulfillment.

Speaking of this, I started to write Alvidia right at the moment I awoke to this reality.

...Big world but it can fit through a window open to the sea!

It was in Refuge Bay, Pittwater, twenty miles north of Sydney, Australia. One half of me was dazzled, in a trance, thinking: I have made it; Alvidia is beautiful. Delirium was bursting out of my chest, taking over my whole body, while the other half was fighting to rationalize about our reality. But what was this reality all about?

Going out of the bar tomorrow we would have the Tasman Sea in front of us, the first step of our journey. We would leave for Brazil, a return trip crossing three oceans, and 15,000 miles, contouring continents and facing seas of different names and humors... We were leaving Australia by boat and this signified a lot because we didn't know how to sail...

Steve Sulis had tried to convince me not to head out to sea. For him I was jumping blind without a parachute over an abyss. "Luís, stay here with us for the season. Let's sail together; try out the boat. Don't go just now Luis! Listen to me..." were Steve´s words, my Viking-soul brother. Later on, he also had said: "Yessss you can".

We had a cheap red bottle of wine opened, a kerosene lamp lit up aboard our yacht, anchored overnight two hours away from the nearest city. We could hear rustling outside, from birds in the woods and from a waterfall. To finish the landscape, stars dotted the sky and reflected on the water. I asked myself: could there be another way to extend moments like this beyond contemplating them indefinitely, holding their memory and most of their effects? The next day we were to leave for an ocean passage but, I was dazzled in this rare moment, one of those moments when we don't want to change a thing.

At the dinner there was silence. What was Helga thinking, with her implacable things to do list on hand? The next day we would face the sea and her nature perhaps was asking her: "You are violating yourself and what if you don't overcome your limitations? Pray. Do you think we will overcome this together and help your husband?"

All of the sudden I realized how we were just ordinary people, and I say aloud, "Two nobodies, lost in Australia, almost in the end of the world…." I laughed and started to tease Helga, comparing her with a character from a movie in which Michael Keaton plays a crazy man who drives a van in New York, followed by three other mentally ill guys. One of them is too attached to checking lists, organization and tidiness, so addicted to standard procedures, that beyond to catch trash from along the streets of the city he follows the most trivial daily things as they were vital for the humanity. Helga laughs back at me, reminding me that on top of suffering from the illness of the Michael Keaton´s character living out of reality, I also have the other crazy man illness: an ex-ad man who has found the path of enlightenment and believes he can perform miracles. I burst out in laughter just remembering the movie...

I began to think aloud and Helga at least could now freely show her anxiety. Together we realized how big the step was that we were about to take; we recollected the previous four years, how tough they were on us; away from our families, in a foreign country, involved with strange people, working 24/7 until exhaustion…

We had lost that feeling of connection with the outside world. We had developed a particular syndrome: that time and space were keeping us away from home, family, friends; we no longer received news from them all; they did not answer our letters; we were living in a place which we were not creating roots, from where we were eager to leave and, paradoxically where I was building my dream, a yacht, right in the Mecca of sailing.

Helga stared at me with a complacent smile, wishing to tell me a bunch of things. I would not listen to her. She had the mystic look of an Indian; of partnership; a look of applause but that was also accusing me of something; a look of friendship that applauded and at the same time condemned and forgave me altogether, with a little sadness, yes, but always letting out a phrase of tenderness that would restore me to a rational mode. The night progressed slowly and my reverie was at a gallop. Now I was remembering the last thirteen years playing a Don Quixote, obstinate behind the making of my dream.

I dreamed of a boat anchored at a white sand beach, a tarpaulin over the cockpit, perhaps some friends over for a tasty meal; Helga next to me and the freedom to lift the anchor and change places if something bothered me. I could have done that right then, just like I had read in adventure books.

Finally we went to bed. The next morning I would start to make a bunch of dreams a reality, except that I had to learn how to sail first, on the Tasman Sea right before me out of Barrenjoey Head.

While in Refuge Bay, we got in the mail a book from Helga´s mother who was a notable librarian and the book was read in a single night. It was The Celestine Prophecy by James Redfield. Thus, to keep up with my one rule, I started to look at those mountains as if they had something to tell me. The novel was absorbed through my pores and flooded up to my heart. A long time ago, unaware I was going through a sort of initiation, I discussed a utopian idea with a group of esoteric people in North Cal - where else? I was trying to convince them that if I could agitate a particle of light, maybe with an ultra-sonic centrifugal force and the assistance of a super camera, after releasing that particle to space, to capture it in the form of images, in order to record the truth about everything, in history, and the present - people's acts, scenarios and even thoughts. And I used to have these ideas without wine, grass, or any dope of any kind except my own will.

Delirium aside, the fact is that, in the midst of my crazy thinking, I stressed the importance of observing the day to day, the natural elements around us. Everything is imbued with truth. According to my theory, richness is all over, surrounding us, the colors, materials, forms, songs, the wind, the invisible end of the sky, the moon, the sun, all the plants, rocks… the energy from and through all of it. So The Celestine Prophecy worked as a big bang inside my chest. And as being just a little crazy is silly, from then on I would not dream of crossing oceans with my toy – come on, I was able to talk with the universe. The mountains around brought me peace of mind; I cherished and loved everything, and everybody, resigned to what could happen to me in the next minute, regardless if I was or was not making any association to Nietzsche or Schopenhauer .

And, if I used to play as if I was in a movie, with books I used to take it seriously, diving deep into them. The most recent cases were by Redfield and three others from Paulo Coelho. So, my own optimistic nature guaranteed I could go on towards my goals - my personal legend - I would achieve whatever I wanted. If anything went wrong, it certainly had to be a sign that I needed to read and understand. So, step by step, I would sail with Helga across three oceans toward our families. All I needed was to leave, make the first move, go out of the bar - if I was able to reach that point…

The one thing I did not pay attention to was that books in general are written in a sort of encrypted language. Those who have achieved something similar to what is being read, take in some information or simply take it as reading entertainment. On the other hand, in my case, someone who never stepped on a boat before, dove into a deep world of fantasy seduced by a mermaid-like song. It was a seduction that changed our lives, both mine and Helga's.

Confined in a data processing center, I was caught on the eve of a long four-day holiday with no plans at all. Work used to eat me up entirely, transforming a young man of 23-years into a stern working person. There were hundreds of students I had to teach a computer programming course to, that I had designed and implemented. I rented rooms and organized all the necessary arrangements for a half dozen clients, from small industries to retail stores for whom I used to develop and implement applications systems (i.e. stock controls, general ledgers, accounts receivable and payable, payroll, etc.); and a weekly article for a local paper. I was a human mill, burning neurons, virtually with no compass. I got out of a meeting and went to the first travel agency I could find. When I arrived at home I shouted to Helga:

"I have two airplane tickets to Espirito Santo (a state bordering Rio de Janeiro in the northeast); I also made reservations at a nice hotel and we will pick up a rented car at the airport. You will like it," I said to Helga.

"But what about my college work I need to get done?" Helga said back to me.

While spread by the swimming pool at the hotel with the beach just across the street, I flipped pages of a magazine with not much interest until my eyes stopped on a picture, and I was instantaneously swallowed.

"How come I never noticed that?" I said out loud.

An excitement started to stir in me, and I read the magazine with solid interest; I even started to read the advertisements thoroughly.

"Amazing! I am amazed!" I said to Helga. "This is what I want," I repeated to myself.

I stared at a picture of a small yacht anchored in a bay, tarpaulin over the boom and people chilling out all over the deck. The water was transparent, and a white sand beach with coconut trees was the backdrop on one side, while on the other side the horizon beyond the blue sea touched the sky.

"Helga! I want to have a boat."

The desire to have a boat burned within me at once. Soon I felt I was not the same person I used to be. I could not focus on my work. I became a clock watcher to go home, to shove myself into bed to read books about sailing adventures. That same week I bought two, and soon I was going to read all of the available books of their kind published in Brazil in Portuguese, then I would start to buy the ones in English, from abroad.

Helga watched all of the excitement of mine, and noticed I was no longer that introspective person dipped in the square world of computers.

Before the end of that same year I made the decision to downsize my materialistic ambitions. To take care of several clients, to teach, to utilize a hybrid English-Portuguese vocabulary, and live in a flowchart – it became my past. I did not want to grab the world with my hands – instead I wanted to embrace it, sunbathing on a Pacific island. From then on I became a frozen dinosaur. "That the computer evolve, I won´t", was my motto.

So that is how I kicked the tent's pole and I think it was right then when I started my private revolution. Helga without being aware of it followed me. To begin with, we said goodbye to a significant piece of our wedding trousseau, selling our flat up state, going back to the city of Rio, near the beach where I could woo the sea, my dream. I found a job across the bay and I could feel the sea by taking the ferry twice a day. Of course it wasn't enough and soon I migrated from system analyst to marketing then to advertising, thinking I had changed from a rational-mind landscape to a creative boiling pot. All I could see in front of me were sailing boats and coconuts trees. Such was my state of feverish.

Thus it was on the very holiday, in the state of Espirito Santo (Holy Spirit state) that I started to write my first book, about my dream of building a boat, become a sailor and making long passages.

That magazine I read had an article about this book, From Rio to Polynesia (Do Rio a Polinésia), by Roberto Barros, a Brazilian yacht designer who got the nickname "Cabilho" (small rope, thin tie) after wrecking a snipe trying to reach a cape near Rio de Janeiro. Eventually he and his wife restored a small wooden yacht and made it good all the way to the Pacific Islands. Why a wrecking story inspired my dream I would never know how to answer.

Time was going by fast and I was still lounging in front of the beach without a boat. Although, every time I used to take one of those books from the shelf and read it again and again, my animus to build a boat at any cost would get me on fire the same way it did during that holiday. I would build a boat, would live aboard, become a boating person, in touch with the sea life, cruising - this was my permanent desire. While nothing happened I used to display a big banner like on my forehead "I am a sailor" and even started to lie to friends, telling them I was sailing already. And it was so easy for me to throw myself in a trance. My thoughts would get me lost in old wooden piers with pelicans, longitudes, latitudes, compass cards, islands and rolling waves under the hull of a wooden boat. A world full of stereotypes which I created of my free will, mixing a Nordic painting with a harbor and marina altogether.

It was not very hard to find Barros' phone number, a Brazilian yacht designer. And unbelievably I acquired the building plans of that boat without ever being aboard an yacht of any kind. Well, this is not entirely true, I met Cabilho on a Saturday morning aboard his boat at the public Marina of Rio de Janeiro and, to have met the man and mingle myself with that environment - it was somehow an accomplishment to my childish state of mind. And it was real.

Ten years later I would learn that on that very weekend Cabilho and some friends were setting sail towards the South of Africa, crossing the Atlantic, and that they would end up stranded near the Falklands Islands, a terrible ordeal sponsored by a lack of attention from the skipper.

When I got back home that Saturday, I spread all the sheets of the plans on the floor. Now it was serious business. I used my Systems Analyst methodologies to organize the plans, draw a pert cpm flow chart for the building process and made a spread sheet (on paper) for the would-be budget. I started with "chimarrão" (traditional mate from deep in South America), and switched to coffee. Saturday evening got fizzy; the streets of Rio's south zone were getting in the summer night mood, and I stayed put, consuming beer after beer.

That night I started my logbook. How could a person be so passionate? I didn't know, but I was. Oh that very night I baptized my boat as Helga II, after my Helga, my lovely wife. I called a friend and told him the news. The next morning I took "my boat" to his house and told him all about it. I became the only knowledgeable person among my friends who was a sailor and they would ask me about this and that and I would answer every single question with self-assurance – based on the books I had read so far and the ones I would read in the future.

Laying in bed the excitement would not let me sleep. I would dream with open eyes of abandoning the nine-to-five working life and cruise jumping from one island to another. I used to carry an imaginary picture of the two of us, Helga and I, together on the cockpit, Helga II with her sails full of wind crossing the sunset into the night… following the moon mat in the immensity of the sea.

"The world is big and fits
 In this window open to the sea
 The sea is large and fits

In the mattress of love
The love is big and fits
In the short moment of a kiss"

(Free translation of a poem by Drummond de Andrade)

...There is no right time to start to dream.

I tried twice to build my boat with my own hands; "it's gotta be that way". The first time was on a Saturday morning. I was driving so happy, like a Don Quixote horseback riding in the fields, digging out against imaginary enemies. I was going to discuss the building of my boat. Happiness was bursting out of my chest, so I turned the volume of the radio up at its highest and started to sing loud, to the limit of my lungs. For few miles I was really crazy. I went to visit this boatbuilder at Barra da Tijuca, with the boat plans under my arm and lots of ideas to discuss with him; after all I was a system analyst, with an abundance of ideas and methods. Half an hour or just a little more of a nonsense chat, the man nodded his head only once, when I showed the plans and said I would like to build my boat. Then he couldn't help but shake his head side to side while I was talking, making no sense at all. I did not have a clue what boatbuilding was all about. I was sweating, nervous, and afraid that he would notice I was ignorant, had no knowledge at all about boats. And he noticed right at the very moment I started to talk, making assumptions and questions, projecting steps and elaborating a building calendar. So I went back home frustrated and depressed, but spent the rest of that Saturday restudying each plan. There were more than thirty sheets with designs and detailed descriptions, few in 1/1 scale, so real size, all of them spread on the floor of the living room.

To own a boat was my irreversible dream. A virus took over me and I would not rest until I was building my boat. Deep inside though, despite all my positive thinking and optimism, an increasing anguish was bitter. I used to stare at the horizon from the beach and, if I saw a boat crossing the horizon's line I would lose myself in thoughts until the languor set in. By this time I was used to wandering around the Marina da Gloria, the only public marina in Rio, reaching out as close as I could at the boats. However, I was not able to distinguish what exactly those many cables, ropes, wires, and pulleys were; I could barely distinguish a power boat from a sailing vessel.

I did not have a minor inkling of knowledge about boats, and did not know anybody I could talk to about boats. If I had I did not know what to ask first either - up until then I had never stepped aboard a boat, never even touched a pair of oars. But J. Slocum's *Alone Around the World*, considered a bible among newcomers and old salties, had been read twice already and would be reread again and again in the near future. Around that time I was nurturing the romantic notion of the living aboard atmosphere, going through a storm - it seemed to me it was cool, adventurous, and I dreamed to be there...

The second time I tried to build my boat was when I discovered a boat building course. So I thought: I grew up listening my father's story that he built our first house all by himself, after hours; and on a few occasions I helped relatives build their houses in a pull-together way, cousins and aunts, brothers and uncles, *et cetera*. So I thought, well then, I guess I can built a boat.

Sure I was going to build Helga II. The classes were at night, out of the city in a suburb. Around this time I had migrated to marketing, living behind the computer field and self employed pace, and I was working for a multi-national company and did not drive my sports car anymore. Thus, once enrolled in the course, I had to face a commuter bus packed with workers, on a hot summer three nights a week. The classes were given in a small dusty room, poorly lit, with no air conditioning and, on the third day, I gave up.

In my mind things developed at a fast pace, as if each day was a year, and everybody in my circle knew already that I was an old sailor and was going to build my boat, my main interlocutor being the oldest waiter of this fly bar I was a frequent flyer.

"How is the boat building ?" he used to ask while bringing me a draft beer.

"I am working on the budget. You know, such a major project I need to be meticulous, " it was me playing a fiction movie based on a would-be real future.

Thirteen years went by since that weekend in Espirito Santo, while I was rehearsing to be the main actor of a movie based on my own comedy. And no matter how much I was reading about boats, I remained a layman on the subject. No practice, no acquaintances or friends of the same trade, no inside ticket, no entrance, only to realize much later that too much vanity and pride, mixed with shame to unveil I did not know anything about boats were keeping me from what I was in love with.

Helga tried to help and found that Germano, Lilia's brother, one of her old friends, was building a small wooden catamaran, so I was introduced to him. But again, we never could schedule a meet up, time was drifting away and I was still boat ignorant. Besides, the folder with the Helga II plans made a drawer a tomb, but I myself was the one buried under a lower economic social class. Inflation in Brazil that time was crazy, near 10% a month. How would I build my boat if I couldn't project a budget for two or three years ahead, that was the time frame to build a yacht, so I had heard. I became a sad guy.

My reading turned out to be dense and apocalyptic. I wished I had been born before to be able to engage in the cause of Alexandre

Panagulis, so Oriana Fallaci would write my biography too – I wished to be exiled – how romantic it was to imagine myself a political prisoner and escape from a solitary prison tomb like Alekos Panagulis did. Oriana Fallaci showed to me a man I thought I had so many things in common. I was enchanted with our disgrace. But as a matter-of-a-fact I was like a lead soldier toy marching with the wrong foot thinking the whole platoon had to follow me. I loved these comparison and used to scape from any conventional stream. Bakunin, Trotsky and Marx were gobbled with beard and mustache sharing my library with Machiavelli, the Third Wave, and an unruly collection of blue literature from Proust to Madame Bovary, fading out happiness from my chest. My living room was full of books, a pile of prophets on my bedside table and a bunch of philosophers next to the toilet bowl. I started to wear heavy rimmed glasses and smoke a pipe, enchanted to have learnt how to use the tools to clean up my pipe made with a rose tree knot. I did not look my 30-years-of-age at that time.

During my rare surges of lucidity, I used to ask myself: where is my dream? It was when Milan Kundera´s *The Unbearable Lightness of Being* gave me the fatal blow. I melted, yes, melted for real, my golden wedding ring, ordered a golden anchor I designed, to wear on my chest over whatever shirt or jacket and bought a one-way ticket to America.

Just like this, all of a sudden, and I had never thought to go to America. Thus, on the road I was more of a Jean-Baptiste Grenouille, *Perfume*, than a Jack Kerouac.

...A dream can be simply love.

Sometimes a dream is so hard to make true that the path we are searching for looks more like that of a sad detour than a true north. However, if there is a genuine dream one seeks, a permanent wish, there is no detour... All paths will take us to make the dream come true.

I was driving, easy riding, across the United States, sort of aiming for but not to fussy or in a hurry to reach California. While crossing the Arizona Desert something happened to me. I like to think it was THE BEGINNING. I stopped the car in a rest area and decided to walk, walk until I could not see the road anymore. I took with me this book I was reading, *Perfume*, and tucked myself on that arid ground of reddish soil, sometimes like carrara marble that crumbles. And I was amazed at the number of living beings: geckos, small lizards, and snakes - I counted three different types of snakes that ran or stayed still, whispering at me. At nightfall I heard in the distance the howls of coyotes – I felt like I was in a cowboy movie. Then I reached a plateau and sat down.

It was love at first sight, I felt so good and it seemed a place I had been before, as if I knew that place. It was like a cliff but with a gentle and long slope, going down slowly with no interruption to lose sight of. I think that it was right there that the desert really started. I recollected when I was a kid, and used to go to Torres, a deep South beach, and I loved to throw myself from the top of the sand dunes and roll like a ball. I stretched and yawned and almost threw myself down for real. But I started to feel cold, the sunset created in the infinity a theatrical back drop of a variety of golden tones and I stood admiring. All of the sudden I felt as if the time had stopped, that the sunset that usually goes fast did not run.

It got stuck, did not go down; there was no sun, only the fiery horizon, and it started to give me goosebumps. It seemed that the firmament could not support those golden and bronze solid clouds. The plateau once softly became the tip of a deep escarpment, that immense gentle ramp transformed into an abyss, and a breeze wished to push me downwards. Everything static as if there was an universal power holding the time at a check point. A blink, a minor move with an arm, as in a duel, and something would happen to me. I started to turn my head back, disguising it as if I was turning an invisible mask, just to check back from where I came from. And, from the behind, it was solid dark, bringing back in the mask, in front of me, that endless sunset. I breathed deeply, slowly, I did not say it aloud, but as only in thought one can do it, I think I asked to the sunset if I could breathe. I don't remember when I decided to go back to the car. That moment lasted an eternity. I overcame the fear and turned it into a feeling of lightness, unknowingly, as if I did not even realize that I'd had a change of feelings. While I went back to the car, I looked back several times over my shoulders and kept seeing that sunset on the horizon. Ahead of me, that solid pitch dark. I will never forget that vision.

It was always uncomfortable to sleep in my old VW Rabbit, but that night I slept right through, non-stop. I was in a state of peace of mind. Next morning I made myself a cowboy breakfast, with bacon, fried eggs, canned black beans and coffee. Then I decide to reread *Perfume*, and went back to my rock with my sleeping bag. The way to the rock seemed to be longer than it was the day before; I got tired. By the time I reached the plateau my legs trembled for minutes, and I could hear my own heartbeat. The vision that I had the day before was not a mirage, except the sunset stuck, unforgettable; the place was an abyss for real. A cliff like the Grand Canyon without the other side, smaller but still huge and a danger for anyone who as a kid wanted to jump from up there. So I almost got myself killed unaware of what I was going to do. I stepped back slowly, until I got used to the distance and surroundings, and assured myself that I was on safe, solid ground I looked around and... I felt so small and helpless realizing how huge the world really was. It could come and swallow me, if it wanted. I could not run away. I bent down slowly, sat on the floor, opened my sleeping bag and started to stretch myself slowly. I made a pillow with a stone and stood there, thinking. I then started to read and every once in a while threw my neck towards the abyss to make sure it was far enough away from me, or it would come and get me. The more I read about Jean-Baptiste Grenouille, the more I felt we were alike. Aside from his assassin character, disgusting, it turned out that I admired that son-of-a-bitch. I felt sorry by how he was born and his appearance. Like the children left in the streets and all the Misérables born Misérables, he was not guilty. I found beautiful his persistence, obstinate to make the perfect perfume, the essence of love.

I would like to pursue my goals the same way. Not killing virgins, of course, but if possible unseen, almost as if I did not exist. I reread *Perfume* avidly during the day and decided to sleep over on my rock, just for fun, because gradually I became attached to the abyss. I stood until late thinking about my life and fell asleep. That afternoon the sunset came without fuss and the horizon was purple to rose in color. The night came full of stars in the sky and with howls of coyotes. I imagined myself as a cowboy from a Wild West story, Billy crossing the Arizona Desert going to Nevada.

In the morning I got up, packed up my camp and hit the road. Along this leg of the trip I did not get tired and drove straight until I crossed the border into California state. The novel I'd recently read and thrown in the seat was in the back of my mind. The sunset that rescued me from killing myself was as if it was in front of me, while I was driving. Driving along, I was thinking about what I was going to do. I could do anything with my life. I felt able to do anything - to go anywhere in the world. Change professions, renew everything, invent a new behavior, find new friends... Build up another life. I could even change all of this again, if I wanted. I realized that our mind can be conditioned into any direction and this is a powerful weapon. I also realized that a man is a well without end of relative needs. A strange feeling, I foresee that once without certain ordinary needs and conditions a man can disconnect from any piece of his own life, from his father, his mother, his origins...

I drove all night and by sunrise I entered into California state, welcomed first by a forest of giants wind collectors. In the south of California there is an electric wind generation power plant, powered by giant wind vanes. Take off all the leaves of an eucalyptus plantation and place on each of them a wind vane, that's what it is. I carried on through Highway 5 all the way up north then onto 101. Without a map I got lost, and reached a small town called Mill Valley on the other side of the Golden Gate Bridge in San Francisco.

While having brunch in a bookstore, I talked to an Uruguayan I had just met and was invited to a party that night. A party of esoteric people. There were people of all kinds, college teachers, doctors cardiologists, salespeople, working girls and drifters like myself. A nice lady that could be my grandmother pulled me aside for a chat about her study specialty: dreams. We got so excited that a group started to gather around us. From that group arose a tall guy with a funny instrument that I had never seen until then, very similar to the Brazilian "berimbau" but more sophisticated... A zither I learned later on.

He was going to play and before the show started people were watered by beverages of all kinds, as well as weed and other heavy stuff. Milton, my Uruguayan friend told me about Michael Riggs, the American musician fine tuning his zither. He had lived in India and Tibet, seven years among Hindus and a Tibetan master. His actual name was Bhagavan Das. His return to America was in the early 70's when the hippie movement reached its peak. At his arrival at the Los Angeles airport he had discovered that he was a celebrity, and was the inspiration for the best seller *Be Here Now*, by Ram Das or, Dr. Richard Alpert PhD. Another expatriate once upon a time star of the academic world, renowned psychiatrist and millionaire who used to experiment with young drifters along with his no less famous peers Aldous Huxley, Timothy Leary and Allen Ginsberg.

So Michael, or Bhagavan Das, was nothing less nothing more than the guru of Ram Das as well as the guru of an entire generation of beatniks, friend of Swami Bhaktivedanta Prabhupada, the founder of the Hare Krishna movement in the United States, and a sadhu (holy man in the Hindu tradition) initiated by Sri, Sri, Sri (1008) Sri Neem Karoli Baba Maharaji, the creator of the Transcendental Meditation.

After the zither jam session, they placed experimental music to play on an old record player, and Michael, Bhagavan Das, came to chat in our group. Gradually the group dissolved itself and there was only the two of us, me and Michael. I was so disconnected or relaxed that all his past and background at first did not impress me. We chatted about trivialities and when I mentioned that I did not have a place to crash, Michael said I could stay in his place. Milton was living there too and I could stay for free. The house belonged to an old Swiss man and they lived there to take care of the house, which was built among a forest of cypress. I could not deny, the miracles do exist.

I was given an empty room, just a bed and a small table with a long neck water jar and a basin agate. Michael handed me a blue blanket and the room already had a blue curtain. The next day Milton came back from town with a large rug he had found in a dumpster, and it was also blue. My room was blue. The house did not have a heating system, other then a rustic fireplace and no lack of wood. The toilet room was without a shower, and we had to enjoy ourselves, while maintaining our personal hygiene, taking showers outside under a cold tap, with water that had fallen from the rain gutter. In the living room where the fireplace was there was also a bookshelf covering the entire wall full of dusty old books. And there was an electric typewriter not being used, which I could use as mine.

Where had I ended up? I asked myself this question several times, amazed.

We ate when had something to eat, otherwise we made whole-grain bread cooked on a grill over an electric oven, followed by hot tea and also boiled fruits from the orchard. We did not talk to each other very much, myself, Michael and Milton. Later in life I crashed at a monastery for a while, and realized we had lived in Mill Valley as if we were monks, and life was good.

I stayed home most of the time; Milton used to disappear for a week straight, and Michael used to spend the day out, coming back home at night, when he would sit in front of the fireplace to meditate for a couple of hours. After which he played a zither and chanted. He had recorded this vinyl called AH! And he chanted endlessly: AAAA AAAAAAHHHH HHHHHHHN NNNNN NNNNNNNN AAAAA AAAAAAHHHH HHHHHHHH MMM MMMM MMMMMMMMM onto OOOOOOMMMMM OOOOOOMMMMMMMM, OOOOOOOOOMMMMMMMMM!

Sometimes out-of-the-blue I was told that we would have a party in the house. Then gradually on a daily basis before said weekend, beatniks of all tribes started to roll in, bringing food, beverages and dope although I never saw anything more stimulant than grass. And they did not exactly roll in; they all camped outdoors, some with tents others inside a sleeping bag, just like my already-old one. The leftovers from the parties used to last an entire week. To me the food was fallen from sky, literally. That life was real, but I had to act my character who was living out of the real world and I found a way out. In The *War of the End of the World*, a 1981 novel by Vargas Llosa, there is a character who is a reporter from a small town paper; he was actually a writer for real. Suddenly this reporter found himself in the backwoods following and writing about a bunch of fanatics, beggars and repentant criminals whose history turned out to place them as the touchy story of Canudos, that took place in the northeast of Brazil.

On day I called Michael to have a conversation on the couch. I told him that I was disguising, perhaps very well, that I was being twisted, and tortured - that I was missing and longing for Helga and that I did not know how to make it up, to regroup, to find the plot... I went on to say that I realized that my relative needs had started to crumble and I was disconnecting. I was so in torn between fully redesigning my existence or retaining those engraved in my cells, genes and heart. I wished for a mere hint at which path to follow: the Canudos, meaning, to follow Milton to Colorado and sign in with the platoon of Hare Krishna, or stay in the forefront and learn from the opportunities, negotiating with them...and in that case, would Michael, the guru, help me?

The house had a huge balcony and a wooden deck protruded into the cypresses and there was I on this cold morning, sipping hot tea followed by our rustic homemade bread and I found out I could transform myself into any kind of "actor".

I could go to New York, so I thought, to climb the corporate ladder and approach big shots provided I had programmed myself accordingly with the right scruples to be in the right place at the right time to build up a mega materialistic lifestyle. With this token in hand I would set myself on fire like in *The Bonfire of the Vanities,* the book and the movie. A tiny bird landed on the rail of the balcony and I stared at him for a long time, as if I was a sniper through the sight of a weapon, and I realized I could also become a mercenary, if I wanted. I was going to start right there, training my body and my mind into better shape. Rambo, yes, I could be a Rambo-like killing machine, or survival machine. The tiny bird flew away and it was actually right at that moment that I called Michael, the Bhagavan Das, and told him about my need for help.

And he only laughed out loud at me and said foolishly, "Love is Love, Luis, Love is Love!"

Thank God he had this special way of not taking my confession seriously. Years later I read his book *It's Here Now (Are You?)* and learned the truth about my friend Michael, fully understanding the meaning of his answer to me. Apart from enjoying the friendship of Jimmy Hendrix, Timothy Leary, Allen Ginsberg, Allan Watts, Jerry Garcia (Grateful Dead) and many other celebrities, and having made the "mind" of many people, he was an enlightened person for real. Without more than his few words "Love is Love, Luis", he made me believe I could at least glimpse and flirt with a spiritual initiation right there.

From that day on, when he arrived for his daily meditation, he would meet me in the living room, reading or writing or simply thinking or standing still, and wake me up with a big laugh and the same phrase, "Luis, love is love! Love is love!" And before his zither jam session, he started to play Bob Dylan songs on his folk guitar because I had said I liked Bob Dylan.

After almost a year, the Mill Valley house lost its enchantment for me, and I started to feel old needs, for instance, the need to work as an ordinary human being, as someone who less than two years before had worn expensive suits and silk ties.

Thus I found a job, left the house up on the hill, and went to pay for a room, sharing a cottage this time with normal people, two vegetarian girls. I was paying for my basic expenses and saving all the pennies I could to buy a ticket back to Brazil. That sunset in the Arizona Desert did not leave my mind for a day, and somehow I began to understand what Michael was trying to say, laughing at me. The depressive notion that the man can disconnect from himself or become anything he wished was scratched from my mind, and all I could think of was to go back to Helga. So I accomplished that, "thanks Bhagavan Das, I promise to read your book."

The golden anchor made out of our wedding rings became my trade mark. Helga was in the last year of her Masters in Sociology. I was a different guy; she was different too. I reorganized my books on the shelves and among them I included a boating bible called Chapman – that I would read and reread again and again several times in the future. So Helga and I got married one more time, now on the sand beach of Copacabana. Helga was deeply involved in studying about sexual abuse and violence towards children in poor communities in Rio de Janeiro.

"But it is so sad, Helga. Why you don´t take inspiration in that picture by Bruegel, draw a red smile on the mouth of those kids in the picture and change into a research about children's play?" I said to Helga; we were both in a different mood and state of mind altogether. She almost did, not too hilarious though, but it was a sign that my sense of humor was back home, with ketchup e incense. I had acquired new values and had met crazy people. Those people used to talk about love, dreams, and happiness. I witnessed their daily revolution, as little ants. More important than anything, they made me believe that there were a lot of people pursuing their dreams, missions, and making their own destinies. I went back home with this speech and the fixed idea – to build my boat, to go sailing, and make an ocean passage and, of course after that, write a book. Religiously everyday while dressing myself for work, I pinned my golden anchor on my chest.

...There will be mirages.

My plans were well-defined. I was going to build my boat, period. Now I was serious. I was going to work in the advertising field; I had this idea stuck on my mind, that I was creative. I should first find a job in an advertising agency, save money and start to build my dream. It never stopped beating in my chest. Wherever I went people asked me what was that golden anchor I wore. I did not need a label; I simply used to say, a little ashamed, that I liked boats.

In fact, I found a job in an advertising agency, fourth in the national rank, traditional and well-respected. But it was funny because I was given the title of supervisor, and was never credited for successes, only when something went wrong they remembered me, so the pressure was intense. They used to introduced me to an airline carrier client as "Director of Accounts" who spoke English well, or for another client of industrial machines, for an account that I knew the "dialect of the engineers" (whatever it means and I never knew quite fully). I was called boss by my secretary who used to hear her daily horoscope on the radio, repeating that I should wait when I asked her for some files or something else to do. My paycheck was that of an ACCOUNT EXECUTIVE, with a job description as simple as any outlet salesperson. All this with a corner office exclusive to me. I had to wear a suit and tie – not an ordinary one - it had to be fancy, and preferably I was to behave charmingly, elegantly, and it was mandatory that I was formal and extroverted at the same time. I had to think fast and not forget anything, be aware of all the news and trends, and be expert in the field of my accounts, more cunning than our clients. And I was awarded with six clients: the most popular newspaper of Rio de Janeiro (O Dia), a manufacturer of industrial machines (White Martins subsidiary of the Union Carbide), an Airline carrier in bankruptcy that in ended up disappearing for good (Pan Am), a brand of French mineral water launching in Brazil but without money for an advertising campaign (Perrier), a French manufacturer of leather luggage, whose life story tells the story of France alone, but also without money for advertising campaign (Louis Vuitton), regardless that I did not speak French at the time. Later on the vice-president thought I could spare some extra time and gave me more accounts to "supervise" so I ended up launching a grated cheese, a yogurt, two different magazines (a picture magazine, Manchete, and an European fashion magazine, Marie Claire), and finally a lingerie brand (DeMillus). I was the first Adman to arrive at the office, before 8 am and the last to leave the boat, extravagantly after 22 pm. Naively, I believed I could make money by working hard.

This was my solid reality, visible on my paycheck stub, through my daily routine, my shallow relationships with work colleagues along with the terrorist threat of anyone being fired at anytime due to the country's economical crisis under a daily inflation rate of close to 10 percent, above 100 per year. Unimaginable but the truth.

To me, that scenario was no less than a huge Kafkian paradox, a transfusion of the absurd into the real and this back into that previous one. I refused to accept that reality in my old way, working standing around my desk playing as if I was in the *Wall Street* movie... Dreaming about building my boat.

Around that time I used to run on the beach to keep my body in shape, and a lot of reading for my mind. There were no more rides around the marina, but always when changing clothes I pinned my golden anchor onto chest, my rite. How many times I told myself under my breath: There has to be a way to build my boat!

Helga was suffering because of the situation of the poor children, no longer only in Rio, but all over Brazil, in Africa, and in the entire world. As a relief to the both of us, I used to plagiarize a saying of a well known picturesque Brazilian politician (Leonel Brizola): "this is an ocean of complexity". Then with my own words "Helga, when it is too heavy, let it go, the fact that you are thinking about and wishing for a better world for these children is already a lot, one day this will be fixed."

But even I thought the chaos was yet bigger; my perception was of an exaggerated complexity intrinsic to the current state of humanity.

Bombed by the most recent Science & technology discoveries and suffocated by the top ten list of new books released, I used to read with an incorrigible appetite taking from the bookshelves all sorts of goodies to cuddle. I used to eat anything, everything. Leaving leftovers all over the house. One day the illustration of an article in a newspaper caught my attention - there was a human head without eyes, no ears, with a mouth wide open to the sky as if it was catching the rain, but with a torrent of letters and special characters falling down into that mouth. I had just read half of *The Brief History of Time*, by Stephen Hawking and the thought came to my mind of a Brazilian poet from my home town, Mário Quintana, who wrote, "The man is to the apes as the worms are to the man. He mutilates his body, shave the hairs, walk oddly upright, with arms down apparently without function, the apes have a reason to be weird, while the worms are disgusting to the man, the mean where they live, how they feed themselves, their bodies..."

Instantaneously while staring at that illustration I laughed at my own conflict. The world is in fact simple. Bhagavan Das was right. Love is Love. Everything is done, men simply just don't perceive, ignorance makes it complicated to have the false perspective of controlling the script. So I realized I was going to end up with my head upright, hard neck, letting come down into my mouth a torrent of letters and special characters. My passage in the Arizona Desert came to my mind; my wish to throw myself down the cliff, into the abyss ignorant of its depth. I remembered that I was a cowboy, and the image of an Indian came to my mind: his countenance was intense, his face full of wrinkles, clean and with that chocolate-colored skin, no hair, and he looked vibrant. He was looking firmly faraway, well away. He could know everything, even there on that rock, isolated from the rest of the world, gazing at the horizon; he could perceive the fullness of the universe. He did not need to read nor use the internet, a thing I have heard vaguely was coming over all of us heavily. He knew the world as it is for real. The tennis shoe, the jeans, the street wear style of that boy with a baseball cap would represent to him a boy transforming himself from the outside in, from a tribe evolving the same way, nothing else. He would look at the boy for a moment before deploying any gesture, before saying anything. My Indian knew that his own tribe would be amazed seeing that boy, but he would do nothing. While if someone introduced to him a Shakespearean play he would move his lips with a light smile and thoughts that would be important only to himself.

I started to mimic my Indian, or a certain Indian inside myself. I joked with Helga sometimes, trying to stare at her with that characteristic Clint Eastwood-look, but secretly I was rehearsing the look of my Indian.

...We knock at the wrong dream's door, sometimes.

To live in Copacabana became unbearable: the noise, the pollution, the lack of civility, smoke and spit in the elevator, slamming the door in your face - small things to just ruin your day, first thing in the morning. In the supermarket we were horrified by the poor quality of a simple tomato, a bunch of bananas, a head of lettuce that looked more like an old dirty mop than a source of minerals and vitamins. In the theaters we liked so much, people talked aloud, shouting at each other and cursing, and the same aggressiveness existed on the streets: on the sidewalk, in traffic, on the road, bus drivers hallucinated, zigzagging at high-speed and suddenly breaking. People talked at the same pace of those buses, jumping on your next thought before you could even say a word. Beggars and bums were spread all over, shitting right where you pass by, so common that when you see someone pissing you feel it is childish; all this and even more on the sand beach. Through the TV on prime time or through the window, there was more sadness coming in to our ears, eyes and hearts. We used to hear people spilling their minds about everything without a sense of solution or worse, without knowing exactly what was going on around themselves. I felt compelled to introduce them to my fellow Indian:

But what if he stands still just looking at them?

Yes, no way out.

Sometimes I envied people apparently well integrated with that way of life, as if all was normal.

Are they happy?

I gazed straight to the far horizon through the Indian's view. I saw, however, the other side of the street and a huge, tall, solid grey wall. We used to walk up the hills of the South zone of Rio, Alto da Tijuca and Paineiras. What a mix of beauty and dirt, littering and human degradation. We liked to go for weekend drives in the countryside, along roads where we saw cattle, to Mauá to taste chocolate, drink wine and enjoy rustic lodging lighted with lamps, but we never found any poet to talk to us. Out there was no poetry at all, the opposite; the same people's behavior in the city. We were a married couple playing as a boy and a girlfriend negotiating things that we could do together, pretending it was all right. Secretly inside I dreamed away sailing on my yacht, Helga with me on the cockpit aiming to anchor on a far away beach with white sand and palm trees.

Two years and nothing, it was too much. I was working at an advertising agency and thought I was the most creative guy in the world. So on a rainy weekend I came up with the campaign slogan, "Brazil, Land in Sight", to celebrate 500 years of history of Brazil in 2000, which was just about 10 years away. The client would be myself. The goal: to mingle myself with the boating community by forceps. A million dollar project. Well, afterwards I would build as many boats as I wish.

The base line of my crazy project was that I perceived there was a giant pent-up demand in the country. With thousands of kilometers of navigable coast free of hurricanes, cape rollers, roaring forties, and away from el Nino it was a mystery to me why we hadn't had water sport traditions since discovered, or colonized, by the Portuguese, Spanish, Dutch, French, or British – during the boom of the century of great ocean explorations?

I had the insight that we would have to celebrate the 500 years of the country's existence as we know it, the so called Discovery in 1500. Right! This is the hook, the anchor. My institutional idea gained a direction and speed that I could not control anymore. Single-handedly I used to work on it to exhaustion. I added several sub projects with parallel goals supporting each other, with the main goal being "to build awareness of the boating potential in Brazil". "Brazil, Land in Sight", the campaign, was the umbrella promoting a bombing of projects in several social and economic sectors.

I would launch a public contest to create a commemorative stamp, five years before the 500 years anniversary, with prizes and a royalty to the winner. I would open an office for the franchise "Brazil, Land in Sight". Media equity and sponsorship categories would be offered to big players, domestic and abroad. If a cigarette brand, a soda and a soap can have it, why couldn't I?

The major event, in the year 2000, would be a race crossing the Atlantic ocean from Portugal bound for the Brazilian city of Porto Seguro, where Pedro Alvares Cabral supposedly anchored his fleet and declared Brazil 'discovered'. The Navy of foreign countries would be invited. This part of the idea was a contribution of Carlos Duarte, a client. He was an architect but worked as a marketing manager with White Martins, a subsidiary of Union Carbide and who was my direct contact while I was THE adman, so I told him in secret my crazy idea. He jumped into my delirium immediately. He also liked boats and was a sad man as much as I was.

So, on a lazy afternoon while I went to White Martins marketing department to make a presentation of a classified type black & white print ad for a lubricant oil, my friend Carlos Duarte asked me about the golden anchor on my chest. The question set us up to chat for the rest of the afternoon. I discovered that there are many more dreamers disguising themselves as ordinary people, with their eagerness to break away from their ordinary worlds almost bursting out of their chests. Although only a few actually snap and go for it. Creatures should snap out of their delirium sometimes. We are creative by nature - it is our essence - but we live restrained, saving ourselves for some unknown purpose, acting dead, until the danger called "life" has passed.

So I started to foresee the implementation of new courses at a college level, related to boating as a sport, for productive industry sectors, economics and so on. Support from a collaboration of efforts between government and private initiatives. Implementation of areas of environmental protection reserved to outdoor activity and awareness of a new lifestyle inclusive to coastal zones, estuaries, lakes, and wetlands. Incentives to real estate developments inclusive to coastal zones and water-related at large, such as condo complexes with marinas and yacht clubs.

More "cachaça" (sugar cane Brazilian alcohol), and more cigarettes; it was me back home at night, up until so late that I started hallucinating and fell asleep.

But, because I am inveterate and resilient, during the whole weekend my crazy side went truly wild. I created a play: "Caramuru, fuck you" (kah-rah-moo-roo). Caramuru is a character all kids read about in school, about Brazilian history. He was a Portuguese man that acquired the status of a true Indian after being shipwrecked along the northeast coast of Brazil and captured by Indians. He mingled with them so perfectly that he married the daughter of the tribe's chief, and eventually took his new bride to France, then back to Brazil. He became a middle-man of European settlers and his Indians friends.

Yes, Caramuru, give me a break, would you?

The play of course hit nothing but the trash bin. But in the following months I had the chance to contact Mr. Erling Lorentzen, a Norwegian shipowner and industrialist who had lived in Brazil for decades. He founded Aracruz Cellulose in 1968, among other enterprises during the military government. He was the widower of Princess Ragnhild, granddaughter of Norway's King, and after all this background, a yachtsman and winner of five Buenos Aires-to-Rio yacht races. He answered my call in person and said he liked my idea - that he would support it if things developed. Great! Then I contacted Thomas Hohony, the king of the Formula One car race circuit in Brazil. I went to the top of several buildings, so many stairs to climb that I got tired of hearing myself talk about "Brazil, Land in Sight", and the campaign went to the bottom drawer and later on also to the trash bin.

...From dreaming so much.

One day, out of the blue, the chance to build my boat fell onto my lap. An ex-neighbor contacted me with a proposal - to help him to open a business in the United States. It was for an active wear unique components manufacturing. Since I knew a few words in English he thought I could be his partner. Within a month I resigned from the advertising agency and flew to Washington, D.C. to do the first field research and set the first conqueror flag.

On the very night after he contacted me I drafted a master plan; I will never forget - I wrote a full blast road map with a flow chart and a detailed step-by-step time frame, to discuss with him a few days later. My planning included procedures to take care of my new partner's entire family including his wife, two children, father and mother-in-law; the moving arrangements, cargo, transportation, banking, and so on. I could not think of anything else but the business in the Unites States.

In the following week after discussing and making decisions with my partner, I came to a resignation agreement with the VP of my ad agency, ceased my contract in a way that would satisfy Greeks and Trojans because I found out that he was planning on firing me that very month.

"Seriously? How nice of you so let's do it four hands then", I remember I told him.

Our first move was to fly to Washington D.C. to obtain official information about how to register a business in America. We would source suppliers and research the market, all empirical but I had all my pores wide open. No internet those days, I had instead Thomas Register, huge tomes A to Z found in the Library of Washington State University where to dig names and addresses from. And I was on fire, I would blow a point of a knife if needed. I had a permanent smile on my face, that look of incisive and some how threatening if anyone got in my way.

The TV prime time news highlighted boats falling apart, packed with migrants from Tahiti aiming for the American dream. And the family I was helping was serious about doing the same if needed. Bag and baggage they were willing to migrate illegally into the United States; scraping their savings they would fight their way up and being Italian descendants they would eventually try to get legal papers and educate their children in a First World country. A bold project. And I was the rower of the skiff.

After the research trip to Washington I spent an extra month taking care of the final voyage while waiting for my partner solve some personal affairs. Finally we boarded to California. We landed in San Francisco, crossed the Golden Gate Bridge, hypnotized to put up a factory right in Marin County. Where is Mill Valley, a magical place to me.

With the proper Visa in hand from having worked as an ad director of Pan Am's account, I was authorized to knock on doors, register the business and obtain permits. I reached out to a friend in Florida who put me in contact with a real estate salesperson in Northern California and with in a snap we signed a three year lease contract for a warehouse of 3,000 square feet. Holy cow! Within less than a month in a foreign country, the manufacturing business was registered. We could operate.

The experience of living under the same roof with my partner's family was moving, and sometimes threatening. Their habits and behavior however were my karma. They used to scream at each other, offending themselves, arguing all the time for nothing...

Something was telling me that we should have thought about the coexistence aspect of the partnership with people of such different backgrounds and habits. But I could not hear that voice and minded only the idea of pulling it together. There was no use in closing my ears to buffer the screaming. In the morning we would wake up with sputum noises and with someone banging on the bathroom door. The children were fighting and crying all the time. The TV was on from the first light of day to the last boxing fight show late at night.

The food was rationed and it was not the multiplication of the loaves. To me, it was torture. I had to build a manufacturing plant from the ground up. During that time, when we lived under the same roof with that family - for a month that seemed to be an eternity - I invented a Mona Lisa look to wear. It was like this: I did not agree, I did not disagree either, I did not approve nor the opposite but it was my way of condemning them all.

Helga and I tried to hide ourselves in our bedroom and pretend nothing was happening, but the vibe in the house was intense and we always ended up anguished, discussing ways out of that situation.

So, finally, the factory was up and running and, as planned, we rented a flat to live on our own.

The rudimentary process that my partner showed me was truly naive and simple, with no methodology at all. It was a handcrafted process and did not follow any standardization of steps, volume of raw material applied, pre-measurements - it was almost like making bread without following a recipe. The equipment was homemade and in the end, once the products were "manufactured", there was no pre-determined pattern for packaging, no one cared.

To implement a business, even a small business, in the United States, requires at least a basic management procedure, thus I had before me a giant task. I reminded myself of my time as system analyst and tried to rationalize.

The first decision I made was to leave the family of my partner alone. Regarding my family, me and Helga, we set up a meeting and decided that for one or two years we would focus on the business and nothing else. In the end it had to be worth the effort. So we gave up going out to restaurants together, as well as our traditional leisure activities. We adopted TV as the only one anesthetic. Our domestic budget was reduced to the lowest possible minimum and we bought only home brand products at the supermarket. Until I built a sweet wooden table, we ate sitting on the floor. Once a week we used to open the house for guests; we cooked spaghetti la bolognese and invited our friend, singer, and dreamer, Sergio Pedroza.

"Hey Sergio, would you like to eat a spaghetti?"

Our friend would take the joke and show up with a bottle of Bolla red wine. Now with the domestic affairs squared away I could dive deep in the business. The "shed", as my partner used to call the warehouse, was empty. There were fifty thousand dollars in the bank and a business to build from the ground up. A minimum of methods and pre-determined procedures were a must, but the only way my partner seemed to function was with two figures, one on top of the other, with a line at the bottom of them and the result under that line, he called that the "Portuguese calculation". It was, however, a chance to convert that handful of dollars in the bank into more dollars figures. So I thought.

What I could not figure out was the reason why my partner had the mind stuck on the idea that family members should not work in the factory. Ok, it was the chairman's wish. My withdrawals as a partner allowed me to pay the rent, only and not enough even for groceries. Thus, the only way to supplement our income, meaning, to make that domestic home brand budget work, while the business did not make enough money that we could all drive a Mercedes, was solved by Helga. She started to work as a babysitter. And our lifestyle went to the top. We would call Sergio for breakfast once a week at Sam's, a nice place in Tiburon, right in front of Sausalito, watching the Golden Gate from a deck over the water, and completing the scenery was a luxurious yacht moored a few feet away from our table.

...Sometimes they are nightmares, not dreams.

The winter arrived and covered the sidewalk with ice. Frequently it rained, increasing the feeling of cold. To walk my way to work was a torture even for me, a gaucho who grew up stepping on the frost to pick kindling for the wood burning stove. The forty-five minute walk from Larkspur to Greenbrae everyday, was just too much. I never asked my partner why he did not gave me a lift. It was, however, my only chance to think about the situation, to meditate, to reflect and, finally, to try to understand what was wrong with me? Not getting a lift from my partner did not worry me that much, out of my understanding was why things developed the way they did.

September was gone quickly; the month zero. October was month number one; November brought us the first order to full fill. By December we already had a modest portfolio of clients. I was responsible for the marketing, the hunting and recruitment of workers; I was the delivery guy as well. In fact, before I made last minute runs to the UPS or Federal Express distribution center, I helped with assembling products and packaging. Meanwhile I used to speak about the image of the ideal business we were building; flexibility, no frills, on-time management, value added - were concepts I tried to implement towards customers and suppliers as well. I started to co-op reps and they also would be invited to be flexible, no frill, hands on, on time management... I offered volume bonuses for the reps and productivity bonuses for employees, and asked the same from the suppliers. Soon positive results started to be visible and I started an R&D department in a tiny corner of my mind, developing new product ideas. These included zipper pulls, knee pads for ski and motorcycle active wear, coasters, small mats and my mind would blow up with ideas of embossing designs on a plastisol, a plastic substance gelled by temperature in an open mold - that what was the novelty process my partner actually pinched from a "friend" back in Brazil, (something I discovered only later in the game).

A few months ago I was in my office at the advertising agency and my partner introduced to me a couple of rubber labels and key rings plus a proposal to open a business in the USA. Six months later we had a Trade Mark registered, manufacturing labels, key rings, stickers, magnets and ideas of new products coming out of the oven everyday.

I went to a trade show in San Diego and made a blitz at every single booth. Lap top computers were not so common around that time but I had one of the first editions of Gateway and a small portable printer. I researched key people (by sneaking into a couple of booths to obtain names), and then ran to the parking lot to print a template letter addressed to a buyer, director or manager. Then I ran back into the Trade Show and handed each one the letter and a bag of samples. An hour later I stopped at those booths to follow up with, "How about a first order to test out our unique labels and embossing badges?" After all, I'd been a sales person since I was born. And I was thrilled.

After that trade show, orders started to pour in. The iron horse was warming up very quick. We already had more orders than we were able to produce. So we hired more people. I found a handicap agency and brought in a couple of special labor force. I also discovered that prisoners from San Quentin, not too far from our warehouse, could be hired cheap and somehow I was feeling good about it (plus the tax exemption and incentives down the pipeline). And there I was, no more a stern young man but now burning energy to exhaustion.

Summer arrived and Mário Benício, another friend, a plastic artist, gave me a compact old Honda that had fallen apart, that I could drive until it stopped for good. I had a jug of water handy on the floor, for when the car overheated. This, in the United States, while being a VP of a business which was already exporting goods was a sacrilege. But I knew the whole story and knew that would change. And I ended up giving away that little Honda to the janitor of my condo because Angelique, Mario´s wife and also an artist, gave me a Studebaker 60 she thought was scrap. I ordered brand new parts and after rebuilding the engine, people turned their necks to look while I drove by. What joy, and the Studebaker was blue, my color. While the business was in shape, the cash flow however was struggling.

"What´s going on?" I was asking myself. I did not know. The more we produced the more we spent. We had too much waste. That's wasn't right. A hundred thousand dollars in orders per month but we could only produce the equivalent to thirty thousand monthly. We had a work force of 30 and we looked like a manufacturing business but our waste was growing. Too many rejected products. And my ideas of streamline, quality control and methodologies were not in place, not followed at all.

Oh no, I think we are en route to a collision. Ok, I adapted myself. I pretended I was running a market stall. But how? I had reps in UK, Australia and Mexico. Some major clients wanted to visit us, for a tour. I needed to hide the truth.

Ok, I tried to square the situation, it should be way easier than start up a business from scratch. Hey, a problem born in less than a year should be easy to fix. Analytical mind. Let me see, let's try. Then a year was gone. The second year was gone too. Positive figures on my spreadsheets, sales were good, production was improving substantially, financial contributions okay, well known brand names in our portfolio, namely Quicksilver, O'Neal, North Face, NEI Outdoor, FreeStyle, Patagonia, lots of not so well known names that soon would be giants of the street wear market such as Mossimo, Rusty and others. We were exporting to England, Mexico, Australia, and China. We should have been implementing important changes, preparing ourselves for the second phase of the business, preparing ourselves to grow; I was thinking these things when I got the news right to my face: "as of the day 12th, Luis, we will not be partners anymore."

The 12th would be next month. And the decision was irrevocable. I could be a sales person or a rep, if I wanted. But the factory would be run from then on as if it was in Brazil, like a backyard business. It was like stopping an iron horse engaged full power downhill. I had commitments with clients, reps and suppliers. It was like a boxing fighter trying to go back for the next round and his own coach blows a punch right on his chin and another on his stomach and a third blow right on the nose. "Stay here, do not stand up, hear me?" shouting the coach.

I went home that day completely stunned, full of questions and no answers. It was so fast. I was surprised and I was so involved with the business that the only thing I could think of were the commitments, with clients, reps, suppliers, and projects in progress. Within a few days my ex-partner would take his family on the road for vacation, he would shut down the factory, the electricity and everything. He had planned it secretly, I could not reverse the process. To sue them? I did not came with this chip.

On another token, if my hands were tied, my brain and heart were now free as ever. My immediate reaction was to unleash a fax to my three main reps telling them the news as rude and raw as it was broken to me. And my spontaneous gesture had three immediate simultaneous replies each with more or less the same point on action:

"Hey, Luís, we are also shocked and puzzled but what to do? Let's build up a manufacturing business of embossed plastic for ourselves. After all, haven't you played the one man show of this business?"

The replies to my faxes came in and I could not believe what was going on. From that night to next day I set up a funny office at home. Sitting on my lazy boy taken from a curb somebody left for free pick up, my lap top on my true lap and that was it. The headquarters of the guerrilla. Cathrine Chapman wanted to know face to face details about the news. Right after replying to my fax she called me on the phone.

"Luis, I want to know this story. See you in Berkeley in a hour, same place as usual. Can you make it?"

"Of course. Right! See you there."

One hour sharp later we were comfortable in a café in front of UCB. Two cappuccinos and I recapped to Cathrine the chat with my ex-partner the day before.

So the guys from Australia, the man from Mexico and my key jewel rep, Cathrine, my American and International forerunner, they all reacted objectively and with good spirit. Then, with that big push from my lazyboy which had a hole in the seat, I was reminded of my bank account balance, three projects were drafted to be discussed on a conference call. It was amazing the speed of the developments. I had not dropped the towel, no way. Instead of a catastrophe, I could see only good things happening for us. Helga looked at me, a bit scared and sorry for me, feelings that were conflicting, but she trusted me and as two pussy cats we still had eight lives to spare.

Nine pages with descriptions, graphics and spreadsheets were sent by fax to Australia, Mexico and to Oakland, where Cathrine lived. I labeled the three projects as "Tequila", "Kangaroo", and "Uncle Sam". My new partners liked my sense of humor and, considering the circumstances they said, again in unison, that I was brave and had a positive attitude. However, I did not know where from I found so much energy to work, 18 hours per day.

With México the negotiation did not go forward but with Charlie in Australia and with Cathrine in the United States we stepped forward in a hectic pace. We wanted to take advantage of a back log of orders and start up manufacturing right away, so we would not lose clients, Yes, my ex-partner would lose a few accounts – that was for sure. Within five days a transfer of petty cash was made into my bank account for personal expenses and it would be deducted off the principal capital of the new businesses we were putting together. The money was borrowed from Cathrine. I was getting money from people I barely knew over the phone and from two or three meetings face to face, and they already called me "Luis" as if we knew each other a long time ago.

In such terms, I planted my butt on the lazyboy early and got up only for the occasional legwork or late at night to crash.

A few days later, Cathrine found me an investor to finance the Uncle Sam Project. This investor came in the picture as an investor from a Hollywood B movie. Someone tells someone, eventually it reaches your ears and suddenly you are advised the investor will make a stop at the Los Angeles airport on the way to Dallas. So I flew off to LA and there I was now acting as if I was in a movie for real, but something funny was happening with me. The speed of the developments was amazing and I did not have time to assess the extent of each move and what the next one would be. I had to deal with the pace they appeared, judge by my instincts and make decisions right on the spot. I had to show, however, that at least a piece of the bat was in my hand and that I could beat hard back if needed, if a dog fight started for instance.

There was a sense of conspiracy in my favor, as if a magic trick made by angels, and this funny thing was happening to me - a kind of flashback with memories of the sunset out in the desert of Arizona, the figure of the Aztec Indian and the angelical face of my Helga, rescuing me with her look gazing into my eyes. Curiously, instead of feeling stressed with everything happened in the last ten days, or in the last two years or even since I started to work in the advertising field, always under pressure – it was a merry-go-round on a daily basis - I was feeling as if everyday I woke and it was a holiday. That day that you don't need to work and you decide to reach out for your old files, organize things, fiddling around with those ideas you always had and never tried.

Immersed in this astral, I landed at the John Wayne airport, in Los Angeles. An airplane glides over the 405 freeway reaching for the scariest airport in the country. The runway is short; the landing seems a deep skydive onto a bundle of concrete buildings almost in a vertical straight line. While taking off the climb is steep, you feel like you're traveling in a missile. With those flashbacks sparkling in my head I saw the people running in a hurry in the airport, stern, worried. Their faces plump and glossy, I imagined their eating habits based on bacon, jelly, bread, ketchup, peanut butter, hamburger and soda. I saw in the dark circles under each one's eyes on the moving staircase a similarity of worries, anguishes and anxieties. They were in the opposite direction of mine and I felt like praying for them and I actually did. These thoughts occurred to me in a fraction of seconds as only in thoughts it can happen. And I wished some of them to have prayed for me too. I was breathing as if I was consciously feeding myself with air and this was somehow giving me the strength I needed, because I felt the air being sucked into my lungs, doing something I wanted and succeeding. I was making the decision to breathe and was being rewarded. I also tried to smile only with my eyes and succeeded as well. Then I was walking, pretending not to use the brain for it because it needed to rest. Only the rest of my body worked, arms and legs. So in such a half-trance I played a unique way of meditation, my way, and prayed for unknown people. Yes, I could have been turning into a complete state of insanity. The matter-of-a-fact was that I was feeling light. I was going through a rain of sharp arrows against me and none had hit me so far.

Even without getting out of the airport I could see the turbulence of the city about to hit me, the vibe of the city. By the time of take off back to San Francisco I was terrified once again. The airplane shot itself on the runway toward a wall of buildings and I felt it would not lift in time before crashing into them. On the last second it lifted its tons of metal, trembling, vibrating and tangent to that concrete wall. I went back home with the same dark circles under my eyes as those people in the airport. The investor was evasive, reluctant and I would have to sell to him an idea of a profitable business. But I did not want to sell anything. I was looking for an offer. And if in one hand I had to hold a bit of frustration, it was because of the time zone difference between the Unites States and Australia - it did not give a chance to lick my wounds. At night I had to call and let them know my progress. And as soon as I had a cold shower I sat to eat a steak with fries followed by a glass of red wine, the phone rang.

"Hello Charlie, I am in the middle of something. I'll call you in a minute."

I finished my dinner, took a deep breath and called Charlie back. The guys in Australia simply went ahead astoundingly fast. They decided, three partners, that they had clout enough to start up the factory from the inputs I sent over to them. I should send a master check list and they would provide whatever was needed until I could arrive and hold the bull by the horns. I should run with it. The clock was ticking already; they called the major clients and had an agreement of delay tolerance. It meant we would start up the factory with old orders in the house, part of the initial capital would be those orders; they also got upfront payments giving away discounts. Agile, clever, were the guys from Australia.

Wow! I came out of a movie into the real world, I said to myself. Be careful, you can hurt yourself once again.

The phone call was quick; they asked me to kindly hang up because they would call me back so I would not pay for the call. Ok, they knew already that I was poor. Then they gave me the first inputs regarding immigration, it would be easy to get temporary residence since I was taking a business into the country.

"Luís, tomorrow you will get a long fax. We have many questions and blanks to fill out. Please reply soonest. We have no time to waste. Sleep well partner!"

It was hard to sleep that night. It must be like the feeling when a spy does not know with who he is talking to. With KGB? CIA? IRA? I don't know, but open-breasted as always, a straight shooter; they can punch me in the face, I don't care, I won't fall down, I am hard to keel. I was going to Australia. The mecca of sailing. I couldn't believe it. Two years had been gone in a blink of an eye. I had left Brazil, built up a manufacturing business from the ground up in the United States - for the first time in my life I had a five year plan and it just disintegrated, slipped through my fingers, something else fell down in my lap; I was going on a round-the-world-trip. Like that, all of a sudden. There was no Indian look that could have explained what was going on; I could not fix my eyes on the sunset and ask for help, the abyss was faraway and would not hear me.

In the bedroom in the dark, Helga welded to my body and I gave myself slowly to sleep that was fortunately rescuing me. I was feeling myself out of my body, hovering in the air. Spread open legs, belly up, eyes opened I saw myself in a time tunnel; I was going to be ejected faraway and would not break. I was a body made for it. My skinny neck, my exhausted arms, my skin stretched, I was feeling myself clean but it was as if the shower after arriving from LA took not only the dust and sweat but also all my energy. My spirit however was intact, as an umbrella hovering in the air out of my body would follow me until the next continent, over mountains, seas, oceans, but unable to avoid the passage. Once the other side of the world, so faraway that I did not know exactly where it was, it would be incorporated back into the matter.

I thought that imagination too crazy, the soul being reincorporated into the body. I prayed a Holy Mary and thanked God for anything good that could happen to me. Finally I was able to turn on my stomach and was making plans; I had a tough agenda for the next morning. I fell asleep coiled like a fetus.

...False wizards show up.

Frankston. The first time I heard this name it sounded to me as a monster. It is an outskirt town of Melbourne, in Victoria, South of Australia. As per my new partners arrangements we would stay in a nice hotel in this town. The factory was going to be installed nearby in the city of Seaford. And we would have to discuss all the points as quickly as impossible. The wish to implement the operation was so great that we could not waste time disputing, nor even negotiating minor details. I figured that was the name of the game for the Kangaroo project. After all, I and Helga would had nothing to lose. Nothing at all. We had our minds, our hearts and lungs that we would use to exhaustion because from that point on it would be the marathon of our lives. On the "Uncle Sam" Project, I met Cathrine, at the same café in Berkeley, and told her about the arrangement and agreement with the guys from Australia. And I proposed a deal.

"You have my word, Cath! If you still interested to build a factory here in States, I will do it for you. For now, keep being a rep for us. Keep doing what you do best. Let's make it official. Let's register the business here as a branch of the Australia operation, an overseas office. I promise you, within a year, if you get the initial capital I will come back from Australia and put the factory up and running here."

"O.k. Deal!" she said straight back.

Cathrine had that ability to create connections as I have never seen before. She got herself involved in a variety of businesses and transactions, all of them of great scale. Right after we started to work together, she sent me a fax with a single phrase: "Hi Luís, help, I need 74 tons of salt. Brazil??? Answer ASAP!"

On my phone call back to her I would learn her fax wanted to say she would earn a commission from a salt transaction, the supply should be consistent on a monthly basis of forty tons of salt and if I had connection in Brazil we would split the commission and, finally, we should close the deal with in 48 hours. With Cat it was like that: sharp, short and straightforward. Once, when we met at that café in Berkley, she told me a confidence. She had a dream of a two-story house with white columns, Crystal chandeliers and a curly oak stair case and marble. It would be the female version of Scarface, if she did not dislike bad addictions of all sorts. She used to get involved in dangerous business too, once she landed in Panama during military tensions to collect a payment from a client in dispute. It was a real estate deal amounting to millions of dollars. She was threatened with machine guns for two days but came back to America with the money. I met Cath on a trade show in San Diego, the one where I used the parking lot as my mobile office with a printer and pre-set pack of samples and letters templates. She was showcasing products for a Japanese group of businessmen and I approached her with my folder of samples. Without stopping to talk to the Japanese group, she said I should wait but kept turning her head to stare at my folder until the Japanese guys went away bowing their heads. But it was less than a five minute talk with her; I was left with a business card and she said, "Interesting. Maybe we can meet another time. Now I must see someone else."

Amazing the coincidences. We are a mysteriously sewed relationship mesh. Cathrine was living in Australia; she was married to a wine maker. Eventually she showed me four pages of the Vogue magazine highlighting a party in her house in Queensland. Two months before the break up with my partners, we were talking by phone while she was over in Australia and I noticed a sadness in her voice. I took a chance and said to her, out of the business tone, "Hey Cath. You can cry, don't be ashamed. Is anything happening that I can help with? You can unburden with me."

She had just divorced from her husband and had bags packed to come back to California, her home town. She burst out crying over the phone and thanked me later on. Felt good. She had not spilled to anybody before. More curious, was the way I insisted to establish contact with Cathrine. After that trade show in San Diego I had a feeling that we would make good businesses together. I called her a couple of times and no luck until I realized the number was an Australian one. Stupid! I said to myself and placed a correct call, and left a message on her machine twice. Since never accepting no is my way of hunting my wishes I mailed her a package of samples and a short letter that said: Hey kid! You don't need to answer my calls, just sell my products, will you? Follow samples in attached and commission basis.

Her answer was a friendly phone call and again, short one, "Okey-doke, let's do business, my friend!"

It was a movie missed on my inner shelf. And, in the real world, very soon Cath had found me reps in Australia - the ones I was going to meet soon and become partners with – and another one in England. Both started to place monthly orders from well known companies like Coca-Cola, Reebok, Adidas, FreeStyle, Quiksilver, Gul, and many others. The rep I met at the same trade show, from Mexico, was not losing ground to his British contenders; he also placed a good order of assorted designs of rubber labels for a chain of souvenir stores in the Caribbean islands.

So I became a Doc Donald producing faxes and phone calls hectically. From our door in Greenbrae, Marin County, where the factory was, I had taken packages of labels a few months earlier to the UPS distribution center, reaching them by the back door as we were always late. I struck a friendship with the manager and he said he would hang around for an extra hour or so, so I could go by the back door. They were sent to London, Melbourne, Mexico City - many cities in the United States. Also over to Asia, because for those brand names of mass products we were asked to ship to their contractors in Hong Kong, Seoul, Taipei and so on. We were taking over the Australasia market but all this ended before the 12th day as my ex-partner had wished. I was no longer the Vice President of that company; I was just Luis being ejected 300 miles per hour, 3000 feet high to satisfy the expectancy of tigers with sharp claws. And I did not know just yet how to make the products.

...A dream take us faraway.

We took off to Melbourne. The Australian Embassy gave me a floppy disk with a business plan template that I needed to present in order to be granted a Visa, plus other important requirements. Within two days I produced a bundle of papers with projections and passports, including a receipt of deposit for $20,000 in an Australian bank account in my name. My Aussie partners opened the account in my name and this was one of the requirements to be granted temporary residence in Australia. The money came from Cathrine and was to be reimbursed as soon as I arrived at the kangaroo land. A week later the Visas were stamped on our passports. 15 days later, counting from the breaking bad News, with luggage in hand I boarded a plane for a 31 hour economy flight, facing three stops including one in South Africa. I was going to set up the same factory I had set up two years earlier, in California.

Sergio's roommate, Ulisses, worked in the factory in Greenbrae, and as he was a friend of Sergio he was like our brother. He had mastered the thermal process of molding plastic on an open mold. I knew the theory behind it; I knew the raw material since I was the one who negotiated with suppliers. I had even helped to standardize the steps, the management and even the timing of the elementary movements of that hand-crafted process, but I'd never tried to actually "bake" a label. Ulisses was the best and his performance was outstanding. No waste, no defective parts. When I figured the discussion with the Australian was headed to where I was now, I had called Ulisses and invited him to go to Australia with us. After all, Ulisses was a true backpacker by heart. He had been traveling in Europe with his sleeping bag so he accepted without blinking an eye. Especially because I had made a point with my new partners - that we should have a compensation withdrawal. You know that story of being burned once - you are extra careful thereafter...

And it should be guaranteed non-negotiable before we land in the land of the kangaroos. Thus, with Ulisses standing by us it was like carrying on a pet bear. Ulisses was a mellow guy. He was also our friend through everything.

It became routine to pack up our belongings. This was good because we used to take a chance and discard things that we didn't need and would only accumulate dust. On the other hand, we also lost things that we liked. From our marriage gifts I had lost already four barbecue sets. Many little dishes, pictures, spice sets, hand embroidered towels, and gifts from aunts were falling along the way since we became pilgrims. Now, going to Australia we were once again giving up little personal items. One thing I could not afford to drop was my books. Thousands of them among which was a pink folder where the blueprints of my dream yacht. When I'd gone to the United States for the first time the trunk of my little car was full of books as in the back seat that pink folder was always visible. I could not stay away from those objects, or subjects for that matter - it was like being near my dreams all the time. When we came to America for this manufacturing adventure we brought Helga's books too, increasing our library as well as with the ones I used to steal from friends - yes I was guilty – a confessed book thief. For this trip to Australia we sent almost a ton of books, two dozen cardboard boxes full of books. Not necessarily rare works and many could be thrown away but we could not. Helga used to keep papers from college many years back. To abandon them? Never. "Is it in the budget?" She asked me, and I replied, "Yes, take them."

Helga's eyes were full of tears from the day before saying goodbye to her children. She was so attached to them that I was jealous. Their mothers on the other hand got attached to Helga. It was a water fall of tears. She was taking care of a little boy who did not want to get out of her arms. The two of them got so attached to each other that he used to call Helga mom. His true mother liked it. One of the families offered us help to find employment and to stay in America. And there was Ilza, a friend of ours who would take Helga to stroll in San Francisco on her day off, so she could go sightseeing since I never had time for this sort of activity. Ilza even helped Helga to buy groceries and found her first babysitter job.

Helga was sad, and was going to miss her friend. All of a sudden we were departing, after developing a feeling of belonging to people and to that place, Marin County. Only then we realized how deep our roots were growing there. We had a good circle of friends - people that we liked just because we liked to be around them. There were places where we knew the waiters, the Chinese man from the laundry place, even a crazy beggar already knew us by name - we would never stop liking that place.

During the flight I planned on working. I thought I could make a head start, organize ideas, but it was a bad flight, too long. We were going to Canudos, that story told by Vargas Llosa where a reporter was writing the events while they were taking place and this time I was the reporter. At the same time I was the crazy Preach, Antonio Conselheiro, pulling together an army of fanatics. When the time came to fill out the immigration forms before landing, I realized I was responsible for the three of us, myself, Helga and Ulisses and this hit hard on my consciousness and started to punish it. My enthusiasm created that situation and I needed to respond positively. I challenged myself once again, beyond my capacity maybe, and felt as I hadn't before. I hadn't proven even to myself that I was able to make the process of molding plastics work and yet had I a backlog of orders to fill as soon as I arrived, but not before building up ovens and benches. I trusted in the skills of Ulisses, but could not expect him to think the business side with me. It was not part of his nature. His function was only to produce the labels and there were preparation steps to perform, to mix the chemical raw material, pigments, solvents, the deaeration, steps that I was an expert at only in theory in the United States while selling and wearing the hat as buyer and other jobs. I became a little nervous with those thoughts and broke up the silence among us, "Well, if it does not work, at least we can say we saw Australia."

The two of them did not find that funny. They looked at me, puzzled, and we remained in silence. Ok, gliding over our heads was a dark cloud of worries from then on. On top of my list of expectations was now a ghost: the "now what?"

Well, if it doesn't work at least we saw Australia... I thought to myself without finding it funny either.

...For love we flew on flocks.

We landed in Melbourne during a storm of rain and wind that suddenly stopped and restarted again. The clouds would open and the sun would shine down on us and then again the clouds would become dark and rain dropped like a waterfall driven by strong gusts, turning trees inside out. We were dizzy, walking as if we were teleguided. Above us the sky was moving to hide the sun and in between over our heads was the ghost "now what?" They were clouds flying by the bunch, changing color from purple to dark grey, making the daylight dark as a solid night, and then another storm dropped over us. This lasted the entire month of July. To top it off it was terribly cold.

Welcome to Melbourne!

Charlie came to pick us up at the airport. It was easy to find him, correction, for him to find us. The three of us were so unglued from the landscape that would be easily found down under, we did not need a sign on our chests.

While we were on the way to the hotel I noticed immediately the dark green landscape. Dense vegetation everywhere – red earth and, with this rain, wait, this is Australia? I did not know it was like that. I had expected tropical landscapes, palm trees, beaches, surfers, and yachts all over. Where on earth had we ended up? We were on a highway outside the city approaching the suburb of Frankston where our hotel was. There were brick houses, some made out of wood, humble buildings with no architectural appeal, TV antennas on roof tops, grass grown over the sidewalks, loose dogs on the streets, old cars. It was raining. My crew was watching the scenery through the blurry glass with a sad look maybe thinking as I was:

What a wild place. Shit, how different it is from Larkspur!

It was a vision that would later be changed completely. The north coastal line from Melbourne is wild yes, and exactly because of that it is superb.

On that very day I told myself that it couldn't get any worse than it already was. On this land I would build my dream – I had a strong feeling in my chest telling me so. On the same token that same voice was saying it was not going to be easy.

We were staying in a very comfortable hotel flat, with two bedrooms, a full kitchen where I could cook my own meal the way I always liked. It was going to be our home for a while.

We arrived on a Saturday and by Monday we were introduced to the Kangaroo Project. There was no time to waste. A huge list of orders to fulfill was waiting for us so we had to get on it. Immediately the agility and cleverness of my new partners captured by their phone calls and faxes were covered by something else right in front of my eyes. By meeting them in person, seeing their installations, offices and their manners, I felt like saying to them: welcome to the club of poor.

At least I had assumed that status. Why British people never do? I might have not met enough British people by then, that's all. The first impact on me was the accent. My ears were used to a nasal sound, with r's coming straight from the inner ceiling of the mouth without ceremony. I was responding to certain American expressions that demanded a reply also without ceremony, as well my attitude before daily trivial situations had been designed by the habit of getting along with a pragmatic fashion. I learned to be practical, demanding, self-sufficient, deliberate and even insolent sometimes, especially while doing. Now, suddenly I was wrapped with a silk veil that slid from over my shoulders, cold, smelling mold. Charlie could not say simply "sure", or "of course". He twisted himself all over with hand gestures as if he was screwing a lamp just to show me where to sit.

"Certainly you shall sit there. You may wish to choose the window, it will be more pleasant."

His office was a mess. A huge room full of papers and samples of made in China products of all sorts were spread on the floor. A cubicle next to the restroom was multifunctioning as a kitchen and shop. His business was a representation and his marketing policy was "to not have prejudice for anything that could be sold". I shouldn't have been upset, after all I was being treated well so far. But I was upset, pouted. It upset me as if I was being held with a strait jacket. We had discussed a huge list that they gave to me, and many items of that list should have been available to me on my arrival. I made a point that we should make decisions about everything related to the new company, before starting the operation. But with the exception of three things, nothing, absolutely nothing was arranged. The first thing given to me was a spreadsheet with financial projections - how much we would spend, how much the revenue would be. There was a column with general ledger terminology that to me was nothing more than two figures with a line under with the total at the bottom. The second thing was a 3000 square foot warehouse that they had purchased to set up the factory. I could not believe it. They were crazy. They had purchased a huge warehouse. We were a mad bunch.

One of the partners was a liquidation lawyer. He knew all the details of the bankruptcy businesses. He knew which people were the ones with one foot in the grave. He used to share the same restroom as judges and auctioneers, who chatted about the next gavel hit while peeing next to each other. It was easy. They discovered a company, which according a local bank, was dying and they came up with an agreement. I did not understand it very well, but the result of the transaction was that they renegotiated the mortgage and won the warehouse on a short sale. We (I was involved in the contract) would pay the loan to that bank without money down - in installments for three years - a blue bird, cash cow hell of a deal all together. My new partners were clever sons of guns. The third and last arrangement was the registration of the business, including my name as the major partner and, per say, the first liable partner. It was easy because in Australia as in some countries you can buy a company off the shelf. Yes, some places have packages of companies pre made and ready to operate with the basic numbers and permits, at the local, state and federal levels. You need to pay the related fees and you are out the door with the company under your arm, including business cards.

Several times on that afternoon I had called Charlie to talk, telling him we needed to have a meeting. He was always busy, walking from one side to another in his office, sometimes with the phone on his ear, sometimes just grabbing paper pretending to be doing something, and then he was out to pick his daughter up from school and so on. Also there was no indication that I was going to meet up with my two other partners. Very weird. I was jumping over that big mess on the floor, trying to find the best spot to use my lap top. I also had my own projections. Then Charlie gave me a pile of Yellow Pages books from the entirety of Australia and from some Asian countries and spent the rest of the day saying out loud:

"Luís, that order from Quiksilver, if we deliver it by the end of the month it will be a good injection of cash."

"Luís, when you need to visit a supplier just let me know because I know everyone and everything in Victoria."

"Luís, there is an auction depot near by, we can go there and we mark whatever we want to set up the production line."

"Luís..." At one point I interrupted him, throwing a heavy Yellow Pages book on the floor. My blood was boiling out of my veins. We had just arrived in the country, our bones were soaked of so much rain and cold, our minds were yet getting used to the jet leg... The secretary of Charlie, wife of one of the other partners, already had Helga with her to help changing fixtures and office furniture around from the old office to the new one in the warehouse. But the things being juggled around were only things to do with appearances, nothing related to our new business. Ulisses was given a brush and he was painting the new office.

"Charlie! What's going on here!"

Finally we had arrived for good in Australia. Down Under the land of the "mate" pronounced "maait"; the land of the G'Day, good day for both Aussies and Pommies. Australia, a portion of land surrounded by water all around, inhabited originally by aboriginals, nowadays almost extinct by the historical discrimination by the British, condemned lifelong exile people. Australia is a country where the folklore is way less diverse than in my country Brazil, where there is a soma of ethnic groups, racial diversity and a huge colorful blend of folklore and original traditions, immeasurable opportunities of idiosyncrasies and the adoption to habits and costumes, a country of so many legends and historical internal conflicts from south to north, a country with so many regional stereotypes, tribes and cultural diversities, variety of food and so many options... So compared to Brazil, Australia is, at first glance, even with all its beauty, lacking of grace. Of course it was just my state of mind at the time, one that would change completely in the near future. Once you are cured from your own problems, Australia is breathtaking all the time anywhere.

But for a long time, the only original thing I thought Australia had was that pie - a kind of greasy pastry with hot stew inside.

...A dream leads us to madness.

After four months I had no doubt that I was going to get myself out of that partnership before it became too late. Once was already too much. Of course it was not going to be as easy as it appeared in the beginning. Within fifteen days I had new partners, money was deposited in my bank account... Hey! Wait a minute. The first dollars were a loan from Cathrine for petty cash, because I was left with empty pockets after the California business. Then twenty thousand dollars was a requirement of the Embassy and should be reimbursed to Cathrine. The rest I discovered with my own eyes right there in Australia. So, that feeling that money was falling from trees was because I lived on the moon. A dreamer, a poet, Bernardo the Zorro's friend, Tonto, the Indian friend of the Lone Ranger. Yes, it is all clear now, I had fallen among scumbags. What was I to do? I knew. I would play Scarface. It was not going to be easy to catch me, they would need to be much more macho to challenge me. Adrenaline started to gush out through my pores, my veins were pumping out of my neck, bursting out of my arms - I became a human bomb. Nobody would stop me. I had enough energy, an iron heart, and stainless steel nerves. I was going to fight with my nails and teeth till I bleed, if needed, and they will need to kill me eight times. Come and get me, get on the line, come as a bunch, I didn't care, it was the movie I was looking for. I was going to scream until my veins exploded and my blood splashed over everyone. I was at war.

I did not know what I was capable of. I was possessed. I walked by Charlie's office and made a signal for to him to follow me, to the parking lot. We walked outside and he was sort of jumping behind on my foot prints. It was the way he used to walk, jumping, and he thought I was going to tell him a secret. I had been noticing an outbreak of whispers lately and it was part of the reason of my wrath. In the parking lot I turned toward Charlie and grabbed his neck with one hand and with the other pointing a finger onto his nose spouting adrenaline and he opened two big blue eyes and trembling lips.

- "Don´t say anything you son of a..." – said I.

I was alternating my low voice with screaming between my teeth, mixing English with Portuguese, sputtering with my mouth only a few inches from his nose. Offending everyone related to him who of course I did not know.

- "Don't fuck around with me! I'm a fucking Latin!"

"Now, you son of a... (another round of cursing) we will go back inside, from now on you will say good morning, good afternoon, everyday as if nothing happened and never, ever, you will even think to cancel an order as you have being doing repeatedly. If you do I will beat the shit out of you! Did you get that?!"

I was shaking with anger. I spent the entire day with a crazy smile on my face but disguising the fact that I was actually feeling completely trashed. When I told Helga she dove into a sadness and immediately developed two giant dark circles under her eyes. Ulisses tried to joke saying I was turned into the character of Michael Douglas in the movie *Falling Down*, but it was no time for a joke - our lives were in chaos.

It was not only one thing in particular that triggered my madness. In fact, it started right when we first stepped into Charlie´s office. Four months went by but it was still too soon and it would be possible to replan the whole thing, a new route all together... with no partners. Once alone I was sure we could purify ourselves, or so I thought. We could work day and night and turn things to our favor. Our nature was intact, our consciousness were clean, we loved each other, we trusted each other; we had faith. If after we tried it our way and it didn't work, okay, we'd drop the towel. Luckily, the molding process was really easy. After assimilating the principle, any person would be able to execute. I was the man who discovered the suppliers of raw material in the United States; I was the buyer. I even paid a visit to the Goodyear manufacturing plant, to follow-up tests and collect samples for our first order. I became a theorist, but with goodwill I was going to be able to perform the production process. And as far as mixing colors, pigments and additives, retardants and hardeners – okay, I read a lot of technical literature and, after all, mixing colors is something we learn at school, like yellow and blue makes green, black and red with a bit of yellow is the color of a dunk when it runs away, and so on. I could do that standing on my head. Ulisses would handle the production line with Helga. This was our master plan anyway, even before we left for Australia.

Thus, recapping what I had done since we had arrived in Australia, I used a bunch of Yellow Pages books and sourced local suppliers. I called them all asking for samples. I went to an auctioneer Charlie recommended – "Hey, my new partners used to recommend me this and that, they were the capitalists - I was the work force" – and brought in working benches, all blue in color - my color. Yes, I was still as romantic as a person can be. Among the used fixtures I bought there was this giant table with low legs which looked like a street circle stage. It became the symbol of our production line. We progressed with leaps and bounds, while in rain and cold, while learning a new language, a new-English all together, and while learning to drive on the wrong side of the street - the factory was up and running within two weeks. That's right - I said, two weeks, in a country on the other side of the planet where I had never even dreamed of being. And we were early birds, having a quick breakfast everyday and off to work. When the three of us heard the train whistle we did not even dare to look at each other, for the train was a signal of a proletariat kind of life during war times, maybe in Russia it was like that or in old Europe, so we thought, because one day drinking wine at home we burst out laughing after realizing we had the same feeling.

Tacitly, we agree to make a sacrifice for a certain time until things got into a groove. Working an average of 12 hours per day, by the time we left the factory we had no place to go but the hotel we were living in. It was in a suburb and bars and restaurants were not so easily accessible. By that time we were tired anyway, wishing only to eat and crash, not to mention by that time the cold and rain - the standard pattern of weather - kept us wet to our bones. TV was as bad as the weather. So this was our routine during the first month and half when we started training employees. Charlie was always pressing me to speed up the production. To add to that, suppliers were struggling to get the raw material right, because we needed a specific unique degree of viscosity and no air in the component.

In the meantime we were wasting good ammunition and the true start up of production kept being postponed day after day. Until one day the first straight production run got the first order done. More orders literally started to pop up, one after another. We started to hire. I was working - dirty apron, on the phone with suppliers, at the computer, walking in and out of the production area, checking the performance of the newcomers, cheering up employees and making friendships while teasing them.

Helga was taking care of the cutting, packaging and production control, plus, at the end of the day she was handling a broom. Ulisses nailed his belly to the oven where we molded the products, 8 to 10 hours straight. When he needed more raw material mixed with the right pigment color he waved to me through the glass of my office and I would run up there to mix cups and pots of resins and pigments.

It was an amazing pace from early morning to late night. At one point we reached 14 hours per day, Monday to Saturday. On Sunday we were like old ragged sandals. Helga could not help herself, and she used to take work to do at home, after dinner. Since I was the cook, she took care of dishes and stayed in the kitchen alone, organizing the production and writing it over her spreadsheets. It was no use asking her to stop. I realized later it was the only way she could put up with the situation, not stopping, because if she stopped once to think about it, it would be her turn to melt the wedding ring to go back home.

There was an assuagement. Summer arrived; we left the hotel and rented an apartment at the beach, where we could witness the most beautiful sunset of the planet everyday. It was on the first floor, had a private garden in front of our living room window, 15 yards from the beach across street and it was in Brighton - the most beautiful neighborhood of Melbourne. A cosmopolitan city with romantic trolley cars, restaurants for every taste and wallet, and a bunch of options for entertainment and nightlife. Not to mention the many green parks which we started to enjoy one by one. So we became busy also on Sundays.

It was all going fine, considering the circumstances, but I felt a lack of many things. We were still operating precariously while fitting the factory with equipment and fixtures. The arrangement was as such: the three Latin-American goofies should produce, while the noble British men were managing the financial side of the business. This was the idea we all agreed. Only that the "factory" was selling products to the "business" of Charlie, Lawrence, and Irvin (my new Australian partners), and then they were reselling the products to the "real clients". It was then that all the problems culminated and I had that 'Scarface' moment, when I called Charlie to talk in the parking lot.

Meanwhile, Cathrine was sending at least three faxes per day from California. She was approaching prospects in Washington, New York, New Jersey, and Colorado... She was attending a Trade Show in Atlantic City. She was personally reaching out to prospects in the Ski wear segment in Canada and also working closely with a rep in England. It was a hell of a lot of dust she was kicking up, with half of her effort to keep linked to the plastic business and guaranteeing that I was going to honor my promise. We had a calendar date to set up a factory in Chula Vista, at the border of Mexico, a few miles from the boating center of San Diego. Thus, she strangled me, demanding sample orders as often as she could. Actually not only to feed her with samples but to reply to hers faxes was suffocating. One thing my partners were right about, I was taking their breath away with my pace, and now I was paying with the same currency to Cathrine's.

Charlie, Lawrence, and Irvin eventually said to me that I was not going to be able to fulfill my promise with Cathrine. That I should hold off, wait until the Australian operation was stabilized.

"Luís, she is stealing your time here at the factory. And after all, we need to review all the prices of sampling to the United States."

"Right. Let's take a chance and review all the prices in general. Because the "factory" sells to your "office" by half of the actual market price. This is not fair. And it's Charlie who sets the price you guys will pay for."

"No, Luis, wait..."

The conflict began. And the pressure from my partners to speed up production started to affect not only myself but my crew on deck. I was working the whole day with a pain in my chest. I was driving back and forth from home to work with that pain in my chest plus the discomfort of a shortness of breath. At night, I used to pray, asking God for a good heart made of iron and my nerves of stainless steel. Three months and we had fulfilled all the back log of orders. I had hired ten employees, including a handicapped man with serious mental disabilities but with whom I was able to quickly make a connection and start bonding. At that point I figured we should have reached the turn over. That is, revenues surpassed the liabilities with profit - the initial capital should have been paid out already.

Hey, we were operating a handcraft process that I just happened to streamline into mass production. We did not need much money to start up, just hard work.

I knew exactly how many cents each fixed asset represented. I adapted all the working benches bought from the auction place with my own hands. I knew the cost structure of the products from the raw material to the bottom line of the final cost. Again, I was the one buying raw material and all the supplies and was I the one who handed the paycheck to each employee on a weekly basis. So it was at least weird to have being called for that sort of meeting.

"Luís, we called you to talk about our need to borrow money from the bank, we need your signature. Look, wait, let us explain..." They were talking as if they were screwing light bulbs up into the ceiling with an entire egg in their mouths and as if they were sitting on top of a golf club, at least at that time it was the way British accent sounded to me

"Humm. Go on," I replied.

"Well, the first phase of the business is done. The factory operates at its full capacity. Now it is time to turn it into a profitable business. With the money we borrow from the bank we will honor the payroll and the overhead expenditures for six months. You will be able to hire more people. There is a line of credit with tax incentives for a certain size of business, you know..."

"Of course. I understand," I interrupted them. "But let me think a bit. Let's meet up again on the weekend."

I went home that Wednesday and worked throughout the night on the computer; I only slept a couple of hours. I went over the numbers of the factory of the last three months, including our travel expenses, and smelled a rat. They never supplied me with the General Ledger with the allegation that they were implementing a new integrated system with the payroll and stock. Give me a break. How many integration of applications had I implemented myself. I didn't catch it at first because we were in the beginnings of a business implementation so why discuss accounting details? But why wouldn't they supply me with at least a summary of figures since I was called for a meeting? I was the major partner, wasn't I? To me the numbers were positive, why borrow money from the bank?

They never touched the subject of borrowing money again, and Lawrence left for an interstate trip. Irvin was too busy; he had some liquidation of companies to take care of. Charlie went to attend a fair of Asian products. So I took the opportunity to start a pseudo-accounting system made out of plain spreadsheets. Helga helped me with inputs and homemade reports were automatically popping out of my Gateway laptop updated manually on a daily basis. It was like a game to me - so sweet was our company. It was simple as it had only three major suppliers, only one client (the office CLI – Charlie, Lawrence and Irvin); it was so easy to control, to manage. Then I asked Charlie for copies of the bank statements to reconcile accounts, since the whole production was bought from his office. Irvin stopped to liquidate companies and made a quick call, feeling offended, asking me if I was suspicious of something. Lawrence called from faraway begging me not to worry about numbers - that he would come back and explain the situation. Charlie, the spineless among them, could not look at me in the eyes and told me that the "master", Irving, was mad at me.

Wow, wow, why so much of an uproar just because I asked for the general ledger and bank statements? Something was smelling bad.

When I called Charlie to the parking lot and unloaded my adrenaline on him, the fact that he had canceled an order after I delivered the goods, was just the last straw. It was that same week that I asked for the accounting reports and they did not give them to me, with the most creative excuses. Some other facts I later recollect would contribute to the smell of rats I had been detecting lately.

"O.k.," I said to my partners once again. "Let's talk about the bank loan that you want, but I need to take a look at the accounting reports of the company."

As if with an entire egg in each of their mouths, the way they talked, they were trying to explain the reason why the company did not have cash flow. I was amazed, looking at the columns of the sweet spreadsheets of my dear little company.

All the expenses of the "sales office" of Charlie were paid by the factory. Worse, our factory already had a giant debit account due to the fact that, in accounting terms, the factory was borrowing money from the "office" of Charlie; it was forged financial engineering, and, the twenty thousand dollars that Cathrine had transferred pro forma was still pending refund. It was accounted as a loan without her acknowledgement. They were sending her small portions of reimbursement, whenever she followed up asking what was going on.

The one fact that upset me beyond the limit was when Lawrence and Irvin invited me for a private lunch without Charlie. They told me were figuring out a way to get a rid of him from the partnership. It was an old issue that had been brewing for a long time between them. Charlie used to generate too high of expenses and recently closed a deal with a client in Africa that could lead them all to bankruptcy - a deal of an international uncollected check. Interpol was investigating the case. They could not understand the numbers that Charlie produced for them; they were managing an already unbearable situation. The "factory" would be a lifeline but they now admitted that they started the business with the wrong foot.

It was not the KGB, CIA nor the ISIS, but I could well think that CLI (Charlie-Lawrence-Irvin) were playing me like a spy in a B movie. It could have been a big joke if I didn't feel a stab right in my soul cutting through my tissues and nerves. Helga said we didn't need that - we could just leave, go away, go home. And she was right. Ulisses was following it all without saying a word. He was a guy of few words. But it was clear that the party was over for him. Soon, very soon he would give up and go back to California.

That afternoon, after that private secret lunch with the other two, I noticed Charlie slyly taking notes of everything on a notepad; he seemed to be doing an inventory of fixtures, tools and material. He spotted the production line and covertly jotted down more notes, then the stock stacks, and as he walked towards each work bench, he pretended to be just thinking and making random notes. I suspected something was going on and it felt off to me. After what seemed to be an entire inventory was complete, he stayed in his office reading the newspaper after hours, contrary to his routine to hit the road to go home at around five. Well, to me and my crew it was easy to carry into the third shift so I told Helga and Ulisses that I had a bad feeling and was going to wait to see what Charlie was doing.

I said to them, "I want to see where this mummery will end."

My blood started to boil. I realized the trap I was in. I would not catch a plane back home before tearing a piece off of them with my own teeth. It was already 10:00pm and the phone rang. I had an impulse and grabbed the extension on the wall of the factory and heard the voice of Irvin.

"Hi Charlie," he said.

"You can send your watchman home because I will not leave tonight," I said, almost going through the wire to deliver the message in person. "If you want to play games come here face to face."

Irvin was so upset that he could not say a word; he sounded something perhaps a folk Aussie-Pommy archaic expression. I hung up the phone and started to walk back and forward aimlessly, irate. These sons of a bitch are setting me up! I thought aloud. Why? Why? I kept saying to myself just like Sean Connery acting as *King Arthur*, Why?! Why?!

A moment later, Lawrence rushed into the factory, sweating and nervous. "Luís, I came in running to try to come to terms with you. Irvin is upset as I've never seen before. He is about to seal the building tonight. He can do this. Tomorrow you will not be able to get in. The situation is delicate. Calm down, Luís. I know how to deal with Irvin. I will call him and try to set up a meeting now. Ok? Easy, Luis, ok, take it easy let's talk, ok?"

The Building

Luís Peazê

...All we want is to go back.

We took over the factory in Australia with fifty thousand dollars in debit to suppliers and only two hundred dollars in our bank account. Solo, with no partners, ten employees and lots of clients. From now on - no middle man. I was going to deal and make decisions directly with each one, supplier, clients and employees. I felt a taste of victory.

I promised to Lawrence to take it easy on the meeting provided we drank wine. He laughed and as a matter of fact it did help to relax tempers. So we signed an agreement.

I adopted a strategy to lose in the retail and win the wholesale. My tactic for the meeting was to make quick decisions, like "this is mine", "no this is yours", "I don't want this", "I want this". Thus, they transferred their stocks in the business to my name and I became a sole proprietorship. The only demand I made was that we should recap and clean up, make the accounting history clear because I wanted to finally know exactly what happened. This way we set apart what belonged to their business and what belonged to the factory. It was my personal play of moral victory.

The beginning of November was the calendar date set for the stocks to be transferred officially into my hands. In February, just two months away I was to be in San Diego to set up the factory for Cathrine who found two investors to put money in the US chapter - the Uncle Sam project I had promised to her. She was horrified following the affair in Australia. I was driving a crazy train downhill with no breaks. But, as they say in plain Castilian in my home town, the Gaucho land of Rio Grande, "não morre quem peleia" (no one who fights dies).

And my first decision as the owner of the factory was to revolutionize the Harvard business management theory. I decided to increase the debts, multiply them actually, almost triple them all. I decided that the only way to remain on the damn island was if I build my dream. My yacht. Just so I could then sail away to quite anchorages with white sand beaches with palm trees. I would be able then to rest in peace with my true and dear partner, Helga, the other side of my own soul, a piece of myself without which I could not have survived that storm. I would sail to a place I could talk with the sunset and gaze at the horizon with my Indian look.

We did not know from where we found so much energy, but the truth was that we were feeling renewed animus. I asked Helga if she would help me build the boat in Australia. Just like that, I asked her without thinking too much; it came out instantaneously as it popped in my mind and immediately we felt a change, a good vibe surrounding us, embracing us. It was like tearing off old notes from a scrap notepad and to start building a new life.

"I will help you, yes, let's build the boat," Helga replied.

From that moment onward we started to live in a different dimension attainable only by dreamers. We decided that we would transform the factory into a profitable business; Helga started to dream the same dream with me, and we would begin building the boat immediately then we would sell the factory and would be free. Happy ending.

I reduced the number of employees to just three. Ulisses and two ladies - the best we had on the production line - a mother and daughter. I also kept the mentally disabled fellow because I had a natural sympathy for him. He did not produce a thing, but also did not disturb; in fact he and I used to laugh out loud at each other, so I used to say to him, while he was trying to assemble key rings: "Stick the scissors in yourself. I want to see if you are crazy." He'd then threaten to do it but then laugh at me while saying like a child of 3 or 4 years old:

"Funny, very funny. "

Crazy and perhaps irresponsible on my part, but the truth is that we established a sort of unique way of communicating; I felt we trusted and understood each other. The institution which brought him to us with several others said he was the most difficult of the group. So I asked them to leave David (his name) with me and it was one of the best rewards I could have had. Day by day I noticed David become more self-confident in the way he walked, asked questions and even sometimes had initiative. His mother sent me a note one day saying he kept talking at home about Luis, his friend. I was touched and rewarded indeed.

The third decision was to call each supplier and negotiate the invoices I had to pay. With each one I put on the table an order equivalent to an entire year, with a time frame for delivery in doses equivalent to a month and signed promissory notes. They agreed. Thus from debtor at risk I became a premium client. Next, I called my clients and offered them a huge discount provided they could pay all the invoices right away as well as pay upfront for the new orders for the next three months. Looking back I did not do anything too fancy as a business manager, but the way it was done and the timing were the perfect leverage we needed. And a win-win solution. We kept on working hard, three shifts, but now we were smiling and on our own feet. The orders started to go out of the door steady and smoothly and, by the third month, we not only broke even but went straight ahead to a true profit status with cash in hand. However, with the accounting reports showing the amounts of the promissory notes there was still so much hard work ahead.

It was the end of January, therefore I had to fly to San Diego. I sent one lady on vacation leave, then called clients and advised them that the factory would be on a slower mode during the month of February. This way I could travel to the United States and leave Helga to take care of basically everything, but at a comfortable pace, considering the circumstances. That image and feeling stayed in my mind and heart forever, boarding the plane with my chest compressed, leaving Helga holding the crazy train, now not on a runaway path downhill but still steaming. That was not for her but she had been handling so much so far, with guts and her characteristic delicacy. On one hand she did not have experience, but on the other hand she did not have the addictions of those who had worked in the trade or main stream. She was used to the academic environment and was not prepared to face that jungle of so-called cynical businessmen and women so I was so proud of her. Ulisses and Dione, the other lady's daughter, were producing an order at a time each; normally it would be a hectic pace of two or three orders simultaneously. Helga, then, would jump in as a one-woman-show to cut, assemble (labels and key chains), packaging, printing invoices and shipping. In between she would make payments and keep me updated in San Diego. We were both missing each other terribly; we would talk for an hour on a daily basis over the phone and from the day I left we were counting the days until we'd reunite. I run that marathon with the tongue out falling down but now we had an arrival point:

"The boat is coming along!"

On each fax, or each phone call that I got from Helga while I was in San Diego, she ended with the phrase: "The boat is coming along!"

With such a push I could move mountains. But from then onward Helga would have all the merits on her account. From this point on I would not be able to build the boat without the dedication and competence of Helga. Each figure was written down with care in our control sheets, especially those personal notes; each initiative that I would take would have Helga's hand and opinion. And we would not make mistakes anymore, or the mistakes would be so naive that would worth to make them.

...A dream cannot split the love.

The trip to the United States was a dramatic one. According to my promise to Cathrine, I was to stay for one month working full-time in San Diego and within that time frame I was to get the factory up and running, operating - meaning making labels, key chains, mattress, parts for gloves and zipper pulls and all the new products that I was coming up as a machine gun of new ideas. Before I went to San Diego, Cathrine played the bugle via fax and phone calls and I was feeling like General Custer going to fight the Apaches.

Any logical thinking or healthy mind would have advised me to cancel that trip, or at least postpone it. But Cathrine understood me; she found the right way to push me and was doing a great job.

"Luís, when you arrive here you will lean back in the chair and put your feet up on the desk. We have everything as per your instructions," were Cathrine's words right before I boarded the plan in Melbourne. She carried on, "You will train employees, and show me how to run the factory and we will visit some clients together in San Diego and Los Angeles. We can even perhaps check it out your "ranch" in Colorado".

And right there, she hit my soft spot. How come I forgot that?

On that very day my ex-partners in Marin County gave me the bad News that our partnership would end the day 12th of that month, I received in the mail a proposal to buy 5 acres in Colorado, in the middle of no where but it was without down payment and only US$30,00 per month. Again, soaked in two or more glasses of wine I signed the papers and put a check back in the mail to Rio Grande Ranches. And as Helga is so picky with bills, we kept paying monthly basis. Well, I had my share of being a little picky too and had asked Brian Kelly, my friend lawyer in San Francisco, to look at the papers and advise me how serious or bad that could be and he said that at first sight nothing looked wrong other than the land would be a long term investment, not a short one, so I kept auto paying and forgot it completely. Now Cathrine reminded me and it became an extra carrot in front of the bunny. I wanted to see "my ranch" in Colorado. Wait a minute: Colorado is the name of my soccer team in Brazil, Rio Grande is the name of my home state South of Brazil, the ranch was in a town called San Luís.

"Habemos una manufatura, arriba muchacho!" she used her Spanish well on me (We have a factory, come on man!).

An old warehouse was leased in Chula Vista, near the border with Mexico, twenty minutes from San Diego. That would be the last commitment with "factories and partners". I would hold on to 15% of the stocks without the need to do a thing but to follow up from Australia. I would honor my word. I would take the time to set up the factory for Cathrine, and would carry it on with my own fate and freedom. Thus I flew to the other continent as a pre-set robot. It seemed strange to be in Australia, then all of the sudden in the US, and then to cross the border into Mexico. One month would go by fast - I was praying – because even before leaving Melbourne I was already missing Helga. On the plane I was looking down through the window at the floor of clouds and could not think of anything else but coming back to Australia. The fact that I was traveling to set up a factory apparently became already a routine to me. The molding process was an old friend; I had mastered it thoroughly. I knew the cost structure and dimension of the business, and the segments of market we could reach and so on. I'd established a streamlined process and had a mental manual to follow, tested, and approved. Finally, my ideas of no frills and flexibility were the trade secret of management and marketing. Helga was left alone, and I felt a bit of guilt mixed with pride seeing her performing many roles so well, and then to hear the great news: "The boat is coming along!" encouraged me. At the X-ray security check point when we left each other I heard these last words from Helga, "I love you; the boat is coming along!"

Feeling impossible to be translated, like a phrase by Rainer Marie Rilke: "there are situations in a human life, unspeakable, they happen in a space that no word has ever entered."

Adding to the psychological effect of the situation, I was exhausted. But the human body is unpredictable. Even entirely healthy, a person may not be able to rise from the living room couch and grab a cup of water in the kitchen. The same body however will cross an entire desert if needed, depending on the circumstances. Definitely we are our circumstances.

So I have learned that one's word is a treasure one needs to nourish and protect; I gave my word to Cathrine and then had to honor it.

With a Passport expired I had to renew it at the American embassy, but the clerk office was relentless.

"You will need to apply for new Visa, Sir."

This now. There were back and forward trips to the Embassy within two weeks. At the first try my application was declined. My situation was too confusing. Arriving less than a year ago in Australia, I intended to go back to the United States, with my last home address in Northern California. In Brazil my last home address dated back two years and the balance sheet of my business in Australia showed solid numbers only on the very month I was applying for a Visa. Even I would have assessed the situation thoroughly before stamping a Visa on a Passport of such a person - a Latino with giant grey circles under his eyes, wearing a suit and tie he lost the swing of for an apron dirty of color pigments. At the last minute I was able to get the Visa only after hiring a very expensive and competent expert lawyer.

San Diego is an American city where people like the outdoor life more than in any other American city, where you see toned young bodies all over, an upscale lifestyle, and at the time the official arena for the America's Cup, the famous millionaire yacht race World Cup.

Speaking of boats, in January, before boarding the plan for the crazy adventure because I'd given my word to set up a factory in San Diego, I had run the circuit of boatbuilders in Melbourne and surrounding areas. It was invigorating to reopen the pink folder with the blue prints of Helga II - the would-be name of my dream boat. Helga and Ulisses accompanied me to talk with local boatbuilders and experts in all the spare time we could afford. From virtually any backyard, a boatbuilder or expert or both would come out and start to assess my dream boat plans. So knocking door by door I found Pompei - a raspy mix of Italian and Greek, well-known all over Down Under and even overseas. His grandfather built boats, his father built boats, and all he knew was to build boats as well. I was in front of a true living legend. It was passion at first sight, and how easily I could transcend my own wish of building a boat and go further, diving deep into a world of fantasy. Pompei was finishing building a 56 foot wooden boat, a traditional design similar to an schooner for charter. I became a frequent visitor; his shop was on the way to the factory, between Brighton and Seaford going up north from Melbourne so a quick stop became a must, but he was pushing me away and never could give me a time frame to build Helga II, and a price. I was impatient and one day he said he would build a stronger boat for me; he would use thicker lumber, with old traditional techniques instead of epoxy, plywood and fiberglass cloth, so not according to my original plans. Thus, contrary to a voice inside my chest I had to decline Pompei. While he seemed to be planing timber with his bare hands, I was introduced to a man who was willing to follow the original plans, a cabinetmaker. I liked the man and we made a verbal agreement.

So with the same pace I used to start up factories, I ordered wood to build Helga II, hearing everyday, "The boat is coming along." The cabinetmaker was hired to work by the hour; he would be building the jig and division panels at the back of the warehouse. He would also buy tools to unfold the wood and then wait for me to come back from San Diego so together we would start building the boat. From that point on I became so anxious, fearing that something could jeopardize the building of my dream. That's not going to happen this time, I used to say to myself, I will build my boat.

Helga wouldn't let me doubt myself. "The boat is coming along," she kept on saying. Every time an order bounced, a client delayed the approval, or a payment was delayed a day or two - any minor incident would make me fear the end of building of my dream. Sometimes the cabinetmaker wouldn't show up for work and my heartbeat would increase. No, I kept saying in my thoughts, that's not going to happen this time, the factory will make the money I need. At all costs, "The boat is coming along." It was our mantra.

With Helga's voice in my mind, I landed in San Diego on the promised calendar date, and one month later I was ejected with no mercy as a package back to Australia. One month as planned but I became simply a sad deception to Cathrine. It was clear since the beginning in San Diego that as in the music by Louis Armstrong, our friendship was yet to be designed. We clashed at everything; it never would be a happy marriage. Even with my bacon for breakfast she implied. From my end, I was not get in her four-wheel drive with her hysterical female dog. Cathrine was expecting me to be charming in a way of managing business, witty and joyful altogether, easy-going in a way. Together we had thought we'd make a terrific couple. She trusted in her atomic power to make connections with great turnover, expecting that I was going to manage many areas simultaneously, under pressure, with an unshakeable temper and being creative even while sleeping. A week later my arrival she had a nervous breakdown, a typical scene from a soap opera, in tears she babbled, "Where did I do wrong? Where? I can't, I can't ..."

I could not believe what I was seeing either. It was the same old movie. There was no working benches, no tools, nothing done in order for me to start hiring guys that were already lined up and ready to train. I would have to assemble the ovens, benches and get raw material, pigments and so on. On top of that, right from the beginning it was clear Cathrine was not skilled in business management. She was more like a blind person in the middle of a street shooting. And more, the two investors she had secured were there with their hands in their pockets, walking like docks out of the pool; they showed up to meet the famous Luís, who "brought the handcraft plastic molding process" and by the time we shook hands they said in chorus:

"We will revolutionize this process, revamp it."

Considering all the previous developments, I was more than hyper and worse, I became mad. I could not believe what I was seeing - those two white collars, wearing khaki pants and social shirts with sleeves perfectly rolled up, one of them carrying a small plastic tool box like a toy, showing up on a Saturday morning to help me to build the ovens, benches and fixtures. The least of my problems was that there were no galvanized metal sheets to build the six ovens, the electrical resistances and fittings, the wool insulation and other pieces and bits – yes, I became electrical engineer too, from day to night. Before assembling them all I designed the ovens cassette type. There is with a tray to slide in and out with the molds full of liquid plastic mix and this was the basics of the said molding process – there was nothing - I had to shop around and buy everything. But before I could begin I had to shout at those two businessmen to go home so that I could work and honor my promise to Cathrine.

Then, I was able to give Cathrine a step-by-step training and asked her several times, "Did you understand? Did you do this and that?"

She was steaming with anger but her money and dream of a house with white column were at stake so there was no time to waste and we engaged the best each of us could. Cathrine even did a great job at trying to calm me down a little by introducing me to a boat builder who had recently built the keel of Dennis Conner's yacht - the famous boat winner of the last America's Cup, brought from Australia back to American hands. We had a dinner in a restaurant where all the hardcore sailors used to hang out. A day later we went to the San Diego Yacht Club to see the America's Cup trophy and the fancy race yachts.

Ah! Now that's what I was talking about, mingling with the boating community - now all I needed was to build my boat and to learn how to sail.

Despite my reprehensible, objectionable, exceptionable, deplorable, faultfinding behavior, I was happy driving all around Chula Vista seeking a welder, iron man, fixtures, benches, tools, supplies and candidates to work in the factory. Within a week I found Ernandes, who was soon going to be the general manager of that manufacturing business. He picked up the process in a snap and while he was practicing mixing colors and resin I was in and out like the Road Runner from Looney Tunes, bip, bip, going to buy things, order materials and solve issues. Bip, bip.

Wow! The factory was finally set up. Ernandes grabbed the process so quick and he was a spectacular human figure. On the side he was an artist, painter of oil on canvas so that's why it was so easy for him to mix colors and to handle the handcraft process. As far as managing the production and deal with employees he said to me, "Well, it is all in the manual you gave to me, Luís, I just need to execute. Listo" ("Listo" is Spanish for ready, like "consider it done, I am on it.")

On the very week before my return flight, the first order was ready to go out the door. The UPS guy showed up without imagining what had been happening in the last three weeks, or the last year, or where I came from, and he handed me a slip to sign while I handed him a package of plastic labels. I was exhausted needless to say; I did not have time to do anything else in San Diego other than a single drive through the border into the Mexican territory to be amazed with the mess and poor conditions of Tijuana.

The budget Cathrine had for my stay did not allow much more than food and a hotel anyway. It didn't matter; my commitment was accomplished. I could return to Australia. Please, Cathrine, do it, dump me at the Lost Angeles airport, don't even bother with kiss and bye, just bye will do.

...Dream and love.

Landing at the Melbourne airport I found Helga anxiously waiting for me and so was I, eager to see her. She was skinny, had lost weight. "What have I done to you my Helga?"

We hugged each other for a long time in silence and then cried. She couldn't have handled that for another day. A storm of guilt, compassion, pride and pleasure took over me at the very moment I saw her in the waiting room - how strong, how fragile, how bold she was, and pretty and weakened. She hung on to the situation and circumstances as much as or beyond what she could; she had not let me know how hard it had been even half of all that she had gone through. I could not do a thing from San Diego, or could I? This question was useless - she would have done anything to soften things up for me, knowing I was in another country away from home as she was too.

"Helga. I am here now? – Look: I felt guilty since I left month ago, I should not have left you on your own taking care of the factory and everything."

"Don´t tell me anything now. It is over. And the boat is coming along!" she said, smiling, the most beautiful smile I had ever seen.

We needed to relax and talk about good things. From then on we were done with commitments to third parties. We were responsible to ourselves only. Let's go home. There was a fish dish waiting for us. And there was also a gift from my friend and production manager Ulisses. He bought me a Windex, an arrow that goes on top of the mast of a yacht to show the direction of the wind. Symbolically he wanted to say that now I needed to build a boat under it and he wished fair winds to me.

On Monday morning when I opened the door of the factory, early before seven o'clock, I went straight to see the woods of Helga II. Mahogany - first class - the color of earth and blood. And I made sure to pass my hand on each pile against the wall of the warehouse and prayed softly. The marine plywood sheets were also of first class degree, clear of imperfections without a single small knot. Once I heard that the difference between a home-built boat and a manufactured branded one is that gradually the home built boat acquires a soul, a bit both from the owner-builder and from the woods applied, more exactly the soul that lives in the trees. For this reason she, the boat, must be built with special care. My boat was being grown with love in a passionate fashion. And I would touch each tiny bit of it since the first scratches on the floor.

I began to alternate between happy and sad moments – sometimes, somehow, both together. I was building my dream and then Helga received a letter from her mother who disagreed with our idea of building a boat and sailing back to Brazil. She was going to visit us in Australia and canceled the trip, next she felt sick because she was stressed about the disagreement. My sister sent a letter telling me she wished to join us in Australia, and about her financial ordeal trying to survive in Brazil, a country more and more stumbling in scandals of corruption, a bad economy and an awkward system. I had just arrived in Australia and opened a factory then a second operation in United States - how would I explain to her my unstable situation and that I was going to live the country back home? My father was producing miracles with his retirement earnings. All these affairs were cutting my flesh and bones and the threat of becoming like a pinball back and forward by making a stormy decision living all behind and flying to meet Helga´s mother, my father, my sister, it was a torture to me... I must be a bit selfish now, I thought, to make something good at least for me and Helga. I needed to be brave. But the news from Brazil did not improve. Within a month we learned that Helga's mother's illness had worsened.

How about the factory that I had left in water bath? Well, I had to wake it up. Start calling clients, shake the bugs out of it.

It's funny. The lack of demand for any company is obviously worse than the overload of incoming orders. But I found a way to have both problems. I had drowned the clients eager for labels, key rings, zipper pulls, rubber mattresses and special projects so I could leave for San Diego; now just two months later I needed to resurrect them all with mouth to mouth. The major segment we targeted was the active wear, clothing and accessories of sports and outdoor gear. There were other segments but this brought the bread and butter. Since I did not have a sales team (I did not want one, each sales person would wanted to become my partner and would ask me to open a factory), I opened my own machine gun over the phone and fax so these were my sales tools. I operated this way since the beginning, cold calls, during two years, and made only a single visit to only one client.

So with the phone and fax firing up I heard from Helga, "The boat is coming along!"

Once I resurrected clients, the factory started to steam up to the top then I would hold the phone calls for a while and would blast them back onward as needed. Perfect little homemade machine. We arrived as early birds, never after seven o'clock. I would go straight to the small lab to prepare color mixing and raw material for the daily production. Then I would make my calls and send some faxes and would dive straight into my favorite nest, my stall of dreams, the boatbuilding shop set up in the back corner of the warehouse.

Helga went straight to the production assembling line to cut, sort, assemble, pack, standing most of the day, non-stop or only for the restroom and meals. At the end of the day I would be the office-boy and delivery guy to drop orders for molds and ship packages for clients via Federal Express and DHL. We were the kings of the last minute and never lost to the clock. Ulisses, like that advertisement of the battery that exhausts gradually until it has no more energy, started to give us the signal that he would soon abandon ship. The winter arrived and it would take a lot of will, an indomitable will to carry it on. Compared to a marathon, we were not yet half-way.

David, our friend with mental restriction, remained pretending he would stick the scissors in his own eyes and I kept saying to him to go on, stick it, just to hear his childish pure laugh. I used to steal a bite from his sandwich, invite him do dance, and asked him to answer the phone. He had a blast, saying, "Funny, very funny."

At the other end of the line people would think we were a bunch of crazies but we were just kids taking life very spontaneously seriously as kids do.

Eventually Ulisses did decide to leave, to go back to the USA. We understood him. We went to drop him at the airport and wished him happiness, to find his dream in California. Yes, at least he got to know Australia.

...Love is to dream together.

We were finally alone. We always liked to be alone, just the two of us, like on a honeymoon. As a matter of fact we even celebrated a second wedding ceremony. I had decided during the trip in San Diego to order a pair of gold wedding rings with the engraving of the three runic deities. My original wedding ring was melted to become my golden anchor pin, so I decided to surprise Helga with a second pair. Later on the same week I carved by hand the same runic deities names on the stem of the boat – if you don't know what it is, you are just like I was at that moment learning that the stem of a boat is the strong wood following the keel and forming the bow, were the Vikings used to hang figureheads supposedly with protective function of warding off evil spirits – so one afternoon alone at the warehouse we got married once again. We drunk a bottle of wine, ate bread and cheese and were silent for a long moment.

Someone said once that I was a dreamer; I also heard that I looked like Don Quixote and Helga was Sancho Panza. I heard that we had a romantic view of what life is, as if those likeness and life perspectives could be negative or worse, pejorative. I actually had been all of that with pride and it was good. I feel sorry for those never tried to free dive into a dream, fighting if needed to make it come true, to get lost in a world of fantasy if that is what it would take, to go beyond where money can buy. That's it, a romantic view of life is to go beyond the horizon, where money can't buy. To dedicate at least once in a lifetime to where you want to go, not where you said to or, worse, stay still in a false feeling of safety until the dangerous called life has passed. Of course, sometimes to accomplish a dream very often you need to work hard to make money, and spend it fast as when you are building a boat, for instance.

Now there has been happened the runic wedding and it would make the difference. That pain in the chest was gone as well as that threat that my heart was not made of iron and my nerves not of stainless steel. They were not but from then on I needed it to be less and less. I started to wake up each morning as if I was going for a picnic. We were going to work hard, each day, but, Hey! "The boat is coming along." I was going to scream at many people but I knew they were just after-shocks. Soon they would disappear. Our problem was only one: money. The payroll of two employees plus the cabinet maker, the overhead of the factory, those son-of-a-bitches and our personal expenses because we still living in the most beautiful and expensive place of Melbourne. After these financial commitments I had to buy material to build the boat. I was writing checks one after another, three, four and five figures, never having done that before especially with that speed and frequency. The cash inward speed was slower than the disbursement. Looking at the bank statement the money was coming out of it the day before it was actually arriving. Deposits and payments were always to cover debit balance. We prayed, peaking at the envelopes of our mail like a poker player wishing badly that a payment from a client was in there. When it was not it was a torture. My cold calls were the way to feed the chicken of golden eggs. Off the top of my head I knew several key client's phone numbers. I also kept on my desk a list of names and the nature of their businesses, the segment of market and the seasonal pre launching trade show schedule all over Australasia and in the USA. So it was like half scientific prospection of order to be with a strong wishful thinking power. I never missed an opportunity to bring in easy orders with easy payments because we did not have the privilege to maintain a portfolio of pending payments. Around that time I liked to believe I was able to pick the brain of each one at the other end of the line and close a sale. It rarely did not work. Ah-Ah! One order, a shout out to the production line. The factory was then performing like a well-greased steam machine.

Sometimes Helga left a quick note on my desk or in my pocket: "the boat is coming along!"

" ... They are many the perils in life

For those who have passion..."

... To live a great love it is very, very important to live always together.

The two being a single defunct if possible.

So no one will die of pain...

...To live a great love it needs permanent care

Not only with the body, but also with the mind

Because any minor down of yours

Your lover will feel and it will cool down the love..."

Vinicius de Moraes

...To sort out what it is from what is not.

The cabinet maker was called Arles and, well, he also used to screw lamps while talking as if he had an egg in the mouth. Yet at the end of the first day of work I had already lost patience with him, and when he called it a day I felt sorry thinking to myself, Oh no! I will need to attack as the Bage Psychoanalyst (a title by a Brazilian author – popular best seller – a comical narrative, the story is about a character who is an orthodox Freudian psychoanalyst, typical from Rio Grande do Sul, a gaucho and his characteristic rustic way of dealing with things in life, no so delicate). The Bage Psychoanalyst usually welcomes the patient with a blow on the chin right when he open the clinic's door.

The plans supplied by the yacht designer were abundant in details since they were made for amateur builders or the BYO Market (Built Your Own). Before Arles was hired and we had started to discuss how to build the boat, I'd called the yacht designer in Brazil and announced officially that I was going to start to build the boat, so I was going to maybe need some help.

Surprisingly, after eleven years, he remembered me and the name of my would-be boat, Helga II. So I asked him if there was any update on that particular design and he said there was an upgraded design - a foot longer at 30 feet, and much more modern in lines and performance. It had the same structural concept of the Samoa 29' but since I was from deep South of the Rio Grande, where winds are crazy, waves are no less, and the cold is as severe as it is anywhere near the Patagonia, and because he thought I was a brave experienced sailor, plus, well, I was living in Australia - I had to have a faster yacht. I felt like changing the bride at the very altar of wedding. The Samoa 30' was like a sister with an extra twinkle that poised me. There I was with the Samoa 30' plans instead of 29' to build Helga II.

Arles did not know how to read blueprints and got scared to the point of not even hiding it. I was going to have the designer at hand on the phone whenever I needed him so it was not going to be a problem. Thus we started to unfold the lumber in strips and scale needed for each part of the boat structure. I became intoxicated with a kind of happiness. One day I took a true shower in sawdust, inebriated with the smell of the wood, as if it was a wine grape harvest; I felt I was a Spanish woman at the menarche kneading grapes with bare feet, mixing my fears unbearable and unknown desires with the soul of the boat while it was being conceived.

On that day Helga thought it was very poetic but made a protest, "Ok, the boat is coming along, but you don't need to exaggerate."

Under Helga's protest I always had a small splinter of wood or a piece of sawdust in my hair, in the office, in the car and even at home 30 km from the boatbuilding shop. And we had a new problem. The sawdust was in fact infernal. It infiltrated in every single little corner everywhere. It became a conflict then between the factory and the boatbuilding and despite that the president of the company and the would-be boat builder was not bothered; we had to sweep those three thousand square feet twice a day at least. And it was sweeping and wiping some areas with a wet rag, starting first thing in the morning. Every day it was the same routine. On the weekends we collected tons of sawdust and dumped out scraps of wood. Those pretty scraps of wood.

One by one my clothes were acquiring spots of resin. We had to impregnate each single piece of wood with at least two coats of West System as they told me it was the best resin. My waterproofing had to be absolute, the durability incomparable. I did not care if my bank account was slim. Let me see. Yes, this one, I will call him and he will place an order. I thought to myself, to pan clients by segment and season and with a hyper optimism the orders would come in and the dollars needed arrived on time. Well, the next day was close enough.

In two weeks we unfolded wood with the proper thickness and width as per the plans of the boat. Following the process we built the jig, a sort of false disposable skeleton where the boat gets its form during the building process. As I read from the manual of building I learnt each step right before actually performing the needed tasks and this became another routine - a true learning on the job process. Each minor step was done like discovering the growth of a child in the womb – to me it was like a burst of speechless happiness. The stem with those runic deities carved by hand, the ribs of the boat, the ballast structure, the bulkheads, or, to me at that moment, the spine. Once they were all together I could visualize Helga II; still it was only a dream just two thirds to the finishing line.

Strip planking and laminating is a process of building with layers of wood, in the case of Helga II, in which one can create virtually any curve or shape. Starting with thin strips, easy to bend, piling them up, glued with resin and fastened with stainless steel screws until the boat reaches its entire ordinary shape according to the plans. It may sound easy but not so much for someone who had never built anything before, other than just recently learning how to build electrical ovens for the plastic manufacturing of active wear components and still amazed with what had been accomplished.

Up until Nathanael Herreshoff, an American legend of the boating industry, who developed the method of building a boat upside down it had been built upright from the ground up. Helga II used the upside down method as almost every single leisure boat is built nowadays. And it reaches a phase during the process that is the great D day, the turn over to work on the interior and deck phase when we are able to say that we almost have a boat ready to launch, a phase that precedes the most delicate and slow future series of phases in the boat building. Of course I did not have a sense of this time table speed and was dreaming of the turn over D day of Helga II.

We established (me and Arles) daily ambitious goals for four arms.

"Let's try Arles, if we fail I assume the failure."

Helga II started to unveil her pretty curves and everyone passing by the factory stopped to check in on the boatbuilding, always amazed, leaving the father of the would-be baby-to-be-born very proud.

"How pretty she is! Her curves! Her spaciousness! She will be fast! Wow! She looks strong... What care in building!"

Boats, for the British and Australians, are named with the female pronoun with a capital letter, 'She', meaning respect and admiration, but they don't blink to criticize a minor mistake. I was flattered. Helga II did not have a single negative comment.

I had a flip chart pinned on the wall showing the major weekly steps. On the same sheet the major parallel steps were on the preparation stage. The daily tasks of management were somehow organized and as much as I could I practiced time management for buying parts, raw material, and general supplies. Finally, I called Arles to talk once a week to discuss the following days' goals and tasks, also to repeatedly walk through our projections of goals, raise questions about details, and a lot of etcetera's.

It was a walk in the park for me updating those projections, switching plans on the wall like leaves from a coconut tree and discussing things with the cabinet maker (promoted to boat builder). At the end of each working day, after Helga and I had cleaned the factory, she would find a way to give one more touch up with a rag, wiping dust while I checked materials and touched parts of the boat, my baby. I had never sailed before and it would be many months until I accomplished that yet but I was building a pretty nice yacht as a grown up. The truth is that I did not know a thing about boating but at the buying department I was doing a great job. On time management methodology in place as a major rule I was buying each item exactly when it was needed. It could not be in any other fashion anyway, money did not come from my freezer. The frenzied pace of managing the factory, fishing potential orders from a list of clients, was also fed by a serious job of researching suppliers for the boat building, calling them up, negotiating with them; I was getting the lowest price I could and closing the purchase at the very last minute, right before I had to use each item or execute each step. I had a queue of suppliers from all over Australia some calling me several times to follow up on my needs.

Looking at my spreadsheet I realized how optimized the final cost of materials were, and so the overall of the boat building. And it was with a sort of an adrenaline rush that I used to contemplate those final figures because the fact was that the initial figures were simply prohibitive, and so a strong dose of an indomitable wish became my daily addiction to make my dream come true. And many times I neglected to let Helga know how doped I was. She would not get that high with me; that is what I was afraid of at least and I never knew the truth because when she saw me sad and concerned about buying something expensive for the boat she encouraged me saying, "Keep searching you will find it; you always do." What a nice drug.

I built a monumental library of yellow pages and supplier catalogs spread all over, including on the small stand next to the toilet bowl, replacing the German philosophers. There were boating magazines, books about boatbuilding, electrical and batteries compendia, electronics equipment, metals and parts of all sorts. A boat takes more items to build than a building - that's for sure. Sometimes Helga knocked on the bathroom door, worried for how long I was in there, "All right? Are you ok?"

"Ah? Yea, I am getting out in a minute!" I had been there for more than an hour.

I tried to outbid my ignorance with efficiency. And it was more and more clear to me that Arles, the cabinet maker, did not like to discuss each step of the process. His method seemed to be learning on the job without minimum prior study, and later I realized he was afraid to fail. One day he complained, almost crying, "Why do you never accept my suggestions? You also make me nervous discussing each minor step all the time."

Well, Arles was paid by the hour and so if we were discussing things it meant that he was actually being paid to just listen to me with a glass of wine – that's the way I liked to discuss important matters. Why then was he so nervous? The first time we met to discuss the boatbuilding I explained to him how important Helga II was to me, almost as important as Helga I, my wife. I told him how many years I had dreamed of Helga II. I told him that around the boat we would never argue; it should be like a sacred place. The pretty wood should not hear a minor swoop – I am superstitious – I told him. The reason why I decided to always talk to him near the boat was so that I would control myself, my temper.

I began to learn how to talk with an egg in the mouth as if I was screwing a lamp while talking to him, trying to be nice, "My friend, I trust the plans. I don't want to change a thing; let's stick with the plans, ok? But if you don't understand a detail, we can talk it through until we both understand."

One certain day, the scene went like this: we were working on gluing strips of wood, the planks, while the two employees and Helga were running the show at the factory, and David, the mentally disabled intern was ready to answer the phone (funny enough, for when he actually had to answer he used to come next to me and place the phone on my ear and approach his ear to a point that the both of us would look like nailed together). On that day Arles decided to lay down on the couch as if I was a psychoanalyst. He started by unraveling family problems and asked me straight - what was my opinion? He was divorced and was about to marry again. He had a ten-year-old daughter from the first marriage and a little female dog he bought the week before. Lessy wished to follow him to work but his ex-wife wanted him to take the dog to his daughter's to play with. When it was his turn to have Lessy he would walk with the little creature on the beach and, according to him, it was the only time he had a little time for peace of mind. He would marry soon and his fiancé was already planning to get pregnant, stop working and stay home to take care of their future kids. Thus my carpenter not only had suggestions to change the plans of Helga II, he also had serious problems to solve at his own end.

I thought for one second and realized his problems were too tough for me, I could not help him but I was curious about one thing, "And your dog, any kids in the pipe line?" Of course it was a bad joke and he did not even disguise being upset, made a face and did not talk to me anymore that day.

Lucky me, Helga II became a celebrity to the neighbors. But on that very afternoon I now call "Lessy day" we had a thing to celebrate. Nothing less than Pompei, the living legend, stopped by to check on the Helga II boat building. Someone told him I was building the boat with the help of a cabinet maker and according to him he paid a visit to make sure I was crazy. Seventy years old and nearly that long around building boat sites, talking with his peculiar way of how he talks without spelling out a word; he let himself be impressed with no ceremony. I could see in his eyes and gestures. Pompei jumped on the scaffolding around the boat and walked along the hull as if it was his ordinary pathway and rubbed his rough hands along the side of the gunnels and hull. Those hands that built so many wooden traditional boats went over the stem while he gave a long look all around and took a long breath. To me it was as if a preacher had come over to bless a mother, father and daughter during the pregnancy.

"And the boat is coming along!" Helga reminded me of that all the time when something threatened to go south. That time it was to celebrate the Pompei visit. If we overcame so many ordeals together we also felt full of joy at a minor achievement; after all we were cruising together for "Navegare necesse est, vivere non est necesse" (Latin for ´to navigate is necessary, to live not so much´).

The next day Arles called me, upset. I was sanding some parts and could see him making notes with a pencil on a piece of wood.

"Luís, I don´t know what is happening. Look, I double checked the calculation, the plans must be wrong. We need to buy more wood."

I bought all the necessary wood at once with a percentage of extra quantity according to the plans projection of waste. We had already bought extra timber, after we unfolded the first lot into strips. I thought I'd made mistake and realized Arles wouldn't be the one to be blamed. Now, he called me saying we needed more wood and I almost asked him to talk away from the boat because I felt my blood starting to boil. But I was able to refrain from bursting out with my bad temper and said, "Hmm... Well, before we start to deflower the Amazon let's make an inventory of scraps to see if we are not able to use some."

I was convinced that we were making mistakes at cutting and were wasting a great deal of fine wood. What to do? I thought, and thought twice and then told Arles that from then on I was going to make the calculation for the cutting all by myself. If we need to buy more wood, I was going to give him a bottle of wine - if it was the contrary, that is we don't need to buy more wood he would have to let me go out with Lessy, his adorable dog. "What you say, Arles?" I asked.

Of course he made a face, pretended was going to be offended but tried to throw back a joke. The phone rang and we went our separate ways. After speaking on the phone I could hear Arles grumble and throwing pieces of wood on the floor.

My God, there is no way to fix this anymore, I thought.

I mixed a batch of resin with pigment, got the production of the factory going, discussed something with Helga and went back to the boat building corner. The first piece of wood I grabbed from the huge pile of scraps ready to be dumped was a nice useful piece for a part of the boat according to the plans. Then the second - the same thing. Not much thought and effort and after less than an hour the pile was almost sorted out. There were also leftovers from plywood sheets and from a small pile I made with plywood, Arles grabbed one and was going to write a line with his pencil to cut a bulkhead, which on a boat is a kind of wall between sections of the boat.

"Wait, Arles, let's give a thought; we might be able to use it better."

"Luís, we will waste time which is also money, and in the end it will be the same any way. Look, Luis, as far as I know building a wooden boat we always waste a lot of wood."

I almost grabbed a crowbar to chase the man.

...To serve a time together, if needed.

Amateur boat building is a heavy task. Not only because one spends a lot of money on it. Not because it takes thousands of hours – in the case of Helga II the plans called for five thousand hours of meticulous and slow jobs. Also not because one is making something requiring extraordinary expertise. It is tough because of all of that - but it is even heavier when one is building a boat that represents a dream. A dream nourished for many years. In my particular case a dream that would come true only after I'd done my time in this particular prison.

To me a prison is the worst punishment among any other kind. I felt like a prisoner of an island; I had the privilege to be with my wife, but that was it. My crime was not a heinous one so I was allowed some perks. But to leave the island? Only after I've done my time? I could escape, break out, but would remain like a prisoner of the same prison, doing time for the same crime. Once I had this vision that while you fight to have a dream to come true it can be like being in prison until the dream is accomplished.

The landscape of my ardent romantic dream was to anchor on a white sand beach with coconut trees, to be on my own boat built all by myself. I was arrested in the action wishing to seduce a fairy so she could make my dream come true. And I was arrested with the bunch of would-be factory investors. Finally, I was a delinquent without rehabilitation.

Once in this kind of prison, one just needs to think of escaping to have the time doubled as a punishment. I'd look around sometimes and it seemed to me that the majority of people are doing a lifetime. Should I have stayed in that advertising agency, poisoned by those snakes? Remained a drifter in America, easy riding with a bag of failure over my shoulders? Abandon the ship in Australia at the first storm? Go back to Brazil as a pinball stainless steel sphere?

That night when I had the impulse to pick up the phone and answer Irvin's call to Charles I did not know who was calling. It was the "fundamental impulse", my intuition, that protected us; me and Helga, and Ulisses. We were the three stooges in a distant country subdued by the gang of manufacturing investors. We would be the first to be arrested because we were naive but sooner or later the greedy and crafty ones would be arrested as well. No matter what in life, everyone will need to manage his or her sins and for each soul a sentence.

I also realized there was another way to put this in perspective, less theologically that is through the restlessness of my fears which I confused as sins – to have dreamed – I was doing my time while building my boat so I was bound to rehabilitation. Along the way admitting my flaws, nodding to my limitations, leaning towards humble, I would get out of the bar out on to the ocean, free.

It was tough to overcome those; in just a few years we had an entangled hank of travels, sudden relationships tied with serious commitments broken all of the sudden, partnerships, adaptations, frustrations, back-to-back changes. From Helga's side it was a sort of particular learning or growing, for she never lived out of her family grid and her mom was always at least next door. I was the opposite in this aspect, always torn apart from the brood but writing tearful letters to my dad and sister, longing my roots.

Now we had our souls sealed doing time together and felt weakened because of the lack of connection. Our letters became more and more disconnected with our true reality because it was impossible to tell our folks back home what was going on. The factories had been built and undone. It was not possible to tell them, "Here in the United States things are..." Next we were in Australia and then not even we knew where we would be next. We could be in China (and actually we almost ended up there). They would never understand, accept, or agree.

So we were disconnecting. To our friends even more, as they would laugh at us or label us as a wild couple. "Hey! Come over to spend your vacation with us!" How could we send out such an invitation, to where? And how would we plan to escape and visit them? We were prisoners and so we faced it.

There is a classic Brazilian romantic poet we read early in school but will only understand him late in life - Gonçalves Dias was his name and he went to study in Europe, and was homesick and wrote long poems. While in Australia I used to reread him only to highlight my pain.

Do not cry, my son / Do not cry, that life it is a hard fight / To live is to fight / Life is combat / That the weak slaughter / May the strong, the brave / You can only exalt...

Eventually Gonçalves Dias headed back to Brazil but his ship wrecked near the Brazilian coast and he died. Avoiding thinking of any such end to myself, I switched my thoughts to memories like when I was kid playing soccer with street boys on vacant lots. We used to take possession of them to build soccer fields. In those soccer games one learns that to be strong is to win, the weak is the one who loses. So I grew up associating the weak with the mediocre, the strong with the virtuous. Doing my time as a prisoner of that island, I started to understand that the concept of strong and weak is so much more relative.

My restlessness of my fears took me to play for the team of the strong. The fear of losing was tormenting to me. So I even learned to walk like a winner, as if every second of life is a World Cup. Yet with another horizon in front of me that was my dream. Thank God I had dreamed, and luckily not too late I discovered how I had been confusing my dreams with my fears. The fear of losing makes one stall. I was afraid to lose, to make mistakes, but this was not my dream - to be the winner. I was just mixing things up, my true dreams with my fears. I used to talk to Helga about these revelations and even I used to get tired of it while she was also engaging in an inner battle of her own. Oh, yes we had titles for everything and at least often we ended laughing at ourselves.

So there we were. Our mouths and minds were full of a salad of fear, strong, weak and winner, losses and dreams. To summarize our lives at that point: we had one third of a boat built, a fairly big bank account but without funds because although the cash income was a lot the outcome was even bigger, a factory at the other side of the world, and three oceans to cross with my dream over my shoulder. Finally, I did not know how to sail just yet; I had never done it up until then.

Of course we considered taking a break. Spend some time in Brazil? How - when we took over the "crime factory" we had so many debits to pay back, and Helga kept pushing me forward with, "The boat is coming along.".

Around this time Arles was upset when I told him I was going to laminate a piece with Helga. It was an important part of the boat a section which supports the bow; it is like the shoulders of an airplane so it is important. It was then when I noticed that a relationship clash was brewing between us.

"Arles, I want to make whatever is possible. It will be the way I cut costs. We have agreed on that since the beginning, remember?"

It was really a delicate piece to build. It must be laminated in place on top of the spine of the boat. And right when I made the first move I felt a flavor of fear in my mouth - the fear of not being able to accomplish such a challenge. Helga noticed my jitters but gave me a strong push. "We will make it," she said, "And if we do it wrong, tomorrow Arles will laugh at us and we will ask him to redo the whole thing again."

It was not the humiliation I feared; my concern were the many hours paid by the weight of dollars to our carpenter. Well, true is it was a bit of both. Whatever - we would make it - I agreed with Helga.

I distilled a little adrenaline but the piece was perfect. What a good sensation you feel when you overcome a limitation of yourself. It ceases to exist; from then on it does not scare you anymore. You become a bit less anxious. In my particular case it helped to have Helga helping me, committed, adding her strength to my effort, throwing in ideas to solve problems even though she was never even close to any handmade task. It was indeed an unspeakable sensation. And the boat was coming along, from our both hands.

Wait a minute: now "we", and this was a great difference. Together we were dreaming, planning, doing. Everything due after the boat is done, of course. It would matter because some of our projects would take too long anyway. For instance, we started to dream of a better world. Exactly. We used to talk for hours about an optimum model for a fair society. We felt sorry about the war, sorry about injustice all over the world, the poor; we entangled with things we would love to change for better in the world. When the bottle of wine would pass half empty we would dream with the planet swamped with happiness. Until we fell asleep awkwardly spread on the floor of the living room to wake up again very early to start up to once again build up a better world, from where we had left the day before, in the factory and the boat building.

☐

...To plan the escape together.

I unleashed the gossip that I would like to sell the factory. Wow! All of a sudden three potential buyers came at me. How many people like to own factories! And it was like in an old popular song we use to sing for children in Brazil, "Teresinha of Jesus / went down to the ground / help three gentlemen / the three of them / begging with their hats / the first was her father / the second her brother / the third was the one Teresa gave her hand."

I don't know how I had time to develop new projects for the already new plastic open molding process. I had rented an ultrasound welding machine to weld plastic parts so I could create new products and also speed up the cutting process. I was making tests to diversify and the man who rented the machine sent me one of his clients who was looking for new venues to invest. We closed a deal in two meetings but first I had two other factory addicts and this is how I came to compare it with the popular children's song, in fact, more like an adaptation by a famous leftist Brazilian singer, Chico Buarque who distorted that into a pop song for grown-ups; one understands when we read the lyrics.

"Teresinha of Jesus" is a name, it was especially common in Brazil in the past century. Chico Buarque used a very similar structure as the original in the lyrics of this song, but with a more romantic/dramatic twist.

Teresinha sings:
The first one arrived like he was returning from the florist
Brought a stuffed toy, brought an amethyst pin
He told me about his journey and the perks he had
He showed me his watch and called me 'queen'
He found me so undefended that he touched my heart
But he denied me nothing, so, frightened, I said 'no'

The second one arrived like he was returning from the bar
Brought a bottle of brandy too bitter to swallow
He asked me about my past and sniffed my food
He searched through my drawer and called me 'lost cause'
He found me so undefended that he scratched my heart
But he gave me nothing, so, frightened, I said 'no'
The third one arrived like he was arriving from nowhere
He brought me nothing and also asked me nothing
I barely knew his name but I understand what he wanted
He laid on my bed and called me 'woman'
He arrived very sneakily and before I could say 'no'
He settled himself like the owner, inside my heart

The world is full of factory would-be owners. Out of those three, the first one came to me like a florist, so he was mellow and smooth talking. He was from Fiji, in the Pacific. He manufactured life jackets for the water ski market in Australia. His partner manufactured surfboards in Queensland and they both would partner in this new plastic molding process. We had a couple of phone calls; I got a fax with a formal proposal to buy my factory. But he was so fast and as the unarmed Teresinha it scared me and I said no. He sounded a trickster.

The second was simply a can of worms. He had gray hair and a kind uncle's blue eyes, and was the top executive at Ford Company; he arrived with his son telling me he was going to transform my small business in a big industry. In that pop song: "he brought a bottle brandy / too bitter / fidgeted in my drawers / ..." And by just talking to me and getting his hand on a good set of samples I gave to him I discovered he was trying to copy my process. So as Teresinha once again "frightened, I said no". Of course not before calling father and son to the parking lot to have a serious conversation with my classic way from old times.

The third one was from Adelaide. Because of my coldness on the phone he said he was flying in to see me in person. I felt he was a serious man so we scheduled a meeting and he landed in Melbourne on time, accompanied by his lawyer. I was in such a way that I did not even bother to pick them up at the airport and adopted a John Wayne style of negotiation - the tactic of a straight shooter. We had two hours of conversation, shook hands and they both went home. Two days later he sent me a fax accepting my conditions of a simple transaction. Money against the active assets like ovens, inventory of raw material, the brand name and a detailed process manual. Bank check in exchange for the business. He tried to go on offering me a commission as his sales representative, offered help to move into his town so I could give him tech support for a certain period, tried hard in different other ways. I ignored all.

Thus "He arrived very sneakily and before I could say 'no' He settled himself like the owner inside my heart."

The transaction was made so quick, just as everything else had happened, in only four months from the time I unleashed that gossip that I wanted to sell the factory. I had a picture taken holding two checks and here is the short story of these two checks: at the very time, he had to make the payment I was handed a check in the amount of 50% of the total value agreed and that check he brought pre-made from Adelaide. So he handed me the check asking if he could wire the other half. – Of course not! – I shouted straight back at him. A long few seconds went by and he asked me to excuse him to make a call to his brother-partner in Adelaide, and right in front me discussed how he would give me the other half which came from his personal checkbook written right there on the spot. By the way, I sold the factory very cheap – it's the reason why I said no for the installment tentative - moneywise, I had only Helga II on my mind.

We were almost free. We just needed to finish the building of the boat, launch on the water, sail back home and write a book. One extra item I did not list but kept secretly almost bursting out of my chest: I needed to learn how to sail.

The factory was sold, and although our bank account got really fat we would not have cash coming in anymore, only outflow, so the next step would be to leave the beautiful apartment at the noblest area of Melbourne in front of the beach with Philip Bay as a backdrop. Another provision we wanted to make was to run away from anything that would remind us of a factory, more precisely of partnerships, at least for a while; specifically we wanted to run away from the first two years in Australia. At that time if we'd been asked where the worst place on the planet to live was, Helga and I would have said in chorus: Australia! Another feeling that we soon changed diametrically all the way across. So we sought to go the other side of the island, to a different Australia.

And the bare hull of the boat built upside down was turned over in August, right on my birthday. A huge wooden canoe pushed against a back corner of the vast empty warehouse - it was a trailer of the ocean passages I would make, a film I could not wait to portrait the main character.

The fixed idea was to sail to Brazil as soon as Helga II was ready. When we dream we have a fixed idea of The End of the dream, often hiding the passage, the actual journey. So as a minor detail our bold course was planned from Melbourne to South Africa to Rio de Janeiro. As rule of thumb, we were ignoring the experienced sailors; we focused on going back home aboard a boat we built with our own hands, we were ignoring the natural course following the trade winds meeting the famous Whitsundays along the Australian coast and the Great Barrier Reef. I was at the helm planning this part of the adventure all by myself answering all the questions Helga asked me with an amazing self-confidence. I thought that after leaving from Melbourne via Taman Sea east bound we would cross the Indian Ocean straight and under Madagascar up to South Africa. You look on the world map and it is natural and reasonably close. Then we had to follow the south Atlantic current and arrive in Brazil. That simple.

Spread on the floor of our living room with Philip Bay across the street calling me to cruise back home I thought of an axiom, or postulate mathematics that says the shortest distance between two points is a straight line. When I ignored the natural route I actually ignored the giant waves, the wind patterns and the cold. I did not ignore my lack of experience because you can not ignore one thing that you don't see. But I have read that Joshua Slocum went through just fine weathering the storms. Once in the open sea, so I thought, I would learn and keep improving my sailing skills. Ah! What if I get tired, or Helga? I would make quick stops, in Adelaide, in Mauritius, in South Africa... I would rest, load provisions and carry it on to Rio. Anyone with a tiny bit of boating experience will nod or burst out laughing at me now and ask if this is a comic story to be. I assure you though; it is all true the way it happened. It's ok to laugh now.

There was only one problem. The Rip. A little stone on my shoe. The rip is the bar out of Philip Bay. I started to read in books and magazines horrifying stories about the conditions of the sea and the wind to get out of the bay. It was when I met the monkeys up in my loft and they kept reminding me that we should make it as easy a passage as possible. These monkeys would help me a lot down the road on my journey. Then after hearing my narrative of those stories, Helga made an appeal:

"Is there any other way to avoid the rip? I don't want to go through the rip."

"Of course, Helga."

If we leave from Sydney, on the other side of the continental island of Australia there is no rip. And, as we planned to leave behind that part of Australia, related to our last two years, as quickly as possible this was our mutual decision. After selling the factory we could not even go to restaurants, everything reminded us the recent ordeal. Thus I started to plan our second route. Once in Sydney, we would go straight across to Easter Island, sailing close to New Zealand, a pit-stop maybe, and we would hop up the South America coast aiming for the Panama Canal westbound; as an already "experienced ocean passage planner" I would take advantage of the Humboldt current. Once crossed through the "canal" Brazil would be just a few steps away. So I started to hear from people that my route was going to be a tiresome one, against the wind all the time and without attractions. Well, we did not have the intention to do sightseeing so I ignored their advice. Our goal was to go as fast as we could then someone recommended me a yet faster route.

"Go under the Cape Horn."

"No. We do not have experience. Cape Horn no." I replied to realize much later they were teasing me, in fact making fun of me and indeed what a joker I looked like to act as "ocean passage planner" by then.

But we decided to gather all our dreams, including the unfinished Helga II and move to Sydney. Change of atmosphere. Enjoy the climate similar to Rio de Janeiro. And finish the boat in Sydney. □

...Dig it out the love tunnel.

Before heading to Sydney, with the hull finished, including two coats of primer paint, we were approaching Christmas. I was going home every day only because Helga would not sleep in the shop with me and the wood and resin, but the happiness could not fit in my body; it was overflowing. To watch that huge bathtub already looking like a boat left me overjoyed.

"You see, Helga, it is almost done. Now we need to cover the top side, the deck, and cabin. After that the mast and hardware. That's it."

She used to look at me with an incredible complacency and said she still could not see the boat.

"How come? Look, here will be the kitchen — which for a boat we must say galley. The bathroom which we call head will be there, see? Our bed will be over there after we glued that sheet of wood out there, it is under the cockpit, very cozy. The dinner table, the dinette, will be right here, see?"

Helga only accepted the boat was done the day before our departure when we made it to the sea for good.

Our carpenter got married and went away for his honeymoon in Bali and when he came back his problems were even bigger than before. He could not focus on the job. He started to apologize for everything, even for crossing in front of me while we were working on the boat. He felt guilty and one day he blew out in tears, "I don't have a life anymore. Only work. I get home and don't have energy for anything else but to crash in bed. I don't go out anymore with Lessy. This is not a life."

His wife was a nurse and worked on Sundays. They barely saw each other. Arles was suffering.

"And then, Luis, look my belly" — he lifted his shirt and showed me his belly blistered — intoxication from this resin, Luis. My wife does not want to touch me."

"Look, Arles, my belly also got blistered."

In the corner of the empty warehouse two grownups were showing their bellies to each other. What if the "Bage Psychoanalyst" sees that. We both got this intoxication because we had started to wear masks but after a while we gave up the proper care negligently.

It was infernally hot inside the warehouse and in order to lift the moral I bought ice cream for the three of us. Arles, I and Helga. The factory has been sold and now we were only producing boats and ocean passage routes. The truth is that my friend wished to be fired and did not know how to say it, and it could be so easy. He got the ice cream the delivery boy brought, thanked me and left the ice cream on the bench melting away.

"What? Don't you like ice cream?"

"I like, just I will have it later."

"It will melt away, Arles, save in the fridge."

He just turned his back on me and left the ice cream right there diving into his introspective mode for the rest of the afternoon. I did not know what to say, what to do. I gave myself a little time to think and decided I should call it a day earlier because I was really tired. Then all of the sudden I heard a cry of dread. I was working on the ladder of the companionway and Arles was cutting some parts for the top sides of the cabin. I quickly ran toward him thinking he got injured and saw Arles facing the cement wall as if he was Hezekiah praying, then he placed his both hands on the head and cried again.

"What happened, Arles? Did you hurt yourself?"

"Luís! Look, I can't, I got to go home, I can't."

"Ok, calm down, of course, go home and get some rest," I said but not knowing what was happening.

He then cried one more time, scaring me but for some reason I found it funny when he turned facing me still with both hands on his head and I figured it was nothing so serious or disastrous and I said, "Arles, easy, look, I will call Lessy."

I tried to make my stupid jokes but he was unsettled nor even heard. "Luís, do you want to know what happened? I cut all the port holes, the windows of the cabin, wrong.

"No shit!" I said. "But can't we use it some way, it is that wrong? Don't worry, Arles. Go home, have a good relaxing shower, tomorrow we will talk. Take it easy, shit happens."

It was then that I decided to go home. I invited Helga who jumped so happy and we bought a six pack of Cascade lager, and went to the beach to watch the night arrive with the stars while we made things on the sand that made the sunset blush with shame.

And the boat was coming along. The next day we would solve the "Arles" case. At dinner, we discussed how to approach the situation and we had to admit that we had been conspiring against the carpenter lately. It was not easy to share the same roof with the creature. Incorrigible romantics we told him that he was helping us to build our dream nest, that we were so grateful he was putting so much care into the job. But lately and especially after his honeymoon, he was too much. It was then when we reached a conclusion that we could carry it on ourselves without his help.

"Right, let's build the boat just the two of us."

The next morning Arles did not show up to work. The second day was the weekend. On Sunday we even forgot Arles was there the week before. Earlier on Saturday, we rolled down the door of the warehouse so we could concentrate on a very important task and avoid any distraction.

We would face our first experience as a solo couple boatbuilders. We would laminate in place the cabin of the boat. In our heads, there was no more Arles. The task was simple maybe for experienced boatbuilders. It was just to glue and fasten two sheets of plywood cut to size on top of the skeleton of the boat so finally to make it look like a boat. As if you top a roof of a house with sheets of plywood. However, a tight fitting including a projection of post trim was a psychological threat. What if I make a mistake; would I cry facing the wall? We had to follow the curves of the Helga II, curves of beauty and hydrodynamics. Last but not least, the task implied to stand on top of that skeleton holding those huge sheets of plywood awkwardly bearing to a disaster.

Once the plywood was cut it looked like a short single bed sheet that won't cover a tall person or a couple. You feel like you have cut it wrong. And the heat of the warehouse was an extra torture not for our already soaked bodies but for the resin gel time. We were using a hardener for hot weather but again we were beginners.

The general amazement when we opened the warehouse was immediate. I started to hear from visitors: it is more and more looking like a boat. Through my smile of happiness, nobody could imagine the auto-scourge on that Saturday. The roof, or, the top side of the cabin was perfect without a gap, nor a problem but only Helga and I could testify our infliction. Our hurry to beat the gel time of the resin and the fear of having cut those sheets of plywood wrong while also trying desperately to avoid my sweat dropping on the coat and contaminating the job were whipping and slashing our bodies and souls.

Helga could not do much more to help me than holding the other side of the plywood when I asked her to but she was there all the time and I could feel an unforgettable face of an angel suffering with me, for me. When I had to fasten those sheets in place, coated with the resin, it was like to have been walking with a heavy cross over my shoulders for I broke all the bids of the portable screwing machine and I had to finish the job with the manual screwdriver. By the time we finished the job my hands were bleeding of blown up blisters. Blood all over from my knees too. I was soaked, lost weight and got lifetime scars and the feeling of having won the battle with myself.

It made me feel good to see the cabin done but it would only make me feel really happy the next day when I was assured the resin had been mixed correctly; otherwise all that effort would have been worth nothing. It was hard, perfect, inspiring confidence.

My blood was left in that cabin. Part of my sins certainly were paid out. My dream to be free from the prison was closer now. My restlessness would soon begin to thin into revelations or saying in another way into learning. Everything soon would start to make sense to me.

On Monday Arles saw the cabin in place and the sheeting of fiberglass cloth we made on Sunday, yes, after all that whipping we worked on Sunday, he could not believe it. He was wearing tight lycra short pants, t-shirt, and sunglasses. Clearly, he was not up to work.

We came to terms and our divorce was without hair pulling. A win-win deal. Page flipped over. Arles wished good luck to the two passionate people who did not have a tiny notion of what they would face next. First off they were left without tools, all the tools or belonged to Arles or the ones bought for the job were part of the agreement that by the end of the contract would go with the carpenter.

Cheer up! This was Christmas. It would be the fifth Christmas away from home, mother, father, sisters... And I could not say to Helga, "It is very close to being finished, we are almost there." But we kept pushing each other forward. The boat was coming along. We would do our time in the prison together and so it was our Christmas dinner, just the two of us and our tears mixed with few laughs.

While we did not get any gifts from anybody, the boat was the lucky one with Santa Claus. Helga II had all her wishing basket items checked: all the deck hardware was Harken, from winches to stoppers, then the top notch of the market for electronics, namely an integrated Autohelm system for wind meter, speed meter, depth finder, GPS and autopilot, VHF and SSB radio of top brand too, professional binoculars, sextant, EPIRB, complete safety set of gears like PFDs and tethers. And as our Christmas tree was too small I left items such as toilet bowl, sink, shower, water pump, oven and a 12 volts fridge at the warehouse. So our summer house was furnished, we just need to finish the building of it.

There is no better atmosphere than the summer. Especially if you are doing what you like. The summer in Melbourne, as a rule of thumb, it is not boiling. It is pleasantly warm with only one or two days of severe heat. A light breeze was always blowing. And when the night arrives slowly the sunset is such a spectacle. So far our experience in Australia had been more like a punishment but as we started to enjoy that summer alone without a factory to run and building the boat by ourselves, everything acquired to our eyes and heart a trace of would-be poetry so in this context the sunset was like if a shy sun started to dress off its daily clothes slowly blushing in front of us. It is so beautiful and we thought that sunset was peculiar to Australia. It was our debut of admiration for the country. The sunset where the horizon mixed its colors, stealing them from a rainbow texture, sometimes metallic, sometimes cotton into a transparent silk. That beautiful.

"Helga, it is so beautiful that is almost like the sunset in the Guaiba River in my hometown."

"Ah, that's all I needed. Are you going to be a gaucho forever?" she replied.

The following week we put in place a logistic master plan to make the Pentagon envy our thoroughness; so taking it as serious as what I like to see in the action movies. We would leave our rented apartment the same way it was when we moved in. Thus we needed to paint walls, clean carpets and take care of the garden and back yard. We would ship our belongings including my books, thousands of them close to one ton in weight, to the deep south of Brazil.

In the meantime, we would promote a garage sale to sell furniture and anything could worth a penny. The warehouse had been already transferred to other hands and so had to be released right away. After all, in the last months, we were renting 3000 square feet to use only the back corner to build the boat. All the above done within three days. Finally, after turning off the lights of our lives in the south of Australia, we would follow a truck shipping our unfinished dare Helga II, 12 hours of driving across to Sydney.

Of course, we considered alternatives, we had been thinking all the time since I decided to sell the factory. How would we do it if all of the sudden we had to manage our belongs, books and everything and how would we move the boat to be finished someplace else and where we would then live?

All the alternatives, however, would imply to stay in Melbourne or depend on someone. Therefore we opted the only alternative in our minds we could unleash without asking for help, that should be fast almost instantaneous as if we were escaping, and that could be less expensive.

I asked Helga to collect all the cargo shipping and boat shipping companies from the yellow pages, the same I used to set up the factory two years earlier. It is amazing how many boat shipping companies are in Australia. I then negotiated the shipment of our belongs and books to Brazil and I reinforced the cradle where Helga II was resting so to ship it to Sydney. We were in an escaping mode - a good taste in the mouth we would never forget. There were a few minor problems to solve: ship Helga II to where exactly? And with all the materials and goods to finish it. Where would we live while building the boat in Sydney? How would we manage the whole plan within three days since all the dates were cramped together? The date to return the keys of the rented apartment and the keys of the warehouse, the shipment of our stuff and the shipment of the boat.

The week before the escape day we worked at a crazy pace (as if we had not already been working at a crazy pace), aiming to get done as much as we could on the boat which would be exposed to weather while being shipped on the road. It was the raining season. In Australia, it rains in the summer as it rains in all the other seasons anyway.

On the very Thursday prior to all the deadlines, we were just two rags but the boat was completely protected and with all the materials and goods down below in its interior. It was like a white giant egg full of Christmas gifts. The remaining three days were a marathon apart.

On Friday we got out of the bed as early birds, had a cowboy breakfast and dashed over to the warehouse. A last minute one-day rented truck was loaded with all the leftovers from the garage sale and our belongings and books and unloaded at the warehouse where we should return the keys the next day. Days earlier I had built a very big wooden container to pack our stuff to be shipped to Brazil. So once that big container was filled we had to go back to the empty apartment. On Saturday again starting very early in the morning we would paint the walls, clean the carpet and take care of the garden. We would then sleep because we were not made of iron, but sleep on the floor like two ragged angels. Sunday would be the great day. Drop off the keys of the apartment, of the warehouse and drive behind the truck which would ship Helga II to Sydney. To where we still didn't know. And where we would live? We decided we would liveaboard Helga II, yes aboard an unfinished boat on the hardstand. From now on we would be boating people.

Apart the tiredness all was going well, although any sound mind would have dropped the towel at any time earlier in the game. We did not and the Murphy's Law acted on us heavily, meaning if something had to go wrong it would even if I was Rambo and Helga was Joan of Arc.

At one point it looked like we were robbing our own things. I parked the rented truck out the back of the warehouse and unloaded our stuff early in the morning – fast, very fast grabbed the wood left aside and started to build the wooden container. Fast very fast. Helga touched for the last time the broom sweeping the entire warehouse to leave a good impression I think. Only Helga. Curiously I always hurt my hands when something not so good was about to happen and I had two barbs in my hand when I finished the wooden container. A rectangular box nine feet long, three feet high and five feet wide. So we put all our things inside that box and nailed the lead. In an hour a truck would arrive to pick it up and take to the port of Melbourne. A break for a quick lunch allowing a beer and that was when all the dwarfs invaded the empty warehouse. The truck driver brought a forklift and while he was trying to grab the wooden container it started to bend and the truck driver grumbled that he did not like it.

"Yes, me too, I wished could have more time to make it prettier," I said back.

The giant wooden box snapped and finally broke in two pieces spreading everything all over.

Helga felt sick and I felt stupid, almost like sitting on the floor and crying. There was no time for defeat. Everything would go badly wrong from then on if I did not act fast and cold. And when you don't give up always something or someone pops in to help.

"At least it was here. Imagine if it breaks on the ship?"

A neighbor, a very nice man who used to come every morning to check the Helga II building found it was a funny and nicely suggested a solution, "Why don't you go to this place I know and buy recycled wooden tea boxes from Indonesia?" He then gave me the address and told me to buy a dozen of them.

So I told the truck driver to take care of my cold beers and I hit the road at high speed. In less than an hour I came back with my car so full of wooden tea boxes that one could see only the windshield. And the warehouse seemed to have a party on with the neighbor, the truck driver me and Helga all drunk packing all the stuff, nailing, singing, shouting, screaming, drinking, hammering.

Our stuff was shipped to Brazil, finally.

However, we were not finished just yet, or ready to hit the road on the way to Sydney; Murphy's Law was still active that day. The rigger who was supposed to deliver the mast, boom, spars, standing and running rigging simply messed it up, did not honor his word to me. The order should be delivered on time, everything should be on time, we had a war scenario going on, nothing could go wrong. But it was, because we could not drive to Sydney with a sail boat without a mast. What were we to do? Well, I had to go there and get my order because the check had been written already.

To get the spars was a story apart. I had to act like John Wayne or Dirty Harry. Ok, relax, what mattered was that the boat was more beautiful each day and more like a boat. Her curves were good to the eyes; she looked like a false skinny that when wearing a bathing suit the whole beach stands up and you hear a wow! Meanwhile, my hands could well be almost compared to the Pompey's hands. My hands were like feet.

And here was I talking to the old man who worked next door - the one who suggested I buy Indonesian wooden tea boxes, I was telling him my route to Brazil from Sydney to Fiji, then to Samoa, Marquesas and onward, yes, that crazy route, and the old man said he would help me to pick up the mast, which was in South of Melbourne, the other side of the city, in the port region. He even liked it more when I told him it could be dangerous because I was mad, that I was really upset with the rigger.

The old man said nicely to me, "Open the glove compartment (of his pickup truck) and see if this will help."

It was a 45 caliber gun, a huge thing that almost fell off on my lap. I closed the glove compartment without saying a word and I don't know if that thing helped or not but after a crispy argumentation of around ten minutes with the rigging supplier, a light frame featherweight gaucho among half a dozen rugby player kind of guys, with the old man quiet, just listening with a subtle smile and his cigarette almost fallen from the corner of his mouth, the 12 meter mast, boom, halyards, everything assembled or not as it supposed to be according to my half upfront paid order, were all put on the old man's pick-up truck and we went back to Seaford, to the once-upon-a-time plastic factory that was turned into a boatbuilding shop and now was going to be empty.

Speaking about once-upon-a-time, after I sold the factory's assets I had to terminate the business, but instead I simply changed the name and the main activity, had to entirely redraw its statement and chapters now as "Build Your Boat" – the name of the new business – building on-demand one-off yacht designs. Yes, since I was learning pretty fast I thought I could build boats on demand too, but secretly I also thought as a business I could get better prices for the goodies I was purchasing to build Alvidia. My buying strategy granted me an appearance in the BoatBuilder Australian Magazine which story lead read: "A passionate Brazilian is the new boatbuilder in town offering building boats on demand." Seriously.

All right, kill us later because we still have a lot to accomplish. The mast was laid down nicely on the floor in the corner of the almost empty warehouse of the new BYO business, and our stuff was shipped; we went back home and left the garden well cleaned so we could then say goodbye to that beautiful place. By the way, the name of the condo Seascape, at the Esplanade in Brighton Beach. Would we live in such beautiful place again? It was past midnight when we crashed on the floor of the empty bedroom and of course, Helga had to give the last go on her things to do list. The truth is that we could not live without her lists from then on.

On Saturday we finished the entire "go to Sydney preparation project" and we spent a little time enjoying a bottle of red wine. So a mix of self-ridicule and hysteria took over of us. We were drinking wine seated on the floor so we started to roll over laughing just remembering the garage sale day. I had promised Helga that I would take care of all the things on the night before. Everything we planned on selling was left in the garage so the house could be kept tidy. People, the buyers, would not be allowed to get in the apartment. But I was too tired and did not honor my promise. Thus early the next morning, those who answered my advertisement in the local newspaper started to stroll in by the bunch. Indians, Chinese, Koreans, Turks, Persians, Germans, Canadians, people from all over the world. Helga asked me to announce that the "store" was not open just yet but it was too late - I was already negotiating the TV with a Turk while explaining to Helga that the Turkish Family would go away soon and before the others came we would have the chance to organize everything out on the driveway. No, it did not happen. My Ad was a success, of course, once an Ad-man you always will be an Ad-man and an avalanche of immigrants invaded our apartment.

Not even a chance to say g'day to each one. Children, a handicap person in a wheelchair, whole families speaking different languages, touching everything, changing the placement of everything - the garage sale suddenly became a big mess. Helga was staring at me with her hands on her waist and that scolding look. I started then to make last minute promotions, a tray goes with cassette tapes, the soccer ball no. Halt! It is mine. Hey! Don't touch the derringer, it is from my grandpa! Helga came in the living room and shouted at me:

-"You tell these people to go away or I will."

"But, Helga, they are my clients."

Throughout the afternoon the traffic slowed down, Helga made me a coffee and set me on a low stool out on the driveway with all that was left to sell. So there I was, pathetically waiting for last minute buyers, and I sold almost everything (but the fact is that I ended up donating things).

Early morning on Sunday we returned the keys of the apartment at the real estate office and dashed over to the warehouse. The truck driver arrived the night before; we had put him in a cozy inn because I made a point to treat our emissary well, after all, he was the carrier of our dream, our boat. He would arrive first in Sydney; he would open the gates of the city to us, two sailors, dreamers - we would be right behind his tail on the road.

I found Rinley in an old article of a magazine. All the boat shipping companies taken from the Yellow Pages were too expensive; they demanded insurance and were not flexible at all. The article I read while researching seated on the toilet was actually a short story telling the experience of the author shipping his boat interstate in Australia, and Rinley was the truck driver. He would be picturesque, moody and rough according to the story teller, and used to drive at high speed. With two phone calls I was able to close a deal with Rinley; he knew all the marinas and boatyards all over the coastal ring of Australia and included in the price finding a nice hard stand for us. There was only one restriction: the shipment had to be made on a certain day, and that was on that very Sunday.

"Ok Rinley. I will be waiting for you."

Including my painful experience with my ex-partners, Australia had not been adored by me up to this point. Independently I had bought all the parts of the boat, equipment, and materials (if not upfront, cash on delivery) and all the suppliers except for one gave me a hard time. Not a minimum of customer service, delays and wrong products, even considering that I was buying well-known brand names. The engine I paid up front A$9.000,00, for instance; it was working perfect but there was a missing part and I had to pick it up because the dealer did not want to deliver the missing item to me. The only exception was the sailmaker. He delivered to me on time and was outstanding.

"Thanks, Shark" – nickname for Mark Rimington, the sailmaker based in Mordialloc near Melbourne. The other suppliers, all from big companies, had their top executive talking to me as if they were screwing a lamp and afraid to fart. This description tells my mood at the time. The boat was coming along. But for, for instance, the stainless steel engineering company from whom I ordered parts, including the anchor support gear, simply could not understand the blueprints, and I had to return all the parts for a second run. I was pulling my hair out. So it was with the aluminum window frames, with the deck gears (the top American brand), and the toilet bowl. When I received the electronics I was like a child in front of a Christmas tree but had a fear something was wrong; I had paid with a credit card and it was coming from another state, so it would be difficult to solve a problem. Well, it did come wrong and I was able to solve it only months later.

On another hand, all the bearded makers that I found, greasy hands, cigarette out the corner of the mouth were spot on with me. All managers of two figures, one on top of each other, a line under, and the result, that kind of guys. On time delivery and friendly. They were the welder, the electrician, and mechanic, and they all lent me their tools and taught me how to finish things up. □

...To have fun even at escaping.

Sydney, a city that breathes boats. I had made so much effort to mingle myself with the boating community and now I was able to jump like Peter Pan, having Helga as my Tinker Bell, making all my fantasies true out of her things to do lists. I just could not believe it was my reality.

We left Victoria heading to New South Wales where you see a bay around each street corner. That was my first impression. And boats all over of any kind, any size. Still, up to that point, I did not know the real difference between a sailboat and powerboat, such was my ignorance, the sail was a small detail. And I was driving behind Rinley's truck watching my white Alvidia half-finished and proud when I noticed someone driving by looking at my boat on the truck. I was driving and wondering if Sydney was like they described to me with many boats and a climate similar to Rio de Janeiro. I would learn to sail by osmosis. And I felt I did not need to grow up anymore; I would be an eternal child playing as Capt. Hook.

The one thing I had not seen yet in Australia after two years was a kangaroo and I thought that while driving along the road one would jump in front of the car. It would take a little longer though.

"Helga, kangaroos must be like cows in South of Brazil. They are everywhere. I don't want to see them in the zoo."

Yes, it is true in Australia cars have bull bars installed for when a kangaroo jumps against it on the highways which otherwise could cause severe damage and human injury. During the day mobs cross highways and at night they tend to jump randomly meaning you don't know which direction they will come or go within the light beam of your car. Crazy. All these lessons I had from Rinley before our departure. Nothing happened though. I did not see a single wallaby, wombat or possum.

After a couple of hours, any sign of civilization was behind us. Rinley was moving farther and farther away from us. I was afraid that going that fast the boat could fall off the truck. At each curve, my heart would burst out of my chest. Half an hour after dusk I gave up to Rinley and stopped at a rest area to sleep in the car. And not a single kangaroo.

Early morning we had a liter of milk for breakfast, a sandwich, and got back on the road. Where was our boat? I was thinking of it while

Helga was half asleep and we were blocked on the road by a herd of cows. They broke through a wire fence and decided to camp on the warm asphalt. I tried to drive around those fat milkies while pushing the horn, trying to shoo them away but nothing; they simply ignored me. Even worse I was now surrounded by cows right in the middle of nowhere.

"Calm down Helga, I understand cows, they will go away, trust me, they will be thirsty. In the meantime, can you feel what a good smell? Cow shit, see, and urine, they smell better than human's" – Helga put that face on and lucky me almost an hour later two cowboys piloting two shining bikes came roaring their potent engines to rescue the creatures. "What did I tell you, Helga?"

Back on the road for good, I was already worried about our ETA. The weather was deteriorating, I was missing my boat and I was afraid that Helga II would not be covered properly and protected from the rain.

Before we arrived around 07:00pm another setback went to our diary. I was driving and reviewing in my mind the next tasks – finish the cockpit, install windows and main hatch, build the rudder, set the keel, the list would go on – and all of the sudden I felt something was not feeling good and I had a quirky gumption to put my hand out over the roof of the car in order to reach the sails bag.

"Helga! I lost the sails!"

I pulled over to the shoulder of the road and had a bitter taste in the mouth. Our brand new sails made by Shark ordered to be bullet proof had fallen from the car and I did not know how long ago, how many miles behind.

"Let's go back. It can't be too far back, I remember hearing the noise of them when we crossed that bridge." So was I speaking to a speechless Helga.

We went back about 10 miles and "voilá": there the two bags were spread on the side of the road. I felt like kissing them. My dear sails. And once I was back driving I thought I already had enough adventure stories to write a book.

It was raining torrentially when we finally found the marina according to Rinley's address and directions. The manager was already closing the gate to go home and greeted us coolly, freezing our hearts. I ran to hug our home, our Helga II. It was placed at the corner of the hardstand next to a giant shed of the marina and the boat was there, prematurely suffering from the first contact with water, from the rain. But it was not enough to hide its elegance and peculiar charm - soon it would be the attraction of the marina.

How come they did not consider covering her up? Considering the circumstances I decided not to act as Capt. Rodrigo (*), I was in an unknown place and ordered to my own brain to cool down; I should not and would not burn my wick. *Capt. Rodrigo is a character from a classic novel The Time and The Wind, ex-high rank from the army in the hey days, he arrives from nowhere in a small town and makes his way as a local leader with a peculiar sense of humor and temper".

In Sydney I should be a sailor, a cruiser per say, gentle and patient. After all, there was no more reason for punches on the table, or for war. I was a happy man. I had a boat. Soon I was going to be on the water, sailing. So I would try to solve all the issues ahead with a sense of humor if possible, with a second thought, just in case, and with a willingness to avoid unnecessary friction. So while saying goodbye to that manager I jokingly invited him to go sailing the next day.

"Hey, do you have a canvas I can borrow to cover my boat?"

After covering the boat with care we did not have the chance to check its interior. It was pouring. We were soaked and dead tired. All we wanted now was to crash so we walked nearby seeking a place to sleep. One block from the marina we found a pub which also rented rooms, to our amazement, only for men. To the drunk that could not go home after hours. We each had a beer and I asked Helga if she would face that dive.

"Of course, I am a rag anyways," she answered back. But it was tough to convince the owner of the pub - a radical orthodox - who did not accept women in the upstairs rooms at all.

"Look, Sir, we are foreigners; we are kind of lost, tired, and I promise, we will leave very early in the morning. No one will notice us, ok?" I punctuate after a funny conversation.

"Ok, but I am not seeing your wife. Leave twenty bucks on the counter and go upstairs and she can not use the bathroom in the corridor; it is only for men. Understood?"

"Of course, sure, she will not visit the bathroom, I guarantee."

And here I admit having broken a local rule. With the excuse of that much rain and beers, I took Helga to the bathroom in the corridor as a bodyguard by the door. Worse was to lay down on the filthy bed.

Welcome to Sydney. Our waterfront home on the most beautiful beach of Melbourne was no more than a recent memory now.

☐

...Pretend to be blind.

We had planned to be on the hardstand for no more than a month. I even told the marina manager I needed two weeks to have the boat ready to launch. I actually could not sleep anymore, dreaming with my eyes open with the launching day ahead.

Later on, when we were sailing on the high seas, Helga confessed to me she could not understand how come I thought the boat was beautiful before it was finished. She was even more surprised, when at the marina, everyone at first sight would say that the boat had fine lines, elegant, and they couldn't believe it was only a 30 feet yacht. I was flattered. How many times I walked backward to admire its shape and look. My boat was beautiful.

I had my things to do list on a clip board. I did not have my wall anymore at the warehouse to place my flipcharts. And my list had columns for major things before launching, things to do in between and after launching, the latter one about installing hardware and adjustments on deck. That simple. In my mind it was all that I needed to keep the boat on the water next to a pier and then finish it entirely. The major list included the building of the cockpit well, the main hatch and companionway, the windows, the keel, the rudder, paint the boat and all the in between. These things fit in my mind within a month of hard work, or two weeks as I told to the manager as I wished to pay as little as possible for the hardstand, which was more expensive than the slip on the water.

I saved that historical list to one day be able to advise someone, case in point not to engage in impossible missions.

Since it was still raining we had to make an agreement with the borrowed canvas, it was too short; a lot of water was taken in and we had extra tasks. We threw ruined material overboard, cleaned up, dried out and improvised a residency shared with all the stuff. I was already blaming the weather in Sydney for the delay of my project. Someone told me that in Sydney it does not rain. They told me many things in Australia. That I would see kangaroos, for instance. Not even a run over so far. Bays as well, I was miles and miles away from the Darling harbor, up on the Parramatta River in the suburb of the west side of the city where I could not even feel sea air. It would take months until I would see the famous Opera House's architectural structure resembling waves or surf boards, or boats half sunken upwards at the entrance of the commercial port of Sydney, around which the Darling Harbour hosts many small bays and basins full of boats of all kinds.

Our pace of work was to use weather windows to get some tasks done. It was January and rain was the pattern. On the other hand, instead of upsetting us we took the chance to adapt ourselves to the new boating life. Sharing the space with building materials aboard a boat on the hardstand that demanded us to step on an 8 foot ladder and crawl under a canvas to actually reach the interior for our home.

"Helga, the weather will improve."

"You mean it can not get worst, right?"

The reason why it was good to be raining that much - each improvement followed with a celebration.

And as it was summer, and summer is full of cyclones; the forecast was strong winds on the east coast all the way up north. In Sydney, we felt some of it. It was announced a few hours before it supposedly would reach us. Scheduled storms. I started to live in an atmosphere of who lives on the ocean, just like I had read in books of adventures from my memory. The first time I heard of such a storm forecast was from the supervisor of the marina whom I discovered later wished to terrorize me and more.

He came to me and said: "If I was you I would stop working and cover your boat. A big blow is coming!"

We were working on the cockpit, with fiberglass and resin perched up there. Minutes before the scheduled storm the sky changed color and I felt a gentle breeze hugging my arm so I told Helga we should prepare ourselves for a big blow. I put a serious face on. I would face my first storm aboard a boat. I remembered well I had sent a precise order to my own brain telling it that it was not a drill, I should not play with, it was a real thing. We started to pull back the canvas, a light breeze would try to take it from our hands.

Helga looked nervously at me ready to follow my order as from a Captain of the ship. I dared to pray in my thoughts, asking for Neptune to bear with me, I would not challenge him, I was going to respect him. The first drops fell from the sky and I thought it would be a white squall

- I read that in ocean passage books. A curtain of rain and a wall of wind would pass over us as if it was a concrete mass. The canvas did not want to stay in my hands and I almost fell off the boat. Finally, I managed to fix it while the sky opened, and nothing else happened until the next forecast or that supervisor came to terrorize me with another false alarm. In fact, that was the forecast - gusts that would pass over way above our heads up with the high clouds. It could be a bit stronger or not, in Sidney it is normal including having rain and sunshine together.

After few days we discovered the marina had an almost universal practice on hardstands - to delay as much as possible the hardstand rent. Good to generate revenue. When they realized we already knew all about hardstands, they applied a different strategy – warning us our boat would have to be moved aside because a bigger boat was coming in.

Well, now they were not dealing with Rambo, I had left my craze for punches on the table in Melbourne.

"Of course," I replied and shouted back that I would help them to move the boats around. And they could not believe what was happening. I stopped my tasks and ran to help them. Sometimes I felt an old impulse but immediately acquired a nice genuine smile, joking with the marina employees that we should protest for better wages. Our setup consisted of an improvised bench, recycled plastic pots spread with resin, our clumsy tools, and concentration on the task. Sometimes it took us an hour just to make the setup. Then that supervisor jerk would come to advise us of boats being moved around. By the second week, I had made friendship with all the other employees, some boat owners, and liveaboard people. I was Lui, and one day it was really funny when the manager was helping a group of employees to push a monster boat and he shouted at me, waving his arm as if I was an employee and should run to help them.

I ran and told him, "This is my job, boss, step aside please."

The whole team laughed out loud and spread jokes in the air. Not being on the payroll of the marina I started to use my diploma from the streets and beach of Copacabana, in Rio. When we finished moving that big boat, I ran back to work on Helga II but stopped at the material stock room of the marina, a place forbidden for nonemployees, and grabbed tools that I needed, rags and acetone for cleaning. I got back "home" with my hands full of stuff, showing it to Helga who did not understand how I got all that stuff for free. From then on they would not handle Lui anymore. First I baptized each employee including the manager and the supervisor with a nickname. To the nice guys, I was creative to dazzle them, to the jerk ones I punished them well. To me it was like creating slogans for an advertising campaign. They tried to bug me a couple of more times moving Helga II all of the sudden but in exchange, I was harder and harder on them. War is a war, right? And I used my secret weapon. While asking the manager to lend me a tool and I looked so poor, with tattered working clothes, bearded but half glabrous; I looked that horrible but at the same time funny because I was always smiley. That softened the manager and he ended up giving me the keys to the room of tools and materials such as rags, acetone and sand paper, to say the least. The weekend manager used to come over and watch me working, bringing coffee. One day I saw the owner of the marina scolding the manager. From then on no perks, no frills to Luis, well, as long as the owner of the marina did not see. That bothered me and I went to the owner who lived aboard a houseboat and asked him to let me store my 12 meter mast inside the shed. He went personally to show me where I could put the mast and spars. Then I told him I was embarrassed that he had to reprimand his employees, I was the one to be blamed.

And he said, "Oh no worries, Lui, you know, an employee is an employee."

"Well, I don't know exactly and sorry anyway and look, since you are here, would you have a bench with wheel I can borrow?"

"Yes Lui, I have!" he said, upset, and pointed me to the bench next to a wall and left the shed nodding helplessly. My secret weapon was lethal. After all, I was paying $60.00 per day to use the hardstand and I felt like was bleeding money. On another hand, although being expensive I was able to learn a lot about boat maintenance, it was like an intensive shipwright PhD course. Each worker of the marina used to give me true lectures about everything related to boats.

Our lives became a construction site. To sleep we had to set aside wood and stuff. One must bear in mind that on a 30-foot boat there is not as much room as in a house even our spacious Alvidia while we sharing the space with paint and resin cans, tools and various other building materials. We had to crawl over to reach the bed. And as the galley was not functional yet, we made our dining room the grass of the marina for meals, mostly consisting of cold sandwiches and the only edible thing close to real food we use to have occasionally was burritos - a five blocks walk away; it went on until we launched the boat. Our wardrobe was the trunk of our car in front of the marina which means when we quit for the day, before freeing the way to our bed we'd run to the parking lot to grab clean clothes, then walk back to visit the shared bathroom of the marina, once again back to the car to stow the bath stuff. Since I was faster than Helga, I used to wait for her on the pier "to go home", so we could relax a bit, watching the finished boats already floating on the water.

"You are pretty."

"You too," Helga used to say back to me.

Caring between us never lacked, unless Helga had begun to lie to me.

On a Saturday we woke up with a frantic movement next to us. A truck - and it was not Rinley's - was unloading a huge yacht wrapped in plastic. It was the first time I'd seen a boat wrapped as if was going to be a gift. It was a brand new 12 meter Beneteau, a French design, straight from the factory in France.

The yacht was shining and had that characteristic new smell. One of the men working to get the new attraction of the marina launched on the water was talkative and had an American accent and several times said to his teammates, "She is so sweet. I wanna take a close look at this one. That's what I was looking for."

Missing the American accent it reminded me of my childish habit of playing as if I was in a movie, and of our time living in the United States, and I started a conversation with that fellow.

To me, Geary was a true copy of a TV character of a children's puppet show made famous by Ed Sullivan, so I frivolously thought and asked if he had been working for a TV show.

"What?" he asked while I said he looked like Topo Gigio, laughing at him and he said, "Funny, I thought you were some kind of replica of Pancho Villa." Ok we were old friends already. Geary had a sense of humor and a permanent smile. Geary was that kind of person that while bragging about himself all the time he was funny. We laughed a lot together, there was no chance for a serious conversation with Geary.

But one thing made me feel flattered. He was saying marvelous things about our Alvidia - "She is so sweet, I wanna take a close look..." He came aboard and said he fell in love with our boat and actually stood on his knees when saw it was wood, strip planking.

Geary was living aboard his boat, also a 30 foot, but a fiberglass yacht. He left the United States many years ago as an ocean drifter making stops where he could work for a while. Lately, when he was not working for the Beneteau company he was making deliveries of yachts. What a job, to deliver a boat sailing! That Beneteau he was working on had a little problem and the launching day was postponed so Geary was around disturbing everyone although it must be said honestly he was, in fact, entertaining the marina atmosphere.

One night the three of us went out to eat pizza and drink wine - I know, not a perfect combination but at least it was red wine and when we returned to the marina Geary invited us to carry on with the red in his boat. He introduced us to his yacht, praising every single detail aboard and he showed us his bunk, saying it was so huge that he could fit himself and three girlfriends and his guitar all at once. Geary played guitar, rock 'n' roll and country music, and while he was doing that I was enjoying and every once in a while looking at Helga like saying: when he will eat or save in the fridge that slice of pizza he saved in the pocket? At the pizza place, Geary grabbed a left over and tucked it in his pocket. It was the first time I realized we were getting into a real boating people´s life.

Fine, with so much wine in the head it was easy for me to get into a trance. I was aboard a cruising yacht that had been all over the world, I was listening to true stories of ocean passages, maybe not all true but who cares; I was there and I was dazzled. I and Helga went to bed that night smashed up and we got a present from Geary, a book about boat building and maintenance. Most important we got a friend and an advice:

"Soon you will have your boat on the water. Do not make the mistake to be in a hurry to reach out for the high sea. Get to know your boat first, get familiarized with everything until you feel you and your boat are one, get some little scratches on your boat, only after that you can make an ocean passage." □

The Cruise

Luís Peazê

... February, the first month.

Each day was a battle. And the feeling was that in each battle we were at a disadvantage. I did not have tools, I did not know how to make things, I did not have the proper set up out on the hardstand and the time was passing by fast. The money being spent was bleeding to the point as if we were going to faint. Living as if permanently camping with that effort to simply get aboard had to crawl under the tarpaulin while inside the boat we had only one place for each other, sharing with material and our stuff yet out of a proper place. The only peace of mind was when we were on our bed although we looked like two abandoned homeless people aboard an unfinished boat on the hardstand of a marina up on the Parramatta river near Sydney, that we had not seen yet. To complete the story, our routine was to wake up with the first rays of sun and crash never before midnight.

Awake, I dreamed of the boat being finished. Sleeping, I dreamed of our flat in Melbourne. The first invoice the marina gave us was like a punch in the stomach. They charged everything including the air we were breathing. They dared to include in the invoice a quotation I asked for welding stainless steel tubes I brought from Victoria for the pushpit and pulpit, I only asked them how much would be – no way, the invoice listed three hours of calculation. They must be kidding, I said to myself and ran into the office boiling, almost losing my new Lui way and after talking, the invoice was reduced by half. I surprised myself realizing I was able to make jokes all the time, diametrically different from the Luis who owned a factory in Melbourne. Certainly, the manager and supervisor of the marina thought I was the most cynical person on earth and I know for sure I was in route of a cure, from then on no more unnecessary fight.

Phew! The stress was going away. Working hard won't kill anybody. It is the stress from annoyances that come when you are doing what you don't like, this kills you. When problems arise while you are doing what you like the ways to solve them are negotiated differently in your mind. Often, behind each problem you end up finding new perspectives. This had begun to happen with me. To start up, it proved to everyone in the marina that I was the most poor yachtsman on earth. They never tried to take my skin off anymore.

And it was the day to assemble the keel on the boat, a ton and half of forged solid iron that should be plugged onto the hull with nine bolts an inch thick. It was a task as intense as its weight. After it was done I took a picture under the boat but it does not show how bad I was. I was so nervous that I thought my heart would not handle it. I placed my arm over Helga's shoulder and asked her, "Get a glass of water for me?"

Poor dear Helga, almost burst out crying because she knew looking at my face I was not feeling good.

To install a keel is a task that only after you get it done you know how easy it seems or really is. However, a week before I started to suffer as if I was going through a meat grinder. I imagined the travel lift, a giant special crane for boats, swinging our dear Helga II while I was trying to fit in the nine four inches long and inch diameter bolts from outside, going inside to screw the nuts over huge washers. Only with Helga helping me. What if the bolts didn't fit in the holes I had to make on the hull and on the keel? The hourly rental of the travel lift was expensive, I couldn't spend more than one hour. If the bolts did not fit it meant the holes would not be aligned, worst than to pay for more than an hour of the travel lift. And what if the bolts fit but got loose? The keel would not be steadfast. All these thoughts terrorized me including the fear that the keel could fall off the boat while sailing if I installed it wrong. To lose a keel is as serious as one losing the mast. Even working in my mind to set aside the worst, what if I didn't feel confident that the keel was solid? It would be a permanent torture.

The matter of fact is that I was contaminated by all the free tips from the neighboring boat owners; each one called my attention to one problem, some trying to help, some I think just having fun scaring me and I would not calm down before I could see the keel in place, solid as if it was a continuous part of the hull in its wholeness. A theory that I developed about my Australians friends, generalizing, is that since being British descendants, they are adept of the vampire culture, they love sinister situations, ghosts, to some extent they think that if it is to go wrong it will go wrong.

Fortunately, at that very crucial moment an angel came to us. Chris, who had been around the world aboard his boat - Feather was its name, built by himself - gave us fundamental advice. The most important - he told us that the job of installing the keel is not a big deal; he noticed my tons of worries and added that I should not worry too much. He stepped back and said, "Wow! I like this boat."

Chris told us that he had two heart attacks during the building of his Feather. He spoke of similar problems that we had with a commissioned carpenter and so on. It was cherishing to hear his story. Any story with true good intentions would be good because being ignorant we did not have parameters. But then again, Chris was a mechanical engineer, ex-Australian motorbike race champion, used to high-risk sports and currently he was building his first single-engine airplane for air acrobatics, so he was not a parameter for us at all.

While I was sanding the hull the day before, I had all these terrible thoughts punishing myself. Helga was also standing next to me and trying to ease the pain saying I was going to make it right and suggested I should call the marina manager and asking him to borrow one employee to help me finish the sanding, otherwise I would not be alive the next day for the installation of the keel. The nights before that week she said I was moaning while sleeping. So I gave in and hired five experts in sanding as a friend once expressed to me about his helpers with muscles in the brain. One was a short guy, blond and bearded quiet as a closed door. Helga made orange juice for all of them, they thanked Helga but the short guy still mouth sealed as a rock. I thought: Hey! What is wrong with you low footer? Why don't you put a smile on your face?

While I had these thoughts I placed an arm over his shoulder and said to everyone out loud, "The best sander will get a key ring of Chuck Norris."

I almost got a punch on my cheek. Later on, I learned the life story of that short man. He escaped from Russia with his wife aboard a small boat of only five meters. A romantic feat, a true hero story. I only picked on him because there was no way to make the compact Russian laugh at my stupid jokes. But anyone would respect his achievement. To escape from his country because he was among those that did not agree with the communist system, without knowing how to sail, set up an escape with the help of friends, certain that no one would believe he would escape through on the sea in that small vessel. According to him, in Russian a person was not allowed to build a boat on his own, it must be a collective building or nothing and should be a member of a club. His boat had two small keels, those we see in comic stories, and one night hidden and silently he set himself free with his wife. Without a passport, without knowing another language he jumped from island to island and managed to reach the United Kingdom. Without support from the authorities, he started to drift from country to country; he reached the Pacific Ocean and finally made to Australia. Up until now, he was ok, the marina owner was trying to get him the legal immigration papers. His life is a book of true adventures; it should be written. Poor

Russian. Or, fortunate Russian, was able to make his dream to come true. On one the very few occasions he spoke he said, "A boat is a problem." His had many leaks. After five years his house was the same small boat he brought from Russia anchored on a mooring buoy.

The "K" day. I woke early as usual and stretched myself with that brave look defeating anything that could jeopardize the success of the installation of the keel - it will not be unaligned, the bolts would fit perfectly, the timing would be spot on, one hour and done. And Helga gave me a terrific idea. We had a sheet of transparent acrylic we used to cut molds so Helga said I should copy the holes of the keel, made in Seaford, onto the acrylic and then transfer from it to the hull of the boat. Millimeter accuracy. And before we could see the keel solid, firm and inspiring confidence, we suffered together, fearing to fail, and I think people around noticed that. But we felt so strong after the whole operation, one hour sharp, wow, we believed we could do anything. But all my knuckles bled while the wrench used to tighten up the nuts on the inside the boat kept slipping and hurting my fingers because I was nervous and in a hurry, running against the rental time of the travel lift holding Helga II, knowing the driver was there just watching with the engine on, and curiously I did not feel pain. I figured out later that I had been numb. One hour and I was a happy man.

At night I was invited by Steve, a liveaboard of the marina for a beer or two in his boat. And what a boat. But I had to decline because, after a shower and a bite, Helga and I crashed helplessly tired. And in the morning Steve came over again, approached our work bench and revalidated the invitation.

After having passed our trial by fire, the mental energy was multiplied many times but the physical was a disaster. And it is incredible when you finish the building of a hull and the deck you think you have a boat or almost a boat. Big illusion. It is at this point that the building really starts or you discover how many thousands little things must be done. Each one essential, in fact, on a boat nothing seems to be superfluous and you work a week and it seems that you have done near to nothing. So I was miles away from the first sailing. I did not have a yacht just yet. And to torture me more people passing by were saying, "Hey, Lui! Each day it looks more like a boat."

They meant to make a compliment but I was disappointed. The balance at this point was: the paint was done and the stainless steel hardware was in place so the boat had a means to be moored on a pier so it could be launched. Still it was without a rudder and the deck was entirely naked, no blocks, no stoppers, no sheets, nothing that could make it sail away. To complete the scenario our wallet was nearly empty. We were irreparably sinking with holes in our pockets. What were we to do? The answer came straight at my chest like a gun shot. We would not stop the "production" as we did not stop during the factory times. We still had alternatives to carry on and finish the boat. We made a quick board meeting, Helga and me, and decided to sell my shares of the San Diego chapter with Cathrine and launch the boat because the slip would be cheaper than the hardstand. We were almost there, we just needed to install all those toys from Christmas, and set up "the boat" for sailing.

Wait a minute! I couldn't believe it. How come? Helga never was aboard a floating boat. Me either, I mean, yes I was when I went to pick up the plans of Helga II from the designer in Brazil, thirteen years ago, yes, I had some experience.

It is all true and my calculation was that I had eighty per cent of a boat and from now on I was going to live aboard, on the water. It was me talking to myself. □

Months later while reading a book by Larry and Lin Pardey, I regretfully launched the boat unfinished and envied the Pardeys, but I also had pride and resignation. They launched their boat Serafin shining entirely finished and dressed with the flags of the nautical alphabet. Our beloved yacht did not go to the water, this great moment of all boats and their owners, as it should go. A boat must be launched only when "she" and "her" owner are ready. Like children should born only when their parents are ready for parenthood and all the circumstances are favorable. Or not? Perhaps if I could do like the kangaroos – retard the labor of their babies if there is an environment of circumstantial inadequacy – and wait until I was ready. The true beauty of nature is that for the conception and birth of babies we can't always wait the proper time. When it occurs to a passionate couple, we start to love our children when they exist only in our mutual ardent desire. The baby will be an extension of love in the making and anytime is time for love.

Again it was daybreak. I crawled under the material from the stern bunk and grabbed my gourd of yerba mate *chimarrão*. It is a must for a gaucho on special occasions. I would not break a champagne bottle because the boat was not ready to leave the pier but would be a special moment. So before five o'clock I was up already and feeding my yerba. I was not wearing bombachas (gaucho garment) however; instead a t-shirt and short pants stained by resin and paint I looked like a Trinity cartoon. No one at the marina understood that yerba in the gourd, the hot water, and the "bomba", a bronze and silver straw used to drink the *chimarrão*. Some thought it was marijuana. What? With hot water?

The travel lift began to move slowly, approaching the pier. Helga held my hand. I was quiet; I felt like was a mutt dog browsing around the marina while it seemed to me everyone was throwing orders at each other on how to move my boat to the water, especially how they would move it once floating because of no rudder just yet. They also made jokes which are the way the shipyard crew worked every day and the marina owner was talking to the manager both watching the action. At least my boat was receiving a great deal of importance and care.

Liveaboard people also came to watch the yacht of the popular Luis being launched. And little by little the travel lift lowered the boat until the fin keel touched the surface of the water while my heart was jumping out of my chest.

"Lui, you can jump aboard as soon as we lower it entirely and before we retrieve the travel lift so you can check that there is no leakage."

What? I thought. My heart burst out fast, beating loudly, and I did not know that was a routine and of the possibility of leakage so the launching could be aborted in a timely manner. And what if there was a leakage?

Helga kept holding my hand and followed me aboard so the three of us were lowered entirely on the water, while I could hear shouts and screams, claps and congratulations, they were making a party out of it.

"So Lui, are you going to pay beers for everyone?"

My voice disappeared, I was speechless, I was goofed. I did not cry, did not have a hiccup, I had that Mona Lisa look trying to pull a smile but half way it could be a threat of tears on the way instead. Under the pier two little happy ducks were swimming, two gray ducks as Helga and I abandoned to our own luck. The difference was that they were on their habitat while we were castaway by choice, potentially shipwrecked. We would now live for a while on a sailboat without the mast, without the rudder, without money, displaying a shabby appearance.

Two marina workers came to help me after I shouted out loud that there was no leakage so we pushed the boat around the pier to locate it on the slip reserved to us. We were moored next to Steve and we were officially residents of the marina next to a noble neighbor. Comforting was the fact that there were two other unfinished boats without masts as ours on the same pier.

Steve came aboard and told me that at night I would not escape from his third invitation for a coffee, since I said I did not like beer.

Two hours later without knowing what to do I was just gaped moving back and forward from the deck to the interior and back to down below. Then Helga shouted that she saw under the cockpit a fine line of water coming in. I jumped and knocked my head on a bulkhead beam. On a boat, sooner or later you will hit your head on a bulkhead beam.

What happened was that the skeg, a small fin-like piece functioning as a pseudo hydrofoil next to the rudder had been placed two days before and with full concentration on the keel I forgot to use resin or Sikaflex, a miraculous sealant while fixing that part. The leakage was right there. "We are sinking! Helga, run! Call..., no, I will call, you get the bilge pump!"

I ran across the patio of the marina and dashed into the office gasping. Very calm, but shitting on my pants, I told the manager what was happening, the little squirt of water and its speed.

"Do you think it is serious?" I asked him.

"Lui, wait a bit, if it does not stop or increase the squirt we will take the boat out of the water."

I thanked the manager and walked very calmly out of the office and as soon I got to the patio I ran again like crazy to check with Helga how was the squirt.

"Helga! Did stop? Did it increase?"

"I don't know, it's still dripping, I mean flowing water squirting, oh my God, check yourself."

"Yeah, let me see it."

I threw myself under the cockpit and came back to the surface quickly and went back like a meteor across the patio. But instead of reaching for the office I aimed for Larry, the shipwright who had helped me by suggesting how to build the rudder. Trying to be chill, controlling my breath I asked him very calmly if it could be a serious problem.

"It seems you are not acquainted with wooden boats, are you, Lui?"

It was a cherishing friendly voice from a near future soul brother I discovered. Larry was working on a delayed task and could not check our boat but promised to check in at lunch time. So I ran back to the boat. On the way, I bumped onto the mechanic, Jeary, who asked about the leakage for at this point the whole world knew about already. But it was another friendly voice who said, "I am coming aboard to check it out. Let me get my tool box."

Jeary became another friend and savior, one of many we would have along the way. The leakage was a minor thing. I simply did not have a parameter to assess its extent. To me, a boat should not have a single drop of water inside. Later on even seeing boats with two or three inches of water on the bilge, even learning that boats have crossed half of an ocean with a hole in the hull the size of an egg and did not sink, I kept my own concept of a dry boat. Ours became a motive of pride on this matter. The problem of leakage was really one with no reason for such worry. Jeary applied a glue that could dry out underwater and tightened it with a professional wrench and that was it. I should check it out next time I hauled the boat out of the water. It was never necessary to do a thing and if Helga has not written it in our diary I would have forgotten that episode.

Once we were rescued from a shipwreck, I sat to organize my thoughts with my feelings. I looked to Helga and she was like someone who had eaten poisoned food. She was not feeling good. In the next minute, she was really bad. Before I asked her anything she gave me the news, "Boating is not for me. I think I'm going to die of seasickness."

Her physiognomy was really scary. And when Helga gives up it is because she is truly bad. And when she is bad the entire world seems to deteriorate as if it was contaminated by a plague. The environment around her becomes so ill that seems even the inanimate objects will rot.

She does not complain but her state of nausea is such that it infects people around.

I felt defeated and the rest of the day seemed not to end. What were we going to do? The subtle swing of the boat moored on the pier was enough to make Helga sick. How would be out on the ocean? It hit me hard, knocked me down. I thought we would reach the end of the line, the end of our adventure, our dream in the making.

"Helga, go outside. Take a breath of clean air, walk a bit."

"I don't want to. I think I will die."

The seasickness never stopped bothering my Helga and during that period of adaptation, it was an everyday state of mind and health of my brave Helga. In the near future, it would improve only by alternate days with seasickness and days without it. Homesick, longing for her mother and now the lack of money threatening the purchase of groceries would advise the crew to abandon ship leaving the Captain alone. Our voyage was safe though, we had only some protests aboard that actually helped to improve our living but mutineers we never had.

... March.

The first decision of the Captain, the day after the launching day was to make an announcement that we did not need a car anymore, so it would be for sale and the cash would make the whole crew happy, we also threw in the basket promo items such as our fax machine brought from Melbourne and an answering machine too. These items were the last sign of mainstream people we once were, from now on we would assume our status of liveaboards and ocean drifters. The second decision made on the same day was to find a part time job for the Captain. The third was to resume the building of Helga II, finish it.

We sold one item on the same day the promotion was unleashed. We could eat an entire week. I pulled back my jokes and became a smiley

Lui once again. I had dreamt to be among boats aboard my own yacht and there I was, so I could not complain. Two days before we were a couple of meters from the water and were not considered just yet boating people, yachties. Now we were. And it was enough to be on the water to begin invitations to go aboard other people's boats and learn the gossips and yarns. For instance, a Danish man who was living aboard an unfinished vessel knew about everyone's lives. Told us crazy stories about the owner of the marina, who also owns a resort for nudists and used to advertise his offers and programs with a splash of his own huge wife naked on a magazine. Ivan was a painter by trade, and accepted orders to paint anything so I was offered a job and accepted as a new labor force in town who would accept any kind of job to survive. My first assignment was to help him to paint a bathroom of a factory. Once employed I and Helga could go back to our daily ritual of a glass of wine at dinner. By the way, we discovered that the Australian learned how to produce a good collection of wine, just like the ones we like most, cheap and decent.

On our things to do list, a task that Helga hijacked for herself with spectacular efficiency, was to mix up errands on the same level of importance like laundry and sanding interior areas of the boat, building the rudder, buy bolts and nuts and call home, purchase resin and call Cathrine in the United States and so on. After all, we were simultaneously many things; boatbuilders, family, ex-entrepreneurs... By me, I would not do anything else other than to work on finishing the boat. Helga, however, had that sense of continuity of normal life.

Thus we established tacitly areas for who would be in charge of what. I handled the most important things on earth - to finish the boat and watch the calendar to make sure we would reach the proper date to start our cruise back home. All the other minor life duties were Helga's business. She handled the catering of the crew, the laundry, the house cleaning, the busy mail business, the budgeting control and in her spare time she helped me, why not? And there was no conflict of management and execution because we always ended up mingled together in each other´s tasks anyway since we arrived in Australia. Even during the factory business every time I had to drive to town to buy raw material or something she would go to the parking lot to say goodbye; if not she would follow me. The trip to San Diego was so painful for both of us because of that, we were ripped apart from each other. Now we would not unglue under any circumstance. And it was the reason why I was able to keep going forward. How many times could we separate? Many. But we did not. It was not funny being apart from each other. So we used to go shopping, get groceries, do laundry, buy bolts and nuts, paint, sand together. This was the fastest way to be free from the prison, escape from the island.

In the meantime, that bathroom paint job was the last job of the season for Ivan after which he had a blank period without customers and I was fired. Aware of that I managed to ask around quickly and found a job in a Brazilian steak house in Sydney. The place was owned by folks from the north of Brazil so it was like someone from China running a Japanese sushi place and all of the sudden comes a knock on the door by a cook from Tokyo looking for a job. Being gaucho I was entitled to lecture about churrasco (barbecue or meat on a skewer with raw sea salt).

Helga tried to follow me, working in the kitchen peeling potatoes while assisting multiple tasks but was fired in the first week due to a dictatorial order from the Captain. Meanwhile, I was absorbing tasks as waiter and cook for a month until I was fired too, I mean, resigned because to work in a restaurant was tougher than building a boat. It was fun. During the day I kept going on the boatbuilding, installing the fresh water pump, electrical system, toilet bowl, sewage system that sort of things. At night I dressed myself up as gaucho with bombachas, white shirt and red scarf around the neck, including that now I was traveling on bus, the car had been sold.

No one could call me a vagabond.

Wait a minute, how did we sell those items so fast? The fax machine was the first item and we will never forget to make sure miracles do exist or that we must believe we are all tied together in this small and non-perennial world. That week we accepted being broke and needed to make some cash immediately to eat and be able to regroup and engage in the next level of life, we went to a convenience store near the marina located at a gas station so I would advertise the car. I was reluctant inside the car, hands on the wheel, Helga glued to my arm and I was thinking how and what exactly I was going to do. That very day we did not have a single penny, exactly that, not a single penny in our pockets. Then I told Helga: "Wait here, I am going to cross the street and sell the fax machine to that man over there."

A man was fueling a car of a client and I went straight on to him, looked straight into his eyes smiled and said: "Do you want a fax machine almost new very cheap?"

He did not want it but suggested I should go inside the store because his boss behind the counter was looking for a fax machine for his wife. He even stopped to fuel the car and walk me to the door while I told him I was going to send him a jersey used by Pelé from Brazil. Within less than half an hour the big deal was closed. And that night we had a glass of red wine bought at that very convenience store.

The car did not have any story to tell other than my phone call to a dealer got a reply, "bring the car here and I will see." So I did and the car was sold within an hour of paper formalities. I must say that I was being a very generous sales person regarding prices, which may be the reason why deals were closed so fast.

To organize the set up to start the building of the rudder took a week of sourcing material and managing to escape from the rain. I was already worried because the building of a rudder's spade-shape is almost as complex as building the hull of the boat itself, with its curves and taper. Then Larry came to our boat and invited us to have a dinner in his place. He was such a nice man. Since we arrived at that marina I noticed he was observing our movement but too shy to approach. When I asked him about the leakage problem I thought I could trust him because he seemed to me the most experienced shipwright at River Quays. So the channel was left open for him and I did not have a chance to decline his invitation. But around this time I became a contradictory person – at the same time popular and anti-social. I was so focused on my own agenda that I owed a visit to Steve, to the Russian guy, to the Beggar, a man I coined this nickname due to his dress and living code, to the son of the marina owner and now Larry.

Meanwhile in the resurrected factory department an action had been taken very seriously. I had sent a friendly fax to Cathrine wishing to know about the financial reports. I did not forget I was appointed Financial Director of the Chula Vista branch although I did not earn a single penny so far nor a general ledger to read either. Ok, because I had set my mind to leave Cathrine running the business the way she wanted for a while and after all, if she wanted to cheat me she would easily. From far away what could I do? That's why her reply was going to be more than laconic. So I was thinking while working on the boat, on the paint job, on the steak house. I understood well the unfolding of the business when I was left in the airport in Los Angeles back then and I accepted it. Cathrine would run away from me, follow my guidelines and manage to have a middle man to deal with me if necessary. But, hey, I own 15% of the partnership and it might be handy now that I am almost starving. So the response to my fax confirmed just that and astute she grasped nor only my state of mind as a liveaboard person but how fragile I was, living aboard a boat without means to come over to the open field as a business man and battle with her.

All that I wanted was some bread in my jar, I did not want to level up with Cathrine or with anybody else. For God sake, I was bootstrapping to build a rudder, looking for a scrap of wood and high-density foam and taking free informal lessons from workers at the marina. Larry, for instance, discussed patiently with me alternatives to build the rudder and tried to convince me to go for a wooden rudder and although it was helpful I decided to stick with the original plans. And my achieved result was superb, according to the grand jury, that were all the marina employees, teachers, and neighbors. This story with Cathrine would unfold completely later on while now I as was just about to reach the time to haul boat (our home) out of the water, to install the newly built piece.

Meanwhile, Steve was pressing on with his hard-to-decline invitation and organized a barbecue in the garden of the marina. He said if I did not attend he would prohibit me from living next to his boat. In fact, all the guests were already present when Helga and I were able to leave the tools and working uniforms to attend the event, hearing everyone shouting and teasing us. As a gift to the host, I brought him a nice noble nickname: "the ambassador of the Parramatta River", which was accepted unanimously. So this was our life, poor of money but rich of things to do and human warmth.

During the barbecue, I started to learn that owning a boat is to be worried about something all the time. Some worries though we enjoy having. And again I lean to compare it with being parents. It really seems that we have children before being prepared and we will be prepared only by having them. So there is no appropriate time, only an ardent desire. Among boaters, everyone talks about each one's problems, with their boats and of course, it is an open forum where we learn a lot. Peter, for instance, was in River Quays to launch his 51-foot homemade iron yacht. To build it he went through five years of hard work and struggled with a lack of money, including having to overcome a tragedy. Half way to finishing the boat a spark of weld caught the whole thing on fire and he lost almost everything. He did not stop and now he was there to see his dream to come true. I had not met him up until then but by observing his movements from a distance I could guess the importance of that moment for him. We sure had things in common. And I noticed some people watching his preparation for the launching of his huge yacht, clearly jealous and highlighting insignificant details of the boat, according to them, not properly done. Human nature. Some even went on complaining about his rock 'n' roll being too loud throughout the entire night. Once again, as if our neighbor had a newborn baby. So I jumped to his political party side without blinking. The day after his extravaganza, I saw Peter nervously walking up and down and asked him as if I was an old acquaintance:

"Hey, Peter! What's the matter with you?"

"Lui. I'm fuck up. Blew up the engine."

If there is one thing that I have zero talent at it is with mechanic stuff, but I ran to help him in some way. What is an engine, Peter? Your boat is like a mansion, you will fix the engine, take a breath, look, I will help you to cry – were the first things I thought to say to Peter including my stupid jokes. Then, "Look, Peter, let's have a beer." Considering that I am not a fan of beer. Helga took off an amethyst stone from one of her necklaces and gave it to Peter to give him luck.

That week I finished the rudder very proudly and stepping the mast was to be the next task because all the quotations around Parramatta River were prohibited to my pocket. So I found a good deal in the Darling Harbour and finally I would get to know the famous

Sydney area. Joe, a rigger at the largest marina of Sydney Harbor, in the middle of the mecca of sailing offered me one of his slips for two or three months and he would step the mast for me in April, so a month later.

With a short-term plan in place, I organized with River Quays marina to haul the boat out the water during a weekend to install the newly built rudder and to get done few other things while on the hardstand which is easier to work on a boat.

It was a bit embarrassing that I followed the maneuver to fish our boat to place on those brackets again and it surprised me that Helga did not sleep well the first night onshore. She woke in the middle of the night saying the water mattress was better and that she was afraid the boat would fall off the brackets.

One month, the first 30 days, living as boating people do and we could not update our families with what was going on with us. Helga tried but could not unveil details of our ocean passage plans... Once the boat was finished.

Ok. All prepared to install that rudder smooth and fine as a blade and a bit of sad surprise: the shaft of the rudder, nine feet of stainless steel, two and a half inches in diameter - the solid tube would not fit in the rubber sleeve. It was too tight. It was when I realized I had already met angels helping me and Steve was one of them and came to help followed by Ron, his father-in-law who was retired and feeling good about life and he was a true impersonation of a legendary mariner taken from a book of adventure. Yes, with the white beard, wearing Greek sailor hat and pipe. Anything for him would be transformed into a rescue mission, invasion of an island, assault to a merchant ship, this was Ron. He was not able to simply say "push a little bit more", he would go with an exaggerated opera shout as if acting in an epic movie. Ron made me feel like a humble stuntman.

Something was in fact wrong. It should not be that tight. I was soaked with sweat going up and down to the cockpit and ground trying to follow the orders shouted from Ron. Steve noticed that it was a serious problem and with his ambassador personality signaled Ron to calm down otherwise he would invent something unimaginable to fix the problem who would know. Ron was a little weird surely and all of the sudden he shouted, "Aaaah! What a sacrilege!"

He left the rudder operation right when Steve made that signal to him and shouted that "it was a sacrilege" pointing to the bow of the boat.

"What now, Ron?" – Steve and I asked him in unison.

"The anchor hardware of stainless steel has been painted instead of being polished for God sake!" – he shouted back to us.

Because we were counting pennies we did not have the means to order a proper polisher for that piece on a boat that inspires seamanship by the look of it, so ours did not. I had a leftover of an anticorrosive paint used on the iron keel and so feeling guilty I painted the anchor hardware mount thinking in the future to strip it off the paint and polish it. And it was just sitting there at the bow waiting to be bolted down.

Steve had not seen the piece and immediately went and grabbed it nodding and followed by Ron went to his boat with my anchor mount. Again I was just a humble stuntman or less of it. I just asked to myself what they would do with my equipment. They returned minutes later and Steve said smiling, "One thing at a time. First let's fix the rudder, later on, we will talk about that anchor hardware mount."

I said nothing. It was an order. Next, we made an extra effort and finally the rudder went in through the rubber sleeve and I had a serious decision to make. Since the rudder was too tight, the shaft of the engine also was tight. I noticed days earlier and the manager of the marina said he would not put my boat back in the water in those conditions because I would not be able to move the boat, I asked myself "what would I do now?"

But I didn't have money for a long term hardstand rental; next month I must to move to Joe's slip at the Birkenhead Marina for free and step the mast – these were my thoughts threatening me. We talked, Helga and I, and made a half decision to launch the boat back on the water and fix all those things when possible and maybe tow the bow to Joe's place when the time came.

"Steve, what do you say?" I asked my godfather.

"Go back to the water. I run the risk," He said that "he" would run the risk.

That was the push I needed. More than that, it was a true proof of friendship while a bunch of buzzards were flying by scaring me that the engine shaft would never unlock, the rudder would not be free. Steve went against them and helped me to make up my mind. The next day, on Monday, we went back to our slip on the water.

A couple of days later, Steve knocked on our hull appealing for us to have dinner aboard Nautilus, his yacht. Invitation nonnegotiable. That first month floating on the water and the River Quays phase could not end warmer. Maureen, Steve's wife, made a Babette's Feast, beautiful and gorgeous and accompanied by wine. One of the hobbies of Steve was to taste wine and his onboard wine cellar was of gods. The main course was baked lamb with whole colored vegetables and an unspeakable sauce on peppermint sauce. The dessert was a homemade ice cream of cherry followed by a genuine, according to Steve, Brazilian coffee. At the end, he produced a cocoa liquor those we pray asking for the second shot. What a dinner. I had no words.

Besides, we had a tour all along Nautilus, a 56-feet tall ship built in 1937 restored by Steve himself; it was a classic masterpiece.

That night had many things reserved for us. Helga was enchanted while I almost cried of emotion. Steve had a company of metal cleaning. Until five years ago he had a classic car's restoration business and was famous in the trade. His expertise was with the Jaguar, Mustang, and Porsche. He showed us one of his pride works sold to a collector by an astronomic dollar figure. His restoration business went from bad to almost bankrupt before his eyes while he could not help himself but to the restoration of Nautilus, his yacht. The boat was indeed an attraction, a 56 ft ketch designed by John Alden. The more we talked the more impressed, and dazzled I was discovering fantastic stories about Steve and boats. He showed me a picture of Nautilus anchored right there in the same spot decades ago before the marina was built. Thus, it was indeed a good title - Ambassador of the Parramatta River. He pulled out a copy of a wooden boat magazine - on the cover had a photo of Tasmania's wooden boat show with Nautilus next to Serafin, the famous yacht of Larry and Lin Pardey. I then realized that Rinley, the truck driver, had brought us to Austrailia's hardcore boat location. River Quays was the marina where the first wooden boat festival in Australia took place.

"So you have met Larry and Lin?" I asked Steve.

"Of course. We are good friends. Here's a picture with them; they love Nautilus," said Steve.

I was shrunken on the couch submerged in admiration. My friend Steve was one of the heroes I read about in books of sailing adventures. I could not believe it - it was a dream. From between some old photos that had fallen on the floor Maureen grabbed one of Steve's family and told us they were descendants from Vikings. It was late already and Helga told me with that look we should go home and I started to say goodbye and thank Steve and Maureen when I heard an order, "Wait! Close your eyes, I have a little surprise for you."

I closed my eyes, thinking it was a joke and, when he said I could re-open, tears came simultaneously - I couldn't avoid it. Steve took from a nice cardboard box the anchor mount hardware that he had taken from me last Saturday. It was wrapped with a red felt as if was a prize; he slid the felt slowly aside and I could not believe the shine of the piece. That night was a gift from heaven to me; I thanked God and realized I never would be able to repay Steve. □

...April.

April was a busy month. Steve tried to turn around the shaft of the engine, I dove in the filthy water of the marina inspecting for any debris around the propeller, we tried everything and convinced ourselves that the nylon bushing should be worked. An out-of-the-water task to be. Regarding the rudder, we speculated if it would be free with time and water lubrication (but confidence was not more than 50%) and I did not have a tiller yet to move the boat. So once again Steve, who seemed to have adopted me, improvised a tiller with a 4x4 pine piece of wood; it was so thick that I used my open palm open to hold onto it and so funny that everyone noticed. I used that improvisation for the next two months. My first sailing experience was with that leg of a dinner table as a tiller.

As the lights of March shut off we left River Quays towed by Joe piloting in front of us with a potent work boat, so we were making our first true cruise aboard our own yacht - our first cruise ever. We went down the Parramatta River toward Sydney Harbour. It took around two hours, turning around each elbow of the river, under bridges, contouring other boats through heavy traffic. Little by little the suburb atmosphere was being left behind and I could see a lot of floating waste as well as on the banks of the river, trash discharged irresponsibly.

Even being towed, the rudder was hard to manage with the engine off; but I enjoyed every inch of the trip. Within my inner secrecy, we were already going back home, by boat, which also meant to me going out of the prison. As recorded in Helga's impeccable diary, I saw huge blocks of concrete on an island approaching Sydney with signs of warning saying "Do not Approach. Explosives!" and I shouted to Joe over his engine noise:

"Hey, Joe! What is it?"

"Nah!" he replied shrugging. Later on, I learned that it was a disabled military deposit and still had dangerous material and the local population used to protest frequently. Wow!

Arriving in Birkenhead, the number of boats and water activity around was exciting. Helga loved the sites around and now we would see skyscrapers again, a thing that a long time ago we forgot the existence. Sydney, a city like Rio de Janeiro, New York, Paris, drumming the next trend to the rest of the country. Joe told us we would be temporarily hooked on a mooring on the other side of the marina and this was a surprise to me. To be away from land, without an umbilical cord. Never thought about that. Joe gave us a tender with a pair of oars and it also was new to me. We would be towed to a pier next day.

"Ok, Joe. I'll see you tomorrow."

As we had never rowed a dinghy before and considering that heavy traffic we made the smart decision to stay home for the rest of the day, contemplating the city skyscrapers from a distance. We had food aboard, drinking water, the galley with stove and with our fridge already operational we could live forever hooked on that mooring buoy. And what a good surprise, a boat swings around a mooring buoy according to the wind and local current it does not bounce as much as on the pier.

The next morning, we stretched our necks out of the companionway like two little mice. The marina seemed to have run away by many yards. "Ok, Helga, to row must be easy, and after all, one day I must start. Let's go?" I said to my first mate aboard. And what an adventure! Apart from the fact that we were almost smashed twice by the ferryboat during our passage it was a success and soon I would become an Olympic rower. But then came another surprise. As soon as I touched the pier, Joe came and threw the keys of a powerboat, said he was busy, and I should tow myself and our boat to the slip that was reserved for me. He definitely must have thought I was a marina rat used to moving boats around.

"All right, no problem, Joe."

Only an insane person would give the keys of a powerboat to someone who had never stepped on a boat until the day before. Worst, to drive a powerboat, I mean, to tow another boat and maneuver the two in such busy commercial and leisure waterway. Needless to say that while you tow a boat it is not like towing a car. In a liquid environment, all the physics are different from a road; the forces involved interact differently. So it was my morning task.

Although I had a happy smiley face like a boy with half of his wishing basket items in his hand, I distilled adrenaline just to turn on the engine of the powerboat and to leave the pier. Then to navigate to our mooring buoy was another story and to finally tow our boat and moor it to the slip was a one-of-a-kind adventure and my strategy was to make each move very, very slow, pretending I was naturally lazy, hoping people were thinking I was just another lousy marina employee who would be fired soon.

For a change, we were once again a curiosity in the marina. Our berth was right in front of the shopping center of the complex so tourists would observe us, take a picture and even stop for a chat, amazed with our accents and some asking if we came from Brazil by boat. And I was so proud when even before the mast had been stepped I received compliments for the boat. We did not have just yet installed the winches and portholes and hatches so the deck was empty like a ping pong table.

Feeling like winners for everything that was happening to us we went for a walk to check things out nearby. It was an old mill with an array of brick buildings gentrified into a modern shopping center complex decorated with maritime motifs and with a retired tall ship right in the middle of it. Commercially, the shopping center was a disaster without anchor stores, and the supermarket and the food area had access by the street so there was no circulation of people and so for my taste, it was a nice place to hang out. By accident, we were frequently caught comparing things in Australia with the United States and Brazil. It was then when I developed a useless theory that Australia is exactly like Brazil but with the majority of the system working more very well than less, contrary to my home country where nothing works satisfactory at all, Australia being with a similar size territory and with only 10% of the population. Then comparing to America was another story. We observed that services were pretty much Americanized, the procedures and layouts of stores for instance but all of the sudden the Australian way would show up. When I was running the factory back in Melbourne, I always noticed that things were going well until an incompatible mix of Pommie and Aussie smack got in the way and things get weird, not functional, but again because the system and the culture are in good terms, all go back to work well fast enough. And of course this was just a hasty opinion of mine to be improved in the future.

Leaving the gooey criticisms aside and accepting the ear pulled by a Social Scientist aboard, the first thing Helga was attracted to in the shopping center was an advertisement for a job position as a cashier in the fruit & vegetable store.

"I will apply!" said my brave Helga, surprising me.

She went there, got herself interviewed and by the afternoon she was hired to start within three days. While Helga was being interviewed by a Greek who at each three words used to curse at something or someone, I went to help Joe to move masts of his clients and he asked if I would like to work in the marina, they were looking a jack for all trade kind of guy.

"Hey, Joe, I have Ph.D. you know."

Next day I had the marina manager for a coffee & cookies aboard our boat and was interviewed around our dinette.

"Well, if you built this beautiful yacht, you are hired. After all, the job is easy, it includes driving the forklift and the travel lift. We will need a temporary license, no big deal. When can you start?" – the manager asked.

"It is easy indeed and I can start tomorrow."

We had been thinking to solve our bank account issues we would sell sandwiches at factories doors and a couple of other enterprises, but none enthused us so much as the employment near our home because, after hours, the major plan was to resume the finishing of our boat and engage the cruise back to Brazil. The route now was: Sydney / Easter Island / Panama Canal / Venezuela / Brazil.

In the meantime: "the boat is coming along". Helga rescued an old mantra which helped to accomplish important tasks in the first week. Install the winches, the main hatch, and the VHF radio. How motivational it was to hear the first buzz of a VHF radio with an improvised antenna since the mast had not been stepped yet. The celebration was with a gorgeous rice & chicken teriyaki followed with red wine and a green salad. Helga made miracles with our domestic budget and building last minute needs, since all the real equipment was still coming from that Christmas tree in Melbourne. Yet about the VHF radio, the first time I heard the weather forecast I transcended the coordinates of latitude and longitude, wind speed, wave height, cloud types, and was confused with what the heck high and low pressure really was. Would I be able to translate all that into decision making out on the ocean? Wow, the wine had been hit my head well and was time to go to bed.

To dream! How nice, definitely the best drug.

My enthusiasm began to bring us problems. Helga tried to warn me, but it was already too late.

Anyone that approached our boat, curious about something (about is a word that fits in any circumstance in Australia) was invited for a thorough tour of our home. To the first three visitors, Helga offered coffee and her killer muffin made in our newly installed oven. But Helga knew "about" my excitement unfolding and curtailed it timely. It was hard to avoid the locals such as Joe who started to shout from his container saying he was coming, and I should put the kettle on, and get ready the muffins. Alan and Ellen from a boat nearby liked our strong black coffee without sugar and they smoked like chimneys. John, another neighbor, started to arrive unexpectedly, bringing donuts and asking for our coffee, and muffins. Trevor, from a racing yacht for disabled people came but did not drink our coffee and declined the muffins, but on the other hand stayed not less than an hour chatting, I mean, talking about races and yachts for races he built. The number of visitors signed into our guest book in the first two weeks at Birkenhead goes over two pages. I was excited with the guest book, a must on any serious cruise yacht. And my excitement was also delaying our departure from the prison.

Joe, apparently thinking I was not in a hurry to leave port, did not bother to delay the installation of the rigging, mast and all that must be provided to make a sailing vessel able to move with the power of the wind. Without my signature, Joe included me in his list of unpaid employees, and called me all the time to help him to move stuff around, including towing boats across Sydney Harbour because I was an experienced boat pilot. Soon I was incorporated into the local landscape, though, building anxiety for not working on our boat and yet somehow happy because I was learning a lot. These controversial feelings and the fast pace simultaneously seemed to be the only certain recurrent pattern in my life lately.

My story started to fly, garbled by word of mouth and within two weeks I was considered an old hand, at least this was my impression because the way people asked me questions. There were three young men splitting the duties of the boat yard of the marina. I was presented to them by the manager as a temporary harbor master and only one of them had a license to drive the travel lift and the forklift. Charles, a guy from Fiji - a lazy but nice person - loved the nickname I chose for him: Coconut (one day I would have to give up the bad habit of placing nicknames, even I started to hate them). During the first three days of work for me in the marina we did not have to move boats with the lifting equipment because it was raining. During that time Coconut, I mean, Charles, did not stop asking me to let him drive the forklift and travel lift to stack powerboats up on the racks and to pull boats out of the water and launch them back. I told him that we were dealing with expensive assets of a third party, that he did not have a license to pilot those things and etcetera:

"Do you know how much these boats cost, Coconut?"

"Of course, Louis. But I will drive them slowly, with care, you will see."

"I don't know, it is too much of responsibility."

At the other side of the shopping center, Helga was gaining the trust of the Greek owner of the green market. During my break times, I used to run to see Helga working at the cash register only to kiss her quickly and come back. During her break times was her turn to come and see me.

And Coconut became an outstanding forklift and travel lift driver. How would he not with that teacher?

It was clear that I was a bluff but at that marina I abused it. My scruples began to tell me that soon I was going to have to prove that I had experience as an old time sailor, fork & travel lift driver, and boat builder; it would reach a point I was going to need to do all that and cross oceans in my own yacht. The first stage of these points just knocked on my door on the third day at work when the manager of the marina gave me a clipboard with a sheet listing boats to take to or from the racks and said to me, "Lui, watch Charles, O.k.? He is too enthused."

"No worries, David," I replied.

So we went to the boatyard with our daily mission under my arm. We walked to a rack of four vertical rows with powerboats sized from 19 feet to 30 feet, on a rack 35 feet high. We had to take down a 23 foot powerboat from the third row up. I was in charge, meaning I should be the driver and Coconut the helper but he did not stop to ask me to try; I was in complete silence, like a rock. Then in front of the rack, I stared at Coconut with that intense look and said, "All right, Mr. You will take down this small boat, to put into the water, but, listen to me. Listen clearly. You will do exactly what I say, at the speed I say you do it; the way I say – ok - understood?"

"Louis, trust me, Louis, trust me."

"O.k. First, show me where the idle is; the forward, the back up, the break. Just point it out to me. Right, now turn on the engine and push the gas on idle, slowly... ok, stop. Lift the fork, slowly, engage forward slowly, slowly, stop. Look both sides. Now, tilt the fork a bit, ok, retrieve the fork slowly, ok, stop.

You are doing well. Relax. Now, imagine that you have a boat on the fork and start to back up, always slowly, turn to your left, stop, look to both sides, engage forward three to five feet, and stop!

Good. Remember: whatever you do it must be very slowly; focus on what you are doing, ok? A minor distraction, it takes only one second, and that's right when shit happens. Letting one of these boats to fall off the fork, or even a simple scratch will be a pain in our ass, we don't want this. Ok? Did you hear me, Coconut?"

"Yes, Lui. You are great, man, trust me, I will do it just like you are saying."

"Right. Don't talk; just listen now and follow me. We are doing this together."

And we spent the whole day taking boats out of the rack to the water and vice-versa. Coconut in the driver seat and I with the clipboard just instructing him. I got back home and told Helga, "Helga. We moved more than twenty boats. I did not touch the forklift nor the travel lift. Coconut is a great driver."

Helga said it was not funny at all and that I could get in trouble twice, both for damaging boats and by letting a person without a license drive those things.

"No worries, Helga. Coconut is a heck of a driver."

A week later, I told the marina manager that Coconut could get a license too, he would pass the exam, it would be an incentive. Before I left that job as a harbor master, very proud, I witnessed my pupil Coconut take the exam for an operator and get his license. He bought me a Coca-Cola. I worked a little over a month in that marina, and did not drive any of those machines a single time. I never drove one of them in my entire life.

Now, living in a busy and crowded town, some of the city slicker habits returned to my mind, including the criticism of other people's lives. Birkenhead was a marina with problems; some of them included clandestine liveaboards, or sneak-aboards. Another problem was the general manager, a lady seen by at least everyone I met there as an accursed person, and she was responsible for the entire complex - shopping center, marina, and condominium. I heard complaints about her way of treating people, from store owners, security personnel, employees, and boat owners. I did not have my own story to share until she called me saying I was a smart ass. I was accused of using one of the noblest berths of the marina to liveaboard for free, pretending I was waiting for Joe to install my mast.

What? That story was never explained properly because, first, I would not have said that Joe made a deal with me; my first thought was that Joe would be in hot water if I told the woman how we had made the deal. I came up with a creative explanation that no one on this earth would understand; I can not even recollect exactly how I answered the woman while I was thinking what to say, or, what I was going to do if I had to face an eviction action with short notice, which actually I had for good. And I was, let's say, discovered when the tough lady called us all from the boatyard and demanded us to clean the marina, to leave it tidy, and shining. She did not want to see a single hair flying around out of place. The thing was that the future owners of the marina would be visiting the installations and according to rumors they would transform that place into a profitable and sophisticated business. They came - a group of Chinese businessmen, suits and ties and walked like ducks just like I and my peers used to walk when I wore my silk hermès ties. Yes, that was another sign I had seen elsewhere down under, tigers and sharks entrepreneurs and investors taking over Australia.

Our preoccupation, Helga's and mine, was our boat. The Aussie and Pommy behavior and much less the Australian business environment were not our preferred subject to talk about at dinner when we got together after a tough work day. Especially because it was Helga's birthday week and we wanted to celebrate accordingly. From then on a magical cloud began to fly over our heads and, without money to buy birthday gift we would go through the special date, hugging each other in the cockpit at night, amazed by the cosmic coincidences making us look to the sky. The mast was installed right on the Captain's wife's birthday. It was a true Greek present to Helga, and I did not have words to thank her for being such a partner, responsible for so many things without which I would not be where I was. From her work at the green market, the much needed cash for us to carry on was guaranteed. From her delicate hands, several parts of the boat were built, her holding things here and there, bringing me tools and water, and food and comfort. She was acquiring self-confidence a thing that she was looking for making me more proud and admired. Helga did not realize how much she was able to accomplish. Congratulations, happy birthday to you my dear Helga. We went to bed after emptying two bottles of wine, eating half a kilo of parmesan cheese and one kilo of Italian bread with olive oil all topped with chocolate truffles. And from that day on I started listening to the buzz of the winds against the shrouds (pieces of standing rigging which hold the mast up from side to side). How tall it was; I was amazed. I couldn't hide the contentment inside myself.

During my brief passage on that temporary job, I was able to install portholes, winches and all the paraphernalia that goes on the deck. Once again, I always like to remember they had been under the Christmas tree in Melbourne. All Harken brand, bow to stern, and that I installed them with no clue of how each one would or should work. Months later, I asked Helga if she noticed I did not know what I was doing and she said that of course anyone would notice, but she knew that after spreading everything out on the floor of the boat, the manual and parts, I would figure it out and get it done right because everything else had been done the same way.

One day while helping to launch a yacht I had a quick deep breath of anxiety. When the travel lift left it to go floating on the water, its owner turned the engine on and moved slowly making a nice gentle wake mingled itself with other boats like a duck. How easy, how natural. When would I be able to do the same thing? The shaft of my propeller was stuck, I could not motor like that. To sail was not possible either, not only because I did no know how, because I did not have time and without being able to use the engine it would be risky navigating among so many boats in the Darling Harbour.

The answer to my distress came sooner than I thought. The manager of the marina let me use the travel lift for free to pull my boat out of the water to fix the shaft on my day off. And it was done by Coconut, following my instructions. Steve had promised me to come over and help but he actually took over the whole task while I was just a useless assistant. It was a Sunday and Steve brought his inseparable friend Ron, the pilgrim from the Himalayas, the intrepid old sailor of the Tasman Sea, the pirate of seven seas, and they both worked hard from 8am to 5pm, nonstop, eating only snacks and bananas. The shaft was taken out and replaced with a fine adjustment. Steve decided it was time to install the depth and speed transducer – a piece of equipment that I would connect to my network of navigational electronics in the near future. The rudder was also taken out and replaced back after an improvisation and even my prayer. The boat was relaunched and on that afternoon I was able to hear my engine making the shaft turning smoothly for the first time. What a joy! Steve did not leave before seeing me driving the boat back and forward in front of the marina; he wanted to be sure the job was done correctly. Only Steve. And it was perfect. I was now another duck around campus. It was the first time I steered my boat and it was right in the middle of Darling Harbour. My dream came true in the mecca of sailing. To make it complete, I had only to anchor in front of a beach with white sand...

It was the end of April and the two months ahead where the worst nightmare of my life.

...May and June, just remembering gives me shivers.

It was pouring rain when Joe gave me that sudden and short notice - the Federal Police were after me. I quit the job as a temporary harbor master and instructor because my back was soaring, the job was not a ride in the park and I decided I should focus on finishing my boat in order to leave port en route to Brazil by Christmas. Yes, ambitious goal. So I went to Joe's container, his shop, to find out that crazy story or to make sure it was a big joke. It was not. Joe was upset, walking aimlessly and throwing things around, kicking boxes.

"Hey, Joe, how can I help you?"

He did not look at me; instead he raved to himself while grabbing a box of tools and threw it in the water right in front of me.

"Joe, easy man, talk to me..."

"The Feds are after you. You need to leave my berth now. That bitch told me if you do not leave she will cancel my leasing. Fucking bitch! I will kill her! Fuuuck!!!"

"Wow! What is it? What happened?"

There was no way to talk to him. And it was worst when I asked him when he would finish the job we had agreed he would do on my boat and which I had already paid for up front. He did not know. He had a line of "real clients", he needed his berth, I had to leave. Cursing and kicking things he said he thought I was going to use the berth for one month only, April, and then he got himself in his car and left burning rubber.

While gaping I saw coming toward me two security personnel from the new security company that had just started to protect the marina, part of the new management, and they asked if I was Luis and if I was the owner of that boat in Joe Riggins's berth.

I felt a bitter taste in the mouth, I was caught by surprise, within a second it looked like a Kafkian situation.

"Yes, that's me."

"You have one hour to leave, to take your boat out. Order from the General Manager," one of them said to me.

"But I have a deal with Joe."

"Liveaboard is not allowed here."

"I will get my notes of the things Joe is supposed to do," I said and I went down below to grab a briefcase of docs, but when I came back to the cockpit the security guys were gone.

I ran to the office but my friend the manager had been fired an hour before and the girl at the reception had a bill against me showing one month of rent. There was also a note to Luis – to leave the marina today or to pay a month of rent. While I was trying to understand all of that the two security personnel came from behind me. I wanted to argue but the two of them approached me. I looked over my shoulders and figured by their attitude that any minor out of tone words from me they would touch my arm and I would react and they would then immobilize me turning my already unbelievable situation into an even more awful one. I had gumption and told them in an amicable way, "All right then, give me half an hour and I will leave and might stop by tomorrow or so to talk with the general manager or I will call her." And I walked past the two tall security guys. But instead of going straight to the boat I ran to the supermarket to let Helga know what was happening. But tell her what? If even I did not know what was going on?

Mid way to the supermarket I made a U-turn and went to the boat starting to undo the mooring lines, my heart almost jumping out of my chest. The truth was that I feared our conditions of expired Visa were going to create a serious problem once unveiled. I should have solved that months before, but living half aboard half working in crazy jobs how could I? The matter of a fact, I realized later on that I was so tired of so many escalating challenges that it was a sort of snap of my nerves. And it was translated into fear, fear of losing my boat, my dream, so I had a reaction of self-preservation - the life of a dreamer. Thus I would leave that place immediately even if I had to hop up the coast endlessly as if I was escaping from Australia. The lack of money and our unconventional condition of allien-building-a-woodenboat-with-a-deadline-to-leave-the-country left us vulnerable.

While I was undoing the mooring lines, an old man in his late seventies who occasionally used to stop by and help Joe, came around and suggested to me to pick up a mooring buoy at the Drummoyne Sailing Club next to the Marina. They would let me stay there for free for a week or so. Weeks later I discovered it was him who had been stolen my battens (inserted strips that help to shape the sails) and the spinnaker pole of a neighboring boat. It all happened while I was there working at the Marina. Son of a gun.

I turned on the engine and got under the way slowly. Backing from the berth and through the channel, I made a curve inside the Marina pool without touching any other boats, like a pro, and aimed for the exit. Done! It was like escaping, a fugitive feeling in my chest. I thought of Helga. I was going to tell her later on; it was mid afternoon and she would leave work at around six, so after mooring the boat I would run to meet Helga. From the Marina pier, the two security personnel stared at me like two trained dogs. The popular Luís, sailor, boatbuilder, a friend of all, would now have another title around the docks. I never heard a thing but for a quite a while I felt like people were suspicious if was true or false that I ran from the Federal Tax Office, Immigration Department, or worst...

I had now to pilot my boat single handedly without experience in that busy water way traffic, feeling like I was a fugitive, picking up a mooring buoy before asking permission to the club. Ok, I thought, I will ask them right after I hook up the boat, that old thief better be right or I would be in more trouble... But wait a minute: how would I identify myself? My Visa was expired, I didn't have an address, I live aboard an unfinished boat and I have to say I am going to cross three oceans to get back home. Would it make it worse, the fact that I did not have anchors and a bunch of things to make it look like a cruising vessel? And, finally, I did not know how to pick up a mooring buoy, considering I was steering alone and had to go to the bow and grab the thing from the surface of the water. Was I going to shipwreck right there?

I started to feel cornered for good. All of the sudden I was in the middle of the Sydney Harbour in those circumstances while Helga was working at the green market. Our lives were upside down and she did not know it yet. Just as I was about to explode with joy because I had the mast stepped and the radio. It was a nightmare, had to be.

Sealed to that tiller improvised by Steve, I navigated nervously, biting my lip. I could not cry, there was nobody to rescue me, so I went for the mooring in front of the Drummoyne Sailing Club, among dozens of boats, moving as slow as I could, and very slowly went around an empty mooring buoy, and noticed that all the boats were pointing with their bow in the same direction. I figured the tidal stream was some how contrary to them according to my theoretical arsenal, then I went against the stream right towards the buoy I aimed to grab, very slowly still, and at more or less one boat of distance from the buoy I geared the engine to idle and run to the bow, the boat now should go straight onto the buoy. If not I would miss it and would have to make another turn, another try. I saw the buoy approaching as if it was coming towards me so I laid down on the deck, sticking my arm out as much as I could with the end of a rope in my hand while with the other arm curled around the pulpit, holding myself and I was lucky to make the end of the rope go through a corroded ring of the buoy so half of the job was done. I had to stand up quick and secure the rope to the bow's cleat. – Oops! The rope rod was too short and the boat jerked, fighting with the buoy and causing my right hand to bleed so I gave it more rope scope, figuring a boat length, again using my ammunition of theories in high speed thinking. Finally the boat started to slowly go around the buoy and placed herself lined up as all the others.

Gosh! I made it. I was moored and I did all by myself. What next? I went down below and unconsciously grabbed two bananas that went straight almost without a bite to my empty stomach without having had lunch, and I drank almost a quart of water. Helga! I said to myself, I will go to see Helga now. But before I go I have to change my shirt; it was soaked and dirty and I didn't smell good, my face must have been terrible too, unshaven, with dark circles and spooky eyes. A dress code to be arrested I guessed. Thinking this I jumped on the dinghy and asked myself what people at the club would say?

There was no problem they said to my surprise I was welcomed with a friendly tone while tying the painter of the dinghy near the ramp and they even offered me a membership application to fill in later on. Wow! Not everything was ruined. They also gave me the keys to the women's room out around the back; it hadn't been used for quite a while so Helga could have it for her own. I think the deference was given to me because I said with strong confidence that I had some work to get done on the boat before setting sail to Brazil so I was en route for a cruise through Australia. Although the next day that story was unveiled as fake.

Until then, I ran to see Helga and tell her we had changed places. At half way to the green market I met Richard, a welder who worked at River

Quays Marina, who had welded my pulpit, rails, and pushpit in River Quays; he was now with his own shop nearby and Helga was with him walking towards me. I did not understand. What was happening?

Helga then ran in my direction. She was scared. Seeing her like that I felt a bitter taste in my mouth but also almost said out loud: No, with Helga, no. Who ever is playing that game will... But I did not have time to finish my thoughts and declaration of war. Richard who normally used to talk with a lisp, twang and with spooky eyes was excelling himself on that, faster and with a white goop in the corner of the mouth.

"Helga, what are you doing here? Richard, calm down. What happened?" Everything seemed too awkward, chaotic.

"How are you?" Helga asked me and embraced. She was devastated. Where is the Rambo inside myself to protect her?

"I am fine. Richard, calm down, slowly tell me what is happening?:

"Luis, Joe stopped by my shop and said terrible things about you, that the police and the Feds are after you. Look, I had these dogs on my neck more than once. They get you and don't let you speak up. It takes years to be cleared. Get on the boat, Luis, get on the boat and hop up the coast up to Cairns and disappear up north as far as you can, quick, go, man! Go!"

The three of us were against the shopping center wall out on the back of it because that was the Drummoyne Sailing Club, so with it being already dark and three untidy persons in those circumstances we well could be arrested for sure for some reason.

"Richard, what is it? I did not do any thing..."

"All right, Luis, to me you don't need to explain, I'm messed up too and I don't care. Take care of your self, Luis, if I can help you, hide you a couple of days in my place..."

"Good, good, Richard. Thanks. Now, I will go to the boat with Helga and tomorrow we will talk, ok? Thanks. Helga, let's go, all is going to be fine."

"Luis. Be careful, mate, God bless you."

We walked in the dark, Helga and I, and went to where the dinghy had been left. It was windy as it is common in the afternoon and the tidal waves were juggling the dinghy against the stone wall of the Club. In the dark it was hard to row the dinghy with those waves, nervous, feeling cold and dropping things awkwardly to Helga trying not to scare her anymore as if it was possible. She was silent though, listened to me and I was getting very close to an uncontrolled mode. Arriving at home, Helga felt the boat aligned with the wind and tide, more comfortable than in the berth banging against the pier. She sat on the bunk and stared at me with those incredible affectionate eyes, asking me, "Tell me now. What happened. From the beginning."

I think I exaggerated the drama and one more time Helga surprised me. We should not be afraid nor ashamed of anything and did not need to fear anything either. We did not owe anything to anybody. An expired Visa for two months was not going to be the end of the world. It was good actually that I removed the boat from the marina and avoided a fight with Joe and the other men. She was afraid that I had the same reaction I had in Melbourne. It was all fine, considering the circumstances. We should leave Joe with his things. I was impressed, a bit relieved, more in passionate. How great she was, noble, strong. How weak and frightened I was. Fearing to lose my boat I became a scared rat.

Helga then was thoughtful for a little while and called my attention to the fact that the boat had not been registered yet. We planned to register it in New South Wales after leaving Melbourne but did not have time up until then. "We should get this out of the way now," she said.

"You are right," I said almost unconsciously, but it was Helga who was at the helm.

We went to bed and would wake up early the next morning, take showers in the new bathroom arrangement and would then execute a plan for the next week. However, there was a surprise: the shower was cold, no hot water and the first signs of a severe winter could already be felt. The second surprise was that the Deputy Commodore of the Club approached me in the hall and told me the lady next door, the Marina Shopping Center General Manager called him saying horrible things about me. I tried to make a joke saying yes I had stolen few boats, he kind of accepted the joke but warned me to stay there no more than a week or so. A bit of slack but not enough to make me feel relaxed.

Helga held firm my hand and told me to trust in God; all was going to be fine. She would go to work and I should stay on the boat working on installing things. Hey, now at the buoy there was no power for the tools. Next day would be Helga´s day off and we would register the boat.

I would never forget that day, how I felt, scared to death of my own shadow, as if a cloud of disgrace was flying over my head I could not even raise my eyes. Stayed the whole day in the boat, one of the most horrible days of my life. A power boat of the Coast Guard was maneuvering near the Club and I panicked. I turned on the VHF radio trying to eventually pick up their conversation and hidden down below I peered with the binoculars trying to figure out what they were doing. I did not see nor hear anything related to me or any delinquency but my heart burst out of my chest when the Coast Guard seemed to move slowly towards me. I imagined myself arrested, the boat confiscated, Helga left alone with that situation in her hands. What if I was deported? I started to pray, confessing and asking forgiveness for my sins I looked around to my dream, my boat, it could be the last chance to see it, its caverns, the woods that I worked on, all the hardship I had been through.

I sweated and had chills. The Coast Guard came very close then made a turn and steered towards the Club's pier and moored over there. Ok, I thought, they will check with the Club about my situation and later on they will come down to me. I can not even escape. To where? If I make any move I make things worse. Worse? It was noon, maybe they are just having lunch. The Club had a restaurant specializing in seafood and its view was, well, on its membership cards it says:
"The Club with a Million Dollar View". From the balcony and its saloon, it was possible to see the skyline of the city, Sydney, the bridge and the famous Opera House. What a view! And what a time to think about a scenic view...

The Coast Guard boat did not leave the Club for the entire afternoon, and I did not leave my boat either. The night came and I risked jumping on the dinghy and picked up Helga at work. They would not confiscate the boat at night. And sat on the bunk as she was the day before, Helga stared at me almost giving up as I had done and, as only Helga can do, she said two things that transformed our nearly disastrous life all around into good vibrations, first, then into a series of true accomplishments. She held my face with her two hands in a shell and said firmly, with a tiny supplication but even caring to warn me I should not be moving by her fragility, she had a great dose of charge in her voice: "Look into my eyes. I need you brave and strong and with courage, as always you were to me. Come back, please."

It was like to exorcizing me. What a relief. I came back. And I came back all clean inside out. In the future I reflected a lot about those two days of my life. It was like a catharsis a cleansing of the soul. And as if it was not enough, Helga woke me the next morning with a surprise idea, another order: we should register the boat reading the signs of the universe; first changing places, finding a nice anchorage to finish the boat, including being more discrete, and get ready to start up our cruise back home; second, register the boat but not named after her anymore, Helga II no, she never liked it anyway. "Let's name the boat Alvidia, after your mother, *in memoriam*. Your sister will like it; she will pray for us." She carried on defending her idea before I could disagree. "I feel only good vibes already calling the boat Alvidia. It is a great name for a boat, it means whitish, cleanliness."

I felt contradicted and happy at the same time. Only Helga was able to do that to me. From then on when people asked me what the name meant I almost recited a poem or a prayer: "Alvidia? White... Clear... Calm as the heaven must be."

After awaking up from the nightmare I went back to the old daily routine. The huge list of things to do on the boat, listed majors as: build a tiller, safety lines, install traveler and stoppers, finish the main hatch, install electronics (GPS, DEPTH, WIND, SPEED, AUTOPILOT, WEATHERFAX, RADIO SSB/HF, RADIO STEREO/ TAPE RECORDER), navigation lights, buy safety and emergency package (EPIRB, PFDs, emergency kit, Flares, weather outfit and gear, boots and safety harness and many etcetera), buy anchors (three) and at least three hundred meters of rope plus twenty meters of stainless steel chain, spare parts for the engine as well as for the water pump and the electrical system, build shelves, the dinette, cover for the bunks and mattress, trimming the interior and paint, making spray protection (dog house and laterals), acquire charts, buy supplies including food and learn how to sail before pull the hook for good and make it to the sea back home.

Three ocean were waiting for us.

Energy? Of course, if we had up until now why we would not have moving forward. The thing was the money to buy all that. And tools to work. I had an electric drill that needed a 220 power to function. I had a cheap hand saw made in China, another 220 electrical saw, a hammer, a file, a chisel and a couple of screw drivers. We were in a mooring buoy and the next power outlet was several yards away with water between us to row the dinghy.

Of course, we can.

While Helga worked in the Green Market bringing home Australian dollars which would be spent on sand papers, food, bolts and nuts, house cleaning products, epoxy resin and even one or two runs to the Cinema and fast food, I stayed at home building the tiller with scrap of wood I found in the garbage of the Club. Two chunks of mahogany and ash, a beautiful reddish mahogany, and a nice and clean white silver ash. The angels should be taking care of us for the wood found in the garbage was just enough to build a nice reddish and white tiller.

With no tools to unfold the wood, I took the scraps to a carpenter shop and asked to unfold them into strips of the same thickness. Then I laminated them alternating three of mahogany and one of silver. The tiller was outstanding after sanding it well and varnish nicely. Needless to say that the job was done down below, inside the boat, on my navigation table, next to the bed, eating bananas.

The day before our deadline to leave the free Club's mooring, we found a paid mooring buoy nearby in a boatyard. At first it looked a bit run down but it was ok since we would not need its facilities, and we were advised the owner was a not so good guy. What a thing to say about a person. For us, the important thing was that we were moving, and each step ahead was a reason to celebrate.

During our stay on that boat yard renting its mooring buoy, we did not have a minor reason to complain about the "bad guy". In fact, he was nice to us receiving fax similes sent out from the USA.

In the financial department of our adventure here, what was going on: when Cathrine got my first fax, she figured that leaving aboard a boat building in progress I was not going to have means to fight her. She was wrong. Helga worked in Marin County for a couple who were lawyers and by the time I had the first break up with my Brazilian partners the couple offered us help which we thanked but did not need. We needed it now. Brian was nothing more nothing less than a partner of a major San Francisco Law Firm specialized among other areas in joint ventures and business contentions.

Well, since our pockets were completely empty, I decided would not hurt more if I invest $15,00 in our way out of the situation and bought two telephone cards. A five dollars one and another worth ten. Using this one I placed an international call to Brian from the public phone installed on the marina's wall.

"Hello! I would like to speak with Mr. Brian Kelly, please," I had to be very objective and specific and pray for the receptionist not to put me on hold, and praying for Brian not being on a business trip and so my plan demanded a great deal of praying. Sweating, I trusted the ten dollar card was going to be enough, standing next to the boat shed wall, covered with dust and hearing electrical tooling at work full power, in Australia connecting to an office at Embarcadero in San Francisco.

"Sure ... Just one moment," was the reply at the other end and Brian came right way to answer.

"Brian! Luís. Helga's husband, remember me?" How I would drop our story to Brian all at once over the phone, would I be able, would any one be able to summarize such endurance?

"Of course! How are you guys? Where are you?" Brian replied.

"We are fine. I mean, very busy here in Australia."

"Australia? You are crazy. So tell me, you two succeeded."

"I don't want to take up so much of your time, Brian."

"Oh, no, we can talk. How is Helga?"

"Thanks. Helga is doing fine, she is next to me now sending you, Trish and the girls a warm hug. Look, I will make it short my story. We came, as you know to open a factory with partners in Melbourne. Well, after a year and a half I went back to the US to open another one in San Diego, to honor a promise I have made to my American partner. I was there only one month, in Chula Vista. Then I split with my Australian partners, became a sole owner for a while and sold the business less than a year later and built a yacht, a beautiful 30 footer of my dreams so we are now preparing ourselves to sail back home, to Brazil."

"Holy cow! I can see you have been really busy my friend."

"Very, Brian. And I called you to ask you a big favor, of course, it is ok if you can not."

"Yes, go on."

"Thanks, Brian. I need an advice. I will offer my shares in the business in San Diego to my American partner. I have 15% of the business. We are in the first year of operation so the value of my shares is correspondent to the initial capital. But officially I am the treasurer of the company and never got any report and I know the factory is running full power, meaning making revenues. Well, I am living aboard a boat and I need cash with a certain urgency. The value of my shares. Mrs. Cathrine, my partner in the business, would not think twice to get me out of the partnership and so I want to sell my share to her but can not afford to negotiate any penny down... Basically that's all."

"Luís, let me see if I understood."

Brian reshaped my words and description much better than myself and added that if I wanted he would personally sound the business in San Diego, meanwhile I should write it down my proposal to Cathrine, fax to her and stay apart because from then on he would contact her. Otherwise, I would expend all my money in international calls.

"But, Brian, I can not pay your fees..."

"Yes you can, Luís. Just send me a post card with kangaroos to the girls, they will love it. I can hear the signal, you must be running out of credits, listen, don't worry, I will help you. Please say hello to Helga and take care of yourselves."

I almost cried. We had true friends.

On that same day I faxed Cathrine:

"Cathrine,

Hope all is fine. I want to sell my shares for the nominal value. I need cash ASAP. Please send me copy of the General Ledger from the beginning of the operation. Thanks! And take care.

Luís"

Next day in the morning, the "bad guy" who rented me the mooring buoy had a fax waiting for me from Cathrine. Thanks to the time zone difference it could be that quick and she replied to me in her best style, straightforward: she was interested but did not have the money and her attorney would talk to me if I wanted to discuss any other matters.

Ok, so let's play this game. And on the same token, I faxed Cathrine's reply, a copy of my original fax and a note to Brian.

Two days later, as if I was waiting an eternity while swallowing bananas and working on the boat, and Helga working at the Green Market, I started to think my joke on my note to Brian was not appropriate. I should stop making stupid jokes once and for all. I compared my case with the Rhode Island law suits seen in the movies... And again, the "bad guy" this time shouting at me from the pier that there was a fax waiting for me, from the USA. Great News! Brian sent to Cathrine a letter introducing himself as an escrow and she should write a check in the amount of my nominal shares, I would sign a disclaimer and releasing all the rights of the process of molding plastic to her and we would turn a page of this story and it was done like these words within the time lapse of three extra days, two more faxes and one last phone call from me with that $5,00 phone card I had kept until then. Just like that, no wasting time with silly disputes, no hard feelings, and I guess everybody was happy. I was and so was Helga - thank you so very much, Brian.

June was just around the corner and we decided to cross the bay. Luckily in Sydney, you don't have a lack of marinas. There are areas that you find three lined up next to each other. Not all of them were high quality but that was good too because it means you could find good deals, including the run downs ones rented as is. So we picked up Woolwich marina. From then on I would watch and be seen from as far away as the Birkenhead Point and the Club and would miss the "bad guy".

Yet another horizon was closer.

...July, Help! Help! Help!

Steve found us in Woolwich. We did not hide from anybody but it made us feel good to stay away from that last terrible month, two miles and they were logged as a matter of fact as part of our cruise. We were beyond the Cockatoo Island which marked, to me, the end of the Parramatta River and the beginning of the Darling Harbour.

All the ferry lines go through Woolwich station, in Hunters Hill, for the aboriginal "Mookaboola", which means the meeting of waters. An up scale neighborhood ironically, in the old days, the site of a refinery of uranium and radium. The marina is inserted in one of the many wrinkles, as I called them, of the Sidney harbor. At this side of the Cockatoo Island, it makes a strait and so the tidal stream and the wind get substantially overpowered. If in any other area the wind is 20 knots, right there it reaches gusts of 25 to 35 knots plus. In July it starts to come in the westerlies, strong and steady winds, as any other breeze down under anyways, especially for beginners. For a weekend sailing you have a ball guaranteed, but for those wishing to install navigation lights on deck and dozens of other tasks while moored at a buoy, I apologize Mr. Neptune but you must be kidding me. To worsen up, it is cold, the traffic is heavy, meaning a lot of wakes, seriously, if anyone asks me to repeat that, I will skip Woolwich. Yet, in the past, Cockatoo Island was a natural habit of birds of a kind so the name. In the XIX century, as a convict penal establishment, primarily as a place of secondary punishment for convicts who had re-offended in the colonies; it also was one of the biggest of Australia's shipyards. Throughout time, the noble birds were expropriated and the crows took over. And crows do not hiss, they laugh. At least those at Cockatoo Island were laughing at me. I swear, their hiss sounds like a big laugh.

In the morning, already adapted to the local landscape as easy as I used to be elsewhere, I was working, hanging out at the stern, being shaken as if I was a horse tail because the waves and the wind and the wakes of the jet skis, ferry boats, water taxis and vessels of all kinds. I noticed someone waving at me from the pier. Steve, always Steve, showed up. He heard gossip about us and came to make sure it was just gossip as he believed. And he was frustrated because we did not ask him for help.

We did not want to bother, Mate, and after all, there were only minor issues with the Immigration, Federal Police, Coast Guard and the half of people in the Darling Harbor, we thought we could handle.

"Who is Alvidia?" he asked, ignoring my stupid joke.

"What do you say, is it a good name?"

He was already used to the original Helga II. Just squeezed my nose with his two fingers as a plier, his way to say I was his younger silly brother and that he likes me.

He then gave me his wide open smile, turned his back and left with his same saying "that's what life is all about" and an order that at night we should show up at his spectacular Nautilus for a dinner which was set to be a Babette´s Feast.

When Steve comes to my mind, I always remember his favorite phrase, and when I faced with what is important in life, I remember Steve.

...Twenty bathrooms.

Woolwich marina was small, had a single pier in El shape, an old shed and a stock of old boats, some nearly sinking, some being lazily repaired. Mr. Ian, the manager, was a nice guy and I think he liked me at first sight. Probably because I succeeded to stop myself from making my stupid jokes, explored a gentle smile and apparently it worked better. It was Helga's demand and I followed through. But one day Helga brought a bunch of bananas that would not last next day in the Green Market and I distributed them to everyone at the marina, to employees, boat owners, manager, neighbors, me with a face of grieving, prohibited from making jokes and so laughter burst out all over. Done. I was once again popular. Blame it on Helga.

Mr. Ian came to help us load our groceries aboard our dinghy, to row to the boat, and gave his compliments to Helga because she worked in the Green Market while I was working on the boat. I took the opportunity to ask him for a bulb for the women's restroom, women's only in the name because it was used by divers to prime their gears due to the fact that it was the only place with hot water. Until then we had experience with four bathrooms in different marinas. In River Quays it was not good at all, and although we had have not seen others and had just arrived from Melbourne noblest place to live, "we" were terrorized by the lack of cleanliness of the River Quays bathroom. I highlight "we" because I did not even think I could try to explain to Helga that we were boating people who were supposed to be adaptable to anything. Later on, in Birkenhead, it improved a bit, at first sight though. Being a public marina, we started to find weird wet substances on the floor, some solid and wet, some indecipherable and smelly. Next, in the club, I need to open an exclusive paragraph.

Helga bought a comprehensive cleaning kit and religiously cleaned "her" bathroom on a daily basis. She even decorated with a nice trash bin protected with a disposable trash bag, colored rubber mat, hand tissues and extra supply for the other tissue purposes. I could well sleep there, the only problem was the cold water. No hot water. The winter was severe that year so to make the trip to the bathroom in the morning or at night from the boat rowing the dinghy, often in the rain, then pull the dinghy over a lime ramp, it was necessary to have a great deal of desire to be hygienic.

The bathroom of the shipyard of that "bad guy" had no comments. We just looked at each other and simply disapproved and continued to use the club next door. We just needed to row a bit more. My arms started to look like two extra legs. Then in Woolich, we had to wake up at around five o´clock, row to the ramp of the marina and get in the line to use the bathroom. Five regular professional divers, men, used the women's bathroom to soak their wetsuit in hot water. If we arrived before we had to be quick about it, if we arrived later, we had to wait and waiting meant to us rethinking our lives, giving up the whole adventure or worse. Luckily we had early entertainment when the divers left naked, one after another, the small bathroom, to dress up outdoors. To save Helga from that show, I shouted to them that they could get a cold, pneumonia or something else. Never worked. This way was our beginning of the day ending around ten o´clock pm. At night we did not have to wait in the line to use the bathroom, but we had to jump over the gate because the security man was already sleeping. I jumped twice, once to go meet Helga at the ferry station, the second coming back with her and her three bags. If you see Helga without bag, help, she is in trouble.

Up until this time, the bathrooms were a piece of self-punishment. From then on, however, they would not leave on us any scars, to the contrary - they became our prizes for gradually we started to wash up our souls and minds with salt water, metaphorically speaking, pure and relaxing. We had in Alvidia a reference of good fluids. She became our companion, our protector and also our child due to loads of affection that we dumped over Alvidia. From then on, without all the building materials in the way at the saloon down below and next to our bed, Helga managed to give Alvidia's interior a cozy atmosphere of a house. Even a jar of fresh flowers was kept permanently on the dinette. And we did not save any effort to wash Alvidia inside and on deck. Her white hull, her interior in varnished mahogany were always shining and tidy.

It was time to leave Woolich. I bought a new dinghy that was meant to be our tender for the cruise, and for those not used to boating life, a tender on a cruising yacht is as important as the yacht itself, you can't do half of what you must to do without a tender. Your life simply is 50% limited. And this new dinghy fitted precisely between the mast and the forward hatch, upside down it would travel with us and serve as a life raft too if needed. Now, the day after we had the new character in our lives, it was stolen from our stern while I was working down below installing the electrical system. It was time to pick up Helga who was doing overtime that day, so it was late, around eight or nine o'clock, and I found out there was only a piece of the rope which ties the dinghy to the stern, the painter as the orthodox called. Ok, the old Luis from Melbourne arose from inside of myself and I burst out in wrath. I started to scream as high as I could with all my guts: Help! Help! Help!

My yelling echoed far way and I could see lights turned on in the houses as a horizontal flasher. The security man at the marina started to make signals with a flash light. So now you wake up, but to open the gate for me you hide. Then I saw a police patrol approaching the marina and by the water the huge Coast Guard boat pointing those potent headlights right onto me with its red and blue lanterns spinning and blinking. What a scene. And I still screaming and cursing in Portuguese and English. Derik, the security guy, came out on a working boat.

"Some stole my dinghy!" I shouted and jumped on the working boat. "Derik, let's search. It must be near by."

"Of course," he said, "but I can not leave the marina…"

"And my dinghy? And my dinghy?" I insisted with rage. "I have to pick up my wife!" I was steaming.

"Calm down, Luis."

Then, that huge Coast Guard power boat approached Alvidia very close and I could also see an ambulance next to the police car on the road.

"Officer! My dinghy was stolen! It must be near by. Hey, watch! Don't let your boat touch mine, it will damage it, watch, drive this thing a bit away!" I shouted to the Coast Guard and heard him ask if I had seen the theft. "No! I did not but I know it was just moments ago; I was working down below and not too long ago the dinghy was tied up at the stern. If you go around right now you will see it. Hey, watch, your boat will damage mine!" I kept shouting, already prepared to push the Coast Guard boat with my foot and told them they should use defenses. I was possessed and protecting my eyes from the headlight with one hand over my forehead.

After a volley of questions and answers, demands and an invitation for me to calm down, it was resolved in common agreement to engage in a search for the dinghy. The officers hinted that I may have tied the painter with a lousy knot and the stream took the dinghy away, but I replied to them by throwing a piece of the painter onto their boat with a clear sharp cut and I heard back: "Fair dinkum!"

An hour later we came back empty handed, this time to the marina pier, and under vehement protest, I had to answer a long list of questions which were meant to be a formal report of theft. Only then I was able to go for Helga. She missed me at the ferry station and walked alone to the marina. When she saw the confusion, the police car and ambulance, the Coast Guard and noticed my body language she knew I was ok, she told me later.

"My heart jumped out of my chest but when I saw you gesticulating and shouting even without hearing it clearly I knew you were fine, my heart then jumped with joy. What happened? Tell me now," she said.

And in the cozy atmosphere of Alvidia, I made a full report followed by glasses of red wine. We emptied a bottle that night.

If that dinghy did not have itself stolen, it would be with us as a great memory of our friend Larry. Two days earlier it was Helga's day off and Larry learned from Steve that we were at Woolwich and came to invite us for a dinner aboard his boat. And I told Helga, "I feel like we have a bond with Larry as an old friend yet we had only quick chats in River Quays. We can not decline, Helga."

And Larry surprised us in many ways. I was already enchanted just being able to go aboard his Raukawa. A classic wooden boat, restored by his wood artist hands, a true unique pro shipwright. Larry chose pastel colors to paint the boat, terracotta tone-sur-tone, and gouache texture. Everything in his boat reflected good taste combined with the classic lines of a two mast yacht. And the visit to his boat was just a grand finale of a half-day program. We were to arrive a little earlier if we could; he wanted to show us a few places before dark. He was at an anchor in Pittwater, a special wrinkle of the Sydney coast line up north. Precisely at Church Point, an hour from Woolwich. Larry took us to a cliff to visit the Barranjoey Lighthouse and contemplate 360 degrees around. A breathtaking landscape. It was a brisk walk on the beach and a hard climb, according to our noble host about 370 feet. Worth every breath. From the top, we could see it was a cape mushroom shaped of about no more than a mile wide at the end of a stretch of low land along the coast line and the lighthouse at the very tip. From up there I was able to shake the hand of the Sir Ocean for the fist time, a solemn secret moment for me. I felt for the first time how huge it was and powerful and pretty. Looking from up there I tried to imagine how I would behave sailing for the first time of my life, how would my future horizons look aboard a boat I built with my own hands on a passage with a precious freight, Helga. How would the nights be, the storms, the calm?

Helga, on her part, whispered to me that the place gave her peace of mind, that she was definitely a land person, not an ocean goer. Larry told us that he used to come to Barranjoey Head, that is the name of the Cliff, to meditate, to think about his life and that it was a way to prepare himself for the week ahead. I thought it was a nice habit to approach the next days ahead of time. While Larry shared that with us I imagined that the habit on an individual basis would be enough to transform the world into a better place – less violence, less egoism, more love.

At night, when we were the four of us with Larry's girl friend, Michele, we discovered that Larry never talked with people about his personal matters, his intimate thoughts. But he had been talking to us the entire afternoon about his life, in fact in an intriguing way as if he was talking only through thoughts in silent without actually speaking. Amazing. Before we went to his boat, we stop over at Michele's gallery, she was an artist and her paintings were on display in Mona Vale. Then we went in a Café & Book Store, and after that, we went straight to Church Point Anchorage. Larry was mingling questions about our lives with personal details and memories from his and yet finding a way to drop valuable boating information about Pittwater, our future Anchorage.

It was like as if I was talking with a character from the book of the legendary Joshua Slocum, the first man on earth to make a passage around the world single-handed. Larry was the second son of a German couple rooted in London, where he was born during WWII. His parents died when he was young. He traveled through Europe, Asia, India, Africa, few times helping scientific expeditions as a guide or fixer. Once he was left alone months in the Antarctic collecting data. He told us he lived more in cabins and tents than in houses or boats. Once, coming down the Australian coast single hand he had to stay four days at the helm weathering a severe long-standing storm. He liked his rustic life and a bit ashamed he said almost whispering and very slow: "Nowadays nature is my best friend, she gives me peace and it is that I want until the end." Confessed, however, that he was too reflective lately, that he lacked roots and links with people and thought himself a bit weird, especially while with Michele who used to bring home spooky friends, artists he said. It was hard to believe we were in front of the Larry we had met in River Quays quiet as a solid rock. He had this naive and childish smile.

The four us took his dinghy to reach Raukawa moored to a buoy like us and Larry had the same care to restore a classy wooden skiff as his tender, also gouache texture terracotta ton-sur-tone. Above all a touch aesthetic sense. And there we were being rowing to an unforgettable dinner.

It was night and I was embraced by a mist of enchantment saying to myself my dream came true; I belonged to the boating fraternity already with such friends like Larry and Steve, and Geary and list would still counting fast.

Around two o´clock we had already emptied two bottles of wine, the entree, main course, and dessert were simply superb, and Larry insisted on taking us and our most recent acquisition home. During the conversation, we told him a used dinghy had been bought and we should pick it up near Church Point sometime when able to bring Alvidia to Pittwater. The dinghy had been advertised on a local tabloid; we had paid already, and we had the key to the shed of the local sailing club where it was stored. By coincidence, it was close from where we were with Larry.

"Larry, you are crazy. Do you know what time it is?"

"Luís, a long time ago I gave up to pay attention to civil time and calendar. When you become more integrated with your boat and the sea you will understand me better and perhaps give it all up too."

Thus he threw on a heavy coat, almost a bear skin, a wool cap, high boots and pushed me out of the boat. "Let's go," he said. Then he paddled to the sailing club, we picked up the dinghy we bought and he placed it over the roof top of his Kombi so easily. He drove us one hour to Woolwich, and of course one hour back to his boat. I was speechless.

It was a full moon and who cared? The watch was just an accessory of a relative usage. It reminded me of Steve's phrase: "That's what life is all about."

When Larry heard that our dinghy was stolen the day after, he laughed out loud and stared at me, waiting for to tell him the whole story. It was his turn to be amazed.

We left to our next anchorage, Sailors Bay, condemned to use our "Blue Mystery", a small fiberglass dinghy we had found thrown away, sinking at Birkenhead. We patched it up and used it to take in water; Helga bailing water out while I was rowing back and forth from the boat and wherever we had to go. During six months we were dependent on the "Blue Mystery". Before leaving Alvidia, we had to empty it which I figure would take 24 hours to sink, never did.

...August, seventh month living aboard.

While leaving Woolwich we realized we were two different people. The pesticides and invisible chemical agents on the vegetables made open rashes in Helga's fingers tips. My tools and precarious work conditions, needless to mention the learning curve, created blisters on my hands and they opened exposing wounds. However, our organic and mental health impressed us. Our legs, arms, and shoulders were stronger from so much effort to climb the boat so many times and to row the dinghy and to carry on bags all the time. We also realized that during showers we felt a massage in our souls. We were digging out self-confidence from our guts and trusted the wind would change in our favor. To name my dream after my mother Alvidia was little by little creating a feeling of cleanliness in our spirits. So it was what we both felt together.

Sailors Bay was strategically very tempting to stop over before leaving Sydney. And Alvidia was almost ready to go to take us back home. With the money that Brian sent to us, we bought safety equipment, that required by law and extras that we learned from boating literature. Helga took over the grocery supply demands, while I was an ordinary cook aboard, and she trespassed into one of my departments, reading about and preparing comprehensive emergency kits placed strategically in three different parts of the boat. One source of research Helga used a lot, even later on during the trip, was "How to Feed a Crew" by Lyn and Larry Pardey, a gift given by Michael, a Canadian we met in Refuge Bay, north of Sydney.

I numbered by item what I should get done: finish the trim of the companion way, for those who don't know what that means - it is the main entrance to the interior of a yacht, a raised and windowed hatchway with a ladder leading below and the hooded slide-in-and-out-entrance-hatch to the cabin. After that I had to install the auto-pilot, build a dinette because we had an improvised one, shelves above the bunks, a legal gas system (that until then I had also improvised in order to cook and for hot water supply), sand the interior and paint parts, varnish others, and finally make cushions and a mattress, things that Helga would not negotiate including curtains. I could keep on with the list, but I discovered that you never finish a boat - ever.

In Woolwich sometimes after the shower, as entertainment, I used to hoist the sails and let them drape to feel them, bringing in the sheets just a little to feel how they would power the boat, right there still securely moored on the buoy, just to break the ice between me and the rigging system. I'd never done that in my life until then. After half an hour I would roll them back, cover and would go to bed sailing in thoughts, making maneuvers close hauled, abeam to the wind, down wind, rehearsing a jibe and trying to execute all the theories I had from osmosis living in Sydney and the monstrous literature I had acquired and actually read during the last 13 years. I would fall asleep tired of sailing, turning myself into a seaman. And there we went to Sailors Bay.

The contours of Sydney Harbour mimic an ear, at least to me. Every wrinkle is a bay. Right in the middle the North Bridge links the South with the financial district, major nautical activities, ferries and the gastronomic and cultural and entertainment center, to the North area to where the city develops. The bridge is the main postcard along with the Opera House, the architecture of which reminds me of boats pointing toward the sky. I established a goal to myself: I would pass under the bridge sailing, with the engine turned off, that's the way I wanted to anchor at Sailors Bay, which is one of the last wrinkles of the Sydney Harbour. It was so close to be out the heads to the ocean, the Tasman Sea, that I felt a cold in my belly. Fear. Goodbye Parramatta River, from now on only salt water.

If I would take the records from my log, this first passage from Woolwich to Sailors Bay, some twenty miles, could well be a short story adventure on its own. As the lack of experience was abundant, being the first sailing experience on a boat built with my own hands, many things were still improvised and being in the middle of the Mecca of Sailing, it was all very exciting, and comical. At a certain point I was taken out of the boat hanging on the tip of the boom and as the counter action of the same accident the boom brought me back aboard as if I was a fish on the hook at the end of a fishing line from a reed, an animated cartoon, right in front of the pier full of tourists waiting for the ferry boat. And honestly, as absurd as it may have seemed, I felt proud of my feat and I would recommend all the dreamers to ignore any possibility of being in an absurdly comical situation, at least it means you are trying. After all, you will laugh a lot too. It leaves an eternal taste in your chest, unspeakable and very intimate. From here on my records in the log became shorter and shorter until Helga took it over entirely up to the end of our story in Australia. I was not able anymore to live and write everything all the same time, I became a happy duck, the character of an animated cartoon I was authoring.

At arriving in Sailors Bay we felt a taste of vacation. We went straight to the bathroom for a shower, a shower of the winners, we won our first race against ourselves. The bathroom was clean, the marina not so sophisticated at all where we rented a mooring buoy was at the top of a hill leaning as if it would fall in the bay and surrounded by trees as the waterfront houses all around. Pretty place. By the way, what a beautiful country Australia is; have I said that before? Finally, I gave up the irrational prejudice with the whole British culture. Why in the first place did I built that idiosyncrasy anyway? Coincidently or not, it was in Sailors Bay where I bought my first Australian flag, proudly to hang over the stern of Alvidia.

We would stay in Sailors Bay only one month, the budget called for that short period on a paid buoy, but it was unforgettable and beyond that, I had a life lesson.

Boats started to arrive from the east coast, escaping from the cyclone season in the north/northeast and I began to feel in the air a cruising atmosphere. For the first time I saw a boat and its crew newly anchored after a passage and I observed their behavior on deck. Three boats of distance from us was the yacht Thai Hoa, an old wooden boat of forty feet built by his owner Lloyd Williams. I noticed that each boat made a quick stop at Thai Hoa to talk to its Captain and until then I did not know I had an illustrious neighbor. Even harder to believe he was eighty years old.

During the first week, we saw Lloyd managing his aluminum work boat back and forward. What energy. And how likable. While passing by he always greeted us with a bold wave as if he was celebrating life every day. One morning we were lazily having our breakfast and heard a knock-knock on the hull. Lloyd came to introduce himself, asking right away if our boat was made out of fiberglass or wood and drew a wide smile when I told him it was strip-planked with mahogany and that we had built it, were actually finishing it, and as if nothing else was important ignoring my full report he said, "At sunset come to Tai Hoa for a glass or two of champagne. Alvidia, hum! I would like to hear the story of this name. It is Latin, right?"

The winter that arrived earlier that year also left earlier in that part of the world. We could now wear short pants and walk barefoot. To row our dinghy was like child's play so around 5pm we started to row towards Thai Hoa. His Captain was already hurrying us up, waving from the deck. And he authorized us to go home only after nine. The more we talked the more we acquired lessons to the rest of our lives and I was amazed by Lloyd's life experience. He went to the Vietnam war as a radio operator expert in code language and an instructor. After the war, he returned to his home city, Sydney, and built Tahi Hoa with his own hands, right there in Sailors Bay. A half century ago and the boat was back to its birth place after having sailed the entire Pacific, Indian Ocean, and China Sea and we could see a picture of our anchorage to find out how little it has changed since then.

Tai Hoa was a sailing school boat and Lloyd showed to us pictures of illustrious Australian students. When he produced to us a picture of Tai Hoa in Fiji he opened a wider smile and gave a long breath, now he would start an interestingly intense story. He told us that parallel to his sailing school and cruising back and forward to the Pacific he started a typing course which later became a business management college. He no longer was involved with it but new chapters were branching all over New South Wales. Then on one of his trips to Fiji, he married for the third time, to Suruj an Indian who was there with us. In Fiji he was so integrated and popular that he used to be consulted when a new law was to be created or even Family affairs and disputes. Also in Fiji, he began a ship freight business, the Williams Cargo Ship Co. with two ships sailing the Pacific, Torres Strait and Philippines, his back yard. All was going well when he lost one of the ships to a hurricane, the Taoniu, and almost his own life and Suruj too. His crew preferred to stay ashore instead of in high sea waiting for the hurricane season to dissipate. With the help of Suruj they tried everything to save the ship and failed, fighting to the last minute; the ship sank.

Suruj told us that she changed out of her sari into overalls to help her husband. The next year they prepared themselves for the worst and once again lost the other ship of the fleet, ending the business but this time for a deceitful enemy. The financial director of the Williams Cargo Ship Co. was involved in illicit operations behind his back while Lloyd was cruising with Tai Hoa. With no chance to win a legal battle, the company went bankrupt. Lloyd said he sued his employee and that he was arrested but then he did not have his business anymore. It was when he learned that "sometimes one needs to lose to win". My first lesson. He had the insight to go back to Sydney and start what in the future would be a slow movement, quality life against quantity, right there where we were drinking champagne.

Minutes before dark we witnessed a profusion of sun rays through the trees down the water creating a surreal picture, a breeze coming from the sea and birds of many kinds hissing and flying through the masts of the dozen or more boats anchored. Every once in a while Lloyd stopped to unfold his tells and pointed to a yacht asking, "You see that ketch over there? It was awarded in the first wooden boat festival in Tasmania." Lloyd then invited us to look to another boat, "That boat over there, see? Won the Sydney-Hobart in nineteen ninety something...."

And so on. I did not know how to sail yet, but let's face it - I was part of the boating community already. My dream was a reality. Shouldn't I be amazed?

When the night arrived for good it was if the sun had forgotten its rays on the water. It was more like the surface of the water was covered by small lights in the form of scales, and I thought Sailors Bay could well be named the Bay of Planktons. I have read a book of Mário Setti Jr., Sea Adventures (in Portuguese) that the author thought he had a mirage in the middle of the ocean seeing a ball of fire, a concentration of phosphorescent organisms. My view was that intense too and I was clapping with my eyes of so much exciting.

We were in the cockpit and Suruj called us to the cozy down below for an Indian three-course dinner followed by a coffee liquor and we remained for two extra hours because Lloyd wanted to show us a book. It was a short encyclopedia of boating, practical knowledge from building information to cruising recipes, like dozens of ways to cook fish if you have only a type of fish for weeks, how to find an island without a map, how to take a shower without water or say one glass of H2O, how to anchor appropriately, how to build a storm anchor with jeans, and between all these important bits of knowledge the book also included jokes. Boating Digest by Lloyd Williams.

Finally, we were allowed to go home. In my chest was a feeling that the universe gave me a gift, it all could be normal, a dinner with interesting people but considering the fact that everything continued to occur with an amazing speed - that environment and experience were more than I have dreamed. Lloyd was a hero like Steve and Larry... And those planktons? That phosphorescence? Would my eyes be deceived? No, Helga too was gapped. As we rowed slowly from Thai Hoa towards Alvidia our dinghy left a symmetrical wake of brightness. From our oars, fallen tears of tiny lights blinking. I got so emotional that I stopped to row fearing to wound those little creatures and I burst out in tears myself. Could not stop crying. In the dark and in the midst of those blaze of small lights on somewhere in a wrinkle of a bay in Australia...

Helga and I went through the following days feeling we were moved by a magical touch. We decided to slow down on the work on the boat, sleep more and squeezed in the budget a movie and fast food to get the feeling of what it is like to be a normal people, just to realize it was already so strange for us.

August brought the birthday of the Captain of Alvidia and a party was set. We would have gnocchi with sea food white sauce, red wine, Captain´s favorite sweet, fig in syrup.

The next Sunday we had Steve aboard. He and Maureen came to pick us up for a ride in the Blue Mountain, one hundred plus kilometers from Sydney, right when we woke up and decided to go back to our crazy pace of working on the boat, but how could we win Steve's strong personality?

"Mate, put away your tools, lock Alvidia and let's get on the road!"

Thank you, Steve. We would not have seen the marvelous Blue Mountains if you didn't take us because we had our eyes and thoughts on our cruise back home only. The road is something that one must to see, no words or picture will describe it properly because it is a feeling. There is also a smell and birds flying and the proportion of the vegetation is something to impress and leave you feeling so small before nature. I was impressed by the giant fern. We were quiet in the back seat, occasionally looking at each other, Helga and I, like two rescued little monkeys when Steve made a sharp turn onto an unpaved side road and a few miles ahead stopped to introduce us to friends of his. A nice couple who left the big city to run a cottage as an alternative motel. We were welcomed with tea, chocolate cake, honey bread and a variety of home made delicacies. It was a rustic log construction with a huge deck inserted into the trees. Helga and I quiet, dressed in our short pants stained with epoxy and paint, t-shirts as well mistuned with the landscape.

The cottage neighbored the Aboriginal reserve and was less than two kilometers from a sacred lake, according to the primitive habitants. On the nights of a full moon, our guests told us there were rituals dedicated to tribal spirits. Even for us coming from a country where a syncretism is a common place and Brazilian Indians and Afro descendants are still practicing primitive rituals it was a quite impressive to be there and Steve did not know his friends were exoteric.

For the next Sunday, we planned to have Steve and Maureen aboard Alvidia and it was meant to be an honor for us and the first official sailing day. Up until then, I hoisted the sails several times without leaving the buoy in Woolwich and had a sailing trial under the Sydney Bridge which was not considered sailing by the grand juries. So it was, we left the buoy without the engine, a light breeze coming in just enough to power us forward and Alvidia started to show off brilliantly. Funny, I was not excited but it was an important day. We hugged Tai Hoa and waved to Lloyd; he waved back like he was blessing us. The Australian flag flying proudly, our brown sails in the groove, Alvidia's white hull among boats of all kinds. In Australia it seems there is a law; if the day is good for sailing all the boats must go out. A yacht approached us from the windward and shouted to Steve. It was the manager of the River Quays marina where we launched Alvidia and where Nautilus was moored. Jeff could not resist and made a thumbs up while jibed, turning around in a half circle he went past us, looking back, admiring Alvidia. She was really pretty. Right in the middle of a flotilla, we saw the exit of the Sydney Harbor to the sea. Steve stared at me and asked if I was ok to go out and I said, "Yes Captain." There we were out the heads for the first time. It was quick, one hour, light wind, short waves a ride in the park. We went back home, had sandwiches, small talk, said goodbye to each other and I was left thinking that it was not a test really. I did not feel I was a graduate. But I realized Alvidia had been initiated and it melted my heart.

One thing after another was completed, consuming the month of August with out hustling - no hands hurt. A technician from the store where I bought the electronics from came aboard to inspect my installation and gave a grade of 100, asking if I would work for him. Lloyd became an indefectible frequent sunset visitor. He would sit in the cockpit talking for an hour or so; he would get up and step in down below the cabin, naturally throwing away for free valuable suggestions, lessons, information, tips, all without pretension or lecturing. Without knowing it was my birthday, early in the morning he brought me pieces of mahogany he found in the garbage of the boatyard and said it would fit well to build a new dinette, if I would not mind using scraps, and also a cushion thrown away that would do good in the cockpit.

"Hey, Lloyd, of course, I don't mind. Thank you so much. You are an angel."

Lloyd smiled. He knew as I did that although there was a huge difference of generations between us it was a minor detail, for we had a natural affinity. We had met each other just three weeks ago and did not have any restraint in our relationship as if we knew each other a long, long time ago. The more I respected his knowledge about boating, in general, the more we had easy going back to back conversation. I never hear Lloyd make criticism to a person and it seemed to be easy for him to give away compliments. A rare attitude. It was a great pleasure to build up that friendship so fast and it was something like that he wrote in our boat diary:

"The start of a valuable friendship."

At sunset, Lloyd brought Suruj to have a birthday dinner with us, gnocchi with sea food white sauce. Lloyd brought his champagne - the only alcohol beverage doctors allowed him to drink, provided it was baptized with apple juice. He brought me a birthday gift, a copy of his Boating Digest. It became a great party of four laughing our butts off like a bunch of kids until late.

"Lloyd, what you are going to do when you grow up?"

He just laughed.

The next day I had a bar of hot iron stuck in my head, the hang over from too much cheap wine was charging an expensive bill. I looked to Tai Hoa and from far away noticed by their movements aboard the crew probably had the same bill to pay out and went there rowing our dinghy.

"Hey, Captain! Did you see the license plate at least? (from the truck that ran over us)"

He smiled and said there was some not so good news.

"Doctors gave me just a few days," he said then, with a sad face and I felt a bitter taste in my mouth; what a thing to hear from someone you were just enchanted with.

I wanted to hear it again and on the same token I did not believe it; did not accept it.

"No shit!"

Suruj had a shawl around her shoulders, she was sad and asked me to come aboard. I told her I was going to pick up Helga. It was with an odd feeling and in silence that I rowed the dinghy with Helga and once with Lloyd and Suruj, around the same dinette we'd had an outstanding dinner two weeks ago we heard the sad story. He had made an appointment a week ago, did not tell us, it was supposed to be a routine screen but the result taken early this morning while his Brazilian neighbors were sleeping, showed his immune system was wrecked. He could not catch a cold or it would be fatal.

"Luís (he pronounced my name correctly), let's prove these doctors are wrong."

"Sure we will, Captain."

"Suruj, let's open a champagne."

...September and October, what randiness!

It was hard to leave Sailors Bay, it was so good but we had to go to Pittwater where we would not pay to anchor and it was 16 miles ahead. The day before we left, Lloyd came aboard, despite the sad news he continued to move up and down as he used to do. He came to drop me a piece of advice; if I had my mind set to make it to the sea, I should do with extra safety, safety out on the ocean is never enough and in regards to the sailing lessons I asked him to give me for free he said I was not going to have patience and he would not have time, according to the doctors, but he would summarize all the lessons in some phrases for me to use wisely. What a man.

"Remember that a boat is designed to be in a liquid environment. To float, to displace, to infiltrate itself between waves, climbing them and sliding down hill graciously affected by the forces of nature and a yacht by the power of the wind. You have a beautiful boat; well built. Now, it is you who needs to adapt to the conditions of this environment and its own laws. Do not fight with them, try at all cost to understand them. The wind will always be stronger than you and so the sea. On another hand, you can be smart by not challenging the wind, just level up. Finally, the first storm is what counts, it will give you parameters. Then on all the others, and they will come, they will be relative."

He was an angel alighting on my shoulder.

"One more thing, my friend," he added, "Save yourself a lesson I learned when I was already a seasoned sailor and I thought I had lost everything: sometimes one needs to lose in order to win."

He had drawn a map and given it to me. It was a sketch showing places along the coast of Australia where I could anchor for free and he said I should go slowly, anchoring at sunset, pulling the hook like an early bird and make this a routine and our passage would be pleasant and enjoyable.

The next day we tried to leave with out making noise, repeating the maneuver Steve made to leave the buoy but Lloyd and Suruj were there standing in their cockpit and waving goodbye to us. Lloyd shouted that we should come back for a visit before leaving for good up north; he kept recommending things as if he was our family. We almost aborted and stayed.

The day was gray and the outfall of the Sydney Harbour had big swells. The forecast was excellent but we learned that in Australia there is always a low-pressure zone disputing territory with a high-pressure zone. The space between them, the trough, keeps changing places day after day, as a giant snake rippling up on the sky. The two macro ocean systems, one on each side of the island country – the Pacific and the Indian –, each with a particular system of waves, currents, and winds, well, any theoretical explanation would not help me at the moment, after all any sea pattern seemed to me a storm anyway. I was right on the Tasman Sea, single handed and Helga, well, she trusted me as she did up until now but did not have a clue either what we were about to face.

For the first time, Alvidia was climbing on a true wave, coming from far away maybe from the very Antarctica. Pure salt water washing our deck and our soul at the moment squeezed, hidden, behind our bones fearing death. All my muscles stiffened. All my cacoethes actively ruling. After two hours like this, half the distance to our way point started a light rain and the swells diminished a bit and Alvidia's engine running like a Swiss watch. I had the main sail hoisted for better balance and I was dipped in reflections about my life, asking forgiveness for all my sins, avowing all my weaknesses and my defects as well as thanking God for all that I had conquered, realizing it was, in fact, more than I dreamed. And before I decided to register to a monastery, we arrived in Pittwater at the very point of Barrenjoey Head, that giant mushroom where Larry took us a month ago. Helga was nauseated and was laying down on the cockpit tied on the safety harness.

"Helga! We made it! Look the lighthouse where Larry took us. I did not even check the chart. Helga, we made it!" I shouted and she managed to lift the dorse supported by the elbows sighting a half circle around.

We then approached the entrance of the bar. Now we had to check the sketch Lloyd made to us and find the place to anchor. All of the sudden we felt like to be diving in a washing machine. The lighthouse was already on our back, the sea was left behind, we were navigating in a river, I could not understand that convulsion of water shaking us all up frighteningly. The difference of depth between the sea and the river berth at its very mouth adding the high tide coming in made that whirl unexpected to us first-time mariners. Alvidia was like a wobbly man with the mast swinging side by side, I thought we were going to roll over and sink. Helga freaked out and I, well, I did not like my reaction. Where was my boldness? And my parameters, I did not have any, would I have them from now on? Soon I learned it was quite normal at the entrance of a river coming from the sea and after almost an hour searching the spot Lloyd made a reservation for us to anchor we found it. Once well secured to a public free buoy, we looked around and thanked God. Not only due to the success of a little over twenty miles four-hour passage, but also for the privilege to be anchored with our own yacht in a true paradise.

Helga, who adapted the same behavior every time we changed places, at arrival she got herself busy putting things away and getting the interior of Alvidia as tidy as a cozy cottage, including fixing a lunch for us and doing laundry in a plastic bucket, it was her way to create her own world as much as possible to look like a conventional world. From my part that all the walls fall down, that all the bills are past due, that my boss fires me I don't care - I stretched myself on the cockpit and that magazine thirteen years ago came to my mind and the book Single Handed by Joshua Slocum...

It had been hard but worth I am anchored in a white sand beach aboard my yacht built with my own hands and Helga's who brought two cold beers and some hot pastries, what else would I want? That water fall to boot. Yes, a water fall. Refuge Bay is one of the dozen bays at the mouth of the Hawkesbury River. And it is the only one though with a water fall right on the very river when the tide is high. The other bays, almost all of them, host water falls too but one needs to find them among the woods. To access Refuge Bay is possible only by boat. The

Maritime Service Board maintains a public free buoy area and you can just arrive and chose one. No need for an application, and a few buoys belong to yacht clubs but you can use them as long as you let it go when a member arrives which happens only weekends and during summer. We were at the beginning of September and there was absolutely nobody in Refuge Bay.

On the third day, without the courage to leave that place, I decided to train with the anchors I bought while in Woolwich. It was one forged Plow of 45kg and two Danforth of 35kg each. I never used an anchor before other than lots of theories about how to throw an anchor, how to measure the anchor rod, how to correctly splice an anchor rope to chain and many other issues one needs to master in order to make the boat safe at any anchorage regardless of its berth type, there is if the bottom is of sand, mud, rock, coral and so on. So I spent the entire morning moving the boat as if I was arriving somewhere and anchoring according to the Pilot Chapman, an encyclopedia one foot high, ten inches wide and two inches thick, my bible. As I did not have a winch, I spent the whole afternoon complaining of my back soaring. And if I did not become an expert I made a conclusion about the matter and at least when I need to face a true situation of anchoring it would not be the first time.

On the fourth day, we left the buoy to navigate the Pittwater area looking for the Royal Prince Alfred Yacht Club about an hour motoring from Refuge Bay. I was hoping as I read in adventure books to get courtesies at yacht clubs since I was a member of a club, the Drummoyne Sailing Club, the one that yielded me the women's bathroom and gave me the authorization to stay a week for free at one of its buoys when I was practically kicked off from the Birkenhead Marina. Well, we were cruisers so the clubs should welcome us with open arms. And of course, the reception was without excitement because Alvidia had an Australian flag and numerals of Sydney. My accent, however, guaranteed the courtesy granted by the pompous Yacht Club. And Michael, the general manager, allowed me to use the pier for visitors for free for three days, any extra hour would carry a charge.

Our plans were not to abuse the club facilities. We went to the busy side of Pittwater to try to find a job. The money from the United States was spent on safety equipment and spare parts for Alvidia. The money brought by Helga from her job at the Green Market we bought groceries for a month. After being irresponsible and lazy for three days in Refuge Bay, I had in my pocket exactly fifteen dollars. Thus we were in a situation, especially because we had decided to accept a job, any job, provided we would be hired together. A temporary job for the two of us. Preferably not too far away from home, the boat. With that in mind, we started to walk around the neighborhood, visiting marinas and boat yards, because that's what we looked like, a boat workers jack of all trades.

Pittwater is located around the headland we visited with Larry. The Hawkesbury river and the sea water feed a valley and form a body of calm and clean waters surrounded by gorgeous dwellings and chateaus hidden behind trees. It is in Pittwater where are located the famous surf beaches, at the ocean side, the Newport Beach, Palm Beach, Long Reef Beach, and some of the most famous surf gear brand headquarters like Quiksilver, Hip Curl, Hot Buttered, Aloha and Mad Dog, all of them my ex-clients. It was very funny to be walking through those streets passing by familiar addresses to where we used to ship our products from California and later on from Melbourne and San Diego. And I never met any clients in Australia. We had it in our memories very fresh how it had been difficult to manufacture each order for those clients, how the payment was negotiated and arrived at the right time when we needed, for instance, to buy the engine for Alvidia, or more resin and other materials. But we had to find a job so entertainment with good or bad memories should be left for another time. And in one of these free tabloids left to be picked up in a convenience store, we saw a small advertisement asking for two boat painter assistants urgently. It is ours, so I thought. Helga was nervous, thinking that after spending our last fifteen dollars what would we do?

"Easy, Helga, I have a good feeling, we will find a job today," I told her.

The address was the McConaghy Boatbuilder, no more no less than the biggest boat builder of Australia at the time, respected internationally. Whoever had seen on the television a news story highlighting a yacht breaking in two parts in the America's Cup of 1995 in San Diego, witnessed the result of a high tech experiment made by the team of McConaghy while building a high profile top notch race boat. Despite that, one would imagine the scene of the One Australia crew slapping their arms after being thrown out on the water during a competition, but it did not cause any trauma or a scratch to the boat builder's reputation. Later on, John McConaghy told me that they went to the very limit or a bit further and broke. The next day the insurance company sent a big check and they started to build another boat for the same competition. It was in this environment that we just arrived to apply for a job as painter's assistant, without knowing what was waiting for us.

"Have you worked before around boats?" asked a blond bloke, noticeably stressed. "It is a tough job and we are running behind schedule, many have worked for me and gave up on the second day; I can't afford this anymore," he said with a couple of bad words thrown in and before I answered he added, "Look inside the shed. Do you think you can sand that boat?"

Inside a warehouse, I saw a roar of fifty men, many with a professional electrical tool at work. Dust, sparks of welding, noise, a giant air compressor cracking out loud, every man geared with a chemical category mask, gloves, and knee pads. All that was happening around a black monster - a carbon fiber yacht of eight feet, almost three times bigger than the white wooden Alvidia.

"We just finished building our boat using the strip plank process and we need a job. Look at these photos," I said and showed him a display of pictures from day one, a year back, up to that day of the Alvidia's gestation.

"All right, if you think you can," he told me after staring at those pictures with a gentle smile on his face, giving me a sign he liked me. But then he stared at me with wide open eyes when I said, "Of course, we can, if the job is just sanding that monster, no problem – I said it highlighting "we"."

Robert – his name – looked at me then at Helga, who was very serious and quiet next to me. It was as if he had seen a nun in a men football team's changing room. Noticing he did not have a word to say I joked that Helga would work for the both of us; I was the spokesman only. Robert smiled, a little annoyed, looked once again at the pictures, took a good look at Helga from head to toe and said we should show up the next day at 7am.

"O.k., Robert!" I said out loud and shook his hand strongly as a true gaucho from the border used to do, almost crushing his bones, and I thanked him.

We were already twenty some yards and Robert shout at us, "Hey, Luis! Call me tonight at around 8!"

"O.k., I will call you around 8!" I replied.

At 8pm sharp I called and Robert cut right to the issue that was concerning him. He wanted to know if my wife would hold out and that she would work among a harsh manly environment...

"Robert!" I interrupted him, "Would you like to ask her or do you want to confirm we are hired starting tomorrow?"

After I hung up the phone, satisfied that Robert did hire the both of us I asked Helga if she would like to give it a second or last minute thought about it and she said she would not let me go alone; it was what "we" decided and "we" would do it together, and if Helga says so, "we" do not argue.

"Ok then, but at any time if you feel like to drop the towel let me know."

The money we would make was going to be good. Thirteen dollars per hour for each of us, and we could do as many hours per day as we wanted, or could hold out to. I was already seeing our fixed idea of sailing back home very attainable. I figured that with one month of work we would have cash enough for the whole passage. We planned to leave by Christmas; our plan was working. Thus we moved Alvidia from the Yacht Club across that small bay of Pittwater to a place called Church Point, right in front of the Scotland Island very close to where Larry kept his boat. The area had its proper charm and the people seemed to be laid back, normally walking around bare foot and most of them boating people. It reminded me a bit of a hippie flavor but after a while, I noticed the pier where it seemed was a common place for the local gossip we heard too; often people were airing dirty laundry. There was a precarious ferry boat with regular service and the pier was the parking lot of runabouts, nearly one per head, small aluminum boats powered by outboards and used to make the trip to the island and the shore and to reach Mona Vale at the end of the bay. So it was kind of crowded and it also reminded me a poem by Mário Quintana (a Southern Brazilian poet): "the man is to the apes as the worms are to the man. The primates wonder our erect posture, our arms hung apparently without usage, our hairless body spontaneously mutilated and that men live in permanent conflict".

At Church Point, we caught a bus at 6am sharp that Sunday which was our first day of many under such torture. In conflict was I reflected about the formula adopted by the Naked Ape, according to Desmond Morris, its endless contradictions, boiling complexes philosophies and variety of behaviors, often weird, full of subjective codes of ethics and moral despite an abundance of frugality and even obscenities. I concluded that my own formula of a romantic dreamer ape was costing me too much. Arriving at McConaghy, we were introduced to a cabinet where we could and should help ourselves with sanding paper as much as we needed. Robert pointed me to a type of sanding paper we should use and that was it. Get to work, get to sanding. At nine o'clock we could take a quick coffee break; at noon Robert touched my shoulder and asked me, "So, tell me, do you think you can handle it? Today it was just a test, tomorrow those men will be here too as you saw yesterday."

Of course, we could handle it, but Robert would like to rest that afternoon and cut us loose.

We went back to the boat quiet, walking, no patience to wait for the bus, and with the moral pending in limbo. We were silently asking ourselves if we would handle that job and for how long. All right, if we couldn't handle it we would just quit. It was our great advantage. We were together, the money was good, we thanked God out loud simultaneously as if it was written in a script.

It was so good to go back to Alvidia. It was re-energizing. Watching her from a distance filled me with pride. It was the first time we left her alone hooked to an anchor like a true cruising boat. The tide was low and I saw that I figured so correctly the extension of rope. While checking the tide and current chart I had considered all the factors before anchoring and I did it right for the first time, otherwise, I would strand us or worse. But Alvidia was floating firmly and nicely. At night came a brisk breeze of twenty-five knots and I left it go with more rope following the book. Down below, lit by a kerosene lamp it was cozy and we had chocolate milk with cookies. Definitely, we already were boating people.

"To row" was my middle name. While Helga was perfectly adapted to a routine of living aboard Alvidia. To go out and back on board, we developed a procedure and it soon became natural. From the cockpit we threw our stuff and bags on the tender, then we would slide comfortably on the stern platform, I would hold the dinghy with a foot so Helga could go aboard. While I undid the painter, Helga set up the oars and started to bail out the water. I would jump aboard so naturally as if I was putting on my tongues; I would touch the hull of Alvidia saying nice things as a father says to a child and I started to oar going away admiring my materialized dream.

That Tuesday, however, our routine was hard to be executed, it was like we were carrying a load of rocks on our shoulders. The day before, the first true working day, we went back home only after ten hours sanding. To board the Blue Mystery was not easy, even calling it by its nickname. No sense of humor; an inhuman working day.

Robert designated a special task for Helga. Several small parts that should have special care. She would work next to the door so with sun light and better air flow to breathe. Well, at least Helga was going to be treated differently, I said to myself and with due respect I decided to give it back to Robert. It was hot, actually unbearably hot inside the carbon monster and I had the stupid idea of wearing a t-shirt. After an hour of sanding, I could not stand the irritation through my whole body. Millions of tiny particles of carbon fiber were traveling on my skin, poking as microscopic sharp steel blades. I thought I was going to run amok but endured the whipping until the coffee break at nine -thirty and when my eyes where red and I could not see a thing. My eyes were blazing and I could feel the toxic dust in my throat. On my way to the restroom to wash up someone teased me: Hey, snow monster! The sweat mixed with white dust from sanding the undercoat covered my whole body with a paste. To finish it off, my back was sore. After cleaning up a bit, my eyes looked like two huge blood spheres. I was a monster. I met up with Helga trying to disguise it and said that I was done and it surprised me that she was excited. I said a few things, hiding that I was in agony and lucky me the "factory" bell rang saying we all should go back to work. One extra minute and I would confess to Helga I wished to be wearing one of my Italian suits and French ties then she would notice how bad I was feeling and surely she would fire us both from that job. Ok, let's go, get up. And how much my eyes were blazing, how much those small blades were poking my skin, and what the shit the sweat and white dust making a humid paste covering my body!

We checked off our lunch time, checked off our afternoon coffee break, and by this time I had turned into a snow monster, cleaned myself, and turned into a snow monster again. I sanded non stop, without thinking, in a lethargic state, a part of my brain under control, exactly the one was saying "do not stop", such was my state of mind that when the factory bell rang again to call it a day I did not hear, I was just a bunch of bones covered with flesh, cloth and paste, no eyes, and full of stainless steel micro blades poking my soul. I would stay there until bleeding to exhaustion. Helga invited me to stop at the supermarket on the way home; Helga said we would need to walk back home because we would miss the bus – off course, no problem – I was going to do whatever she said, anyone said, I was not there. While we were walking back home it started to pour - water and wind - what else did I need? Next to me, Helga was firm, steady walking, upright, apparently her morale was intact, did not complain about pain, nothing, how come I was feeling destroyed? What if we give up this damn job? No, if she can handle it why couldn't I? That was it; I need to handle it. A spark of life arose from inside. Ah! What nice rain, how good it was to walk on the mud, the grass, the mud and the grass. Look at Helga next to you, I told myself, walking on the grass and mud too, I am so proud of her, what a woman, so small, so fragile and so strong at the same time. I was born in the deep south of South America; I was raised cutting wood for the winter to cook and to warm the house. The winter in my hometown was rigorous, I should be prepared for this here in Australia. Do not stop! Now it was not my conditioning brain at work, it was my spirit lifting myself up.

On the third day I went to work prepared, meaning wearing long sleeves, a headscarf and I helped myself with a mask. When I started to sand my body responded with a bit of comfort, to surprise me; I think I was getting used to that. I felt my back at lunch time but it was tolerable. A week went by and Helga, the only woman among fifty some men, was being treated with respect and frequently I heard compliments to her job. And, as it is normal in society soon people start to know about your life story: we built a boat ourselves, we were going to sail back to Brazil with a date set on the calendar to arrive with Santa Claus, leaving Pittwater, going by the north of New Zealand, then Easter Island and up to Panama Canal, Venezuela, Rio Grande do Norte, Rio de Janeiro. They were impressed with these two Latinos.

"Hey, sailor! Hey, skipper! Captain!" They began to encourage me.

We realized that Church Point was too faraway from McConaghy. Thus, with the first week's paycheck we decided to move up to Marina Iron Cove, paying for a buoy, not a berth though, at the end of Pittwater and if we crossed the bay rowing our dinghy, from the other side we could reach out our work place within only a ten or fifteen minute walk. Our life started to improve. And now we would arrive back home earlier and nearby we had a convenience store, the marina had a good shower; it was relatively close to a paradise. There was a minor detail - we had to take our oars with us because the dinghy we could lock by chain but the oars could not be left for someone to grab. It was an interesting impact to arrive at Mc Conaghy that day because it was raining and we went dressed with full storm gear and the oars. So the curiosity from our work mates was inevitable and their amazement when we answered their question where we were the week before: "- yep, last week we walked almost every day from Church Point, now from Iron Cove we just need to row to the ramp of the park and walk through the horse track..." While we described our adventure to go to work, Robert threw both hands on his head and asked why I did not ask a lift. The other mates swinged expressions like: Brave couple! What a hassle! Crazy people!

Feeling very comfortable and adapted to the environment, we ate outdoors seated on the ground. We shared the same enthusiasm for the factory's bell to ring so we were all excited for a break and even more excited at the end of each shift. And, above all, we got involved with the building of that monster of carbon fiber. It was the famous Morning Glory being born to win the Cape Town-Rio of 1996. Its owner, the German Dr. Hasso, billionaire of the Tech industry, head of the SAP company, was paying more than three million dollars to have a winner boat and to outdo its competitor who also was building his own monster. The designer commissioned to complete the project Morning Glory was the acclaimed and trendy office of Reichel Pugh from San Diego, Ca. The team consisted of boatbuilders, fifty men ragged and dusty - half employees picked among the best and half professional sailors whom would be competing aboard the Morning Glory. A group dedicated to the lamination of small pieces of fiber glass were champions of the 18 feet skiff class and during weekends they would be building their own Racing machines right there at Mc Conaghy. Another group of sailors where high performance athletes and they just arrived from the Unites States where they run aboard the One Australia - the yacht that broke apart in San Diego in front of millions of people while the racing was broadcast. There was a worker, Mathew Mason, who still had a big smile on his face for he was one of the winners of the America's Cup, the Team New Zealand which took "the Mug" (how they call the famous Cup) from the United States, and he was elected the Athlete of the Year, not mentioning that aboard the Kiwi Team was Sir Peter Blake, a legend of yachting.

Those men with that curriculum and I had a dream to be just part of the boating community, build a boat and anchor in a white sand beach...

Mathew, or Matt for his close friends, did not stop to tell me and Helga to slow down the pace of work. Smith, or Smitty, dedicated to hardware and rigging was also the public relation of the Morning Glory in Australia, he also raced aboard One Australia. And the 3 million dollar toy of the German businessman had a manager, Charles, posting on a daily basis to his boss on the status of the project. Charles's wife worked with him; both with top notch laptops, connected to the Internet, a new thing for me - a Jurassic of the computer world, and they could be managing the catering for us all, or dealing with logistics in South Africa and financial matters in Sausalito, California - the headquarters of Morning Glory, right in Marin County from where Helga and I came from.

Morning Glory is the name of a dark purple flower, and, in Australia, it is also an expression that means "early morning erection". However, even with that hard on gush to go to work, on the second day at Iron Cove we went beyond all limits. Every night before going to bed, we used to hear the weather forecast via VHF. It was a kind of rehearsal for our ears. And we should expect that morning a front coming in from the southwest with winds up to forty knots and rain, that is squalls. I meant to get up from bed a bit earlier than the other days to make sure we would not arrive at work late. At six o'clock Alvidia was already sailing around the buoy with no sails, of course, and the mooring line was stretched with Alvidia being thrown sideways as if she would like to escape from the big blow of wind and run backwards while it was pouring heavily. Ok, I thought, we are boating people, let's wait for a window and jump in the dinghy and cross the bay. Yes, we got a window but as soon as we jumped in the dinghy the big blow came back. Then the rain. How could I row on a straight line against the wind? It was taking too much time; normally I could have three trips back and forth already. My arms got stiffened. If I don't die now, I die sanding later on, I thought. Thus, realizing I could not go back to Alvidia nor row in a straight line to cross the bay I aimed for a pier of a private house exactly to where the wind was pushing the dinghy. Some yards from the pier I grabbed a line floating and tied to the pier and pulled us safe and sound.

"Helga, what a hassle, huh?"

Helga did not say a word, she was soaked even with full storm gear and long-sleeved boots. Oars and bags over the shoulders, we trespassed across that private house's backyard. From the veranda where one could contemplate that beautiful landscape, the bay and the surroundings, a gentleman well shaved and dressed casually, holding a cup of coffee was smiling, almost laughing actually.

"I don't believe it; you are crazy going out in such weather on a small dinghy," he shouted from the veranda, but wide-eyed amazed when I apologized for trespassing on his property and said that we were going to work. He could not believe indeed, he thought we were playing Indiana Jones.

When we arrived at Mc Conaghy sharp at seven o'clock coworkers stared at us amazed and asked if our boat was fine at the marina. They had heard terrible news about the storm which slashed Pittwater and the entire coast near Sydney. Houses in the Scotland Island were unroof, whole trees were ripped out and thrown away, a Navy frigate sunk, stuck in the rocks under the Barrenjoey Head lighthouse, a tug trying to get out of Sydney also sunk... Sydney Harbour was a chaos, the Coast Guard was not able to handle all the emergency calls.

"We did not see a thing last night other than Alvidia was shaking a bit. But it was hard to row this morning."

At night, Robert asked if it would upset us if he raised our wages up to seventeen dollars per hour. Of course not, Robert, you can also make it retroactive. Then, he said that he was going to abuse us with generosity and lend us his truck so we could drive to work instead of rowing. He would drive his Mitsubishi instead. And we should go with him to his house, drink a bottle of wine to celebrate the promotion. Robert was considered the best boat painter in Australia. A true artist of his kind. He said he painted only the boats he wanted to. He was a perfectionist and his portfolio included a mix of photography and painted boats, literally mixed for he used to click his boats and build surrealist portraits using the water as a mirror. He showed us several pieces of art, waves falling over the image of boats he painted reflected on the water also mixing "before" and "after", a result that invited one to observe for a long time. Then, there was his personality and style, Robert Forbes used to dress up in black, his Japanese car was that trendy for he could speak some orders and the car would respond and he listened to classic music saying it helped him to calm down.

"But that out loud, Rob?"

Around Morning Glory, Rob run the show. Inch by inch had his finger and if it was not perfect he would ask us to sand it all up again, from scratch starting with a gross sandpaper downsizing to the finest paper to make it as smooth as a baby's face. Luis and Helga witnessed in the last days the renovation of the entire crew of sanders and were now the sander masters first mates of Rob. We were responsible to fill in tiny small holes with filler, learned each step of Rob's painting process and knew which sandpaper should be used at each step, from grade 80 to 400 intercalating filler, spray of under coat, sanding in between, always sanding, then Rob would come and check, mark with a pencil spot to redo and we would do all again and again until Rob could actually work, that is paint. Going back home we felt awarded, being treated with respect and driving the truck. But on that first day with the truck our dinghy had been left on the pier of that gentleman who shout at us friendly during the morning storm. Helga didn't have a driver license and so it was her duty to row the dinghy while I was driving the truck around the other side and would wait for her. It was an ambitious plan because Helga had never rowed the dinghy before due to my dedication to handle the muscular task for the family.

It was hilarious and while I laughed I was also proud of my Helga. The night was dark without any stars and very calm after that big storm. Helga started to spin not used to the oars and could not row straight. When she got it right it was in the opposite direction - then she would scream scared to death of pelicans flying near by, those huge birds reminding her of black turkeys in the dark. Her instinct would make her row straight but suddenly she started to spin again until another black turkey scared her. It was impossible not to laugh and later on I let my ears be pulled as a well deserved punishment.

"It was not funny, Sinbad" – Helga was mad.

The cold fronts kept coming one after another throughout the month of October. We worked for Rob until the end of the month and had only thoughts for the last details to finish off Alvidia and get her ready to set sail and make it to the sea, back home. Any way, even with the comfort of driving a truck to go to work we felt like two old rags. As the schedule to delivery Morning Glory was getting the shape of a bottleneck, Helga was acquiring "man's" tasks and I being psychologically invited to work for as if I was four. The other sanders quit and the crew of sanders was reduced to Helga and I to handle the carbon fiber monster.

Helga was the only one could fit in tight corners and to get them smooth by sanding it thoroughly. She became resident of cabinets, drawers, under sink compartments and such places. I was the one with muscles in the place of the brain, paid to leave Morning Glory as smooth as a chamber-pot. One day I got back home and wrote in the diary:

"Zishzish... ZiShzishZish... Zishzishzish... My muscles have this noise, my eyes and nostrils too, my tongue and my stomach and my nails also have this noise... When I wake up I hear the same noise which I had in nightmares as it will be a nightmare like my entire day. Three weeks sanding. I don't know how come Helga has energy to carry it on. Maybe she is just as conditioned as I am to my entrails. I go to work without thinking about what I am doing, who I am, from where I came, or to where I go. Zishzish... Zishzishzish... Zishzishzish... I can't stop, but I don't have strength and yet I keep going. Rob needs help. We need help. But then, and Helga?

Zishzishzish... Zishzish... Zishzishzish... We are late. He whole crew around us work with noise electrical machines, they make noise and dust. And this pain on my back. Zishzishzish... Zishzish... Zishzishzish... Zishzishzish... The sweat runs down inside my clothes mixing with the sand dust and carbon fiber and this stinking undercoat paint... Zishzishzish... Zishzish... Zishzishzish... How much I love Helga, my dad, how much I miss him... my Alvidia... Zishzish... I can sand, I will sand, I sand, now I am Alekos Panagulis, I was condemned by the right and left wing, I am a prisoner. Now I am Rambo, yes, this is a war... Sand, sand, sand, Ziszishzish... Zishzishzish... I will think of everything I like, maybe it helps, gives me strength. Helga, daddy, Alvidia. Zishzish... Zishzishzish. With both hands, force, let's go, yes you can, I will sand everything, well sanded, go, I am a sand machine, zishzishzish, zishzishzish, zishzishzish... Then someone tapped me on the back and said:

"Hey Lui! Are you crazy? Lunch time, man. Stop, you mad man!"

The siren sounded and I did not hear it as I was so absorbed with my mental exercise to acquire strength to sand. I think I went into a lethargic trance while my body kept going inert to pain and brain command, on auto pilot. I showed to Helga what I just wrote and she said, "Just reading zishzishzish hurts my soul" – she then pushed the diary away and we did not have words to talk anymore that night.

The next weekend, finally Rob was able to paint exterior of the hull. It was a violet tone of dark blue ordered tailor-made; Morning Glory was that fussy, and there was an absurd surprise. But before I explain, I must highlight that I was Rob's assistant painter and put that in my curriculum. The day before, I got compliments from everyone to be assigned to assist Rob. A proof of trust. And, after a long and thorough day sanding the last pieces and bits, Rob warned me that he only painted at night, when everyone is gone, the air is cleaner and the environment is quiet, so he could work without being interrupted until the end, that is until the next morning. What a glory!

"Ok, Rob. And I will trust the pizza is on you."

Thus, at show time, Helga wanted to make a run to the supermarket and stay in waiting for me. Rob and I dressed like astronauts went in the greenhouse where the grey monster would become Morning Glory. Until then I did not know exactly what my job description would be as his painter assistant.

I helped Rob mixing five types of solvents, hardeners, anti-bubble agents and color fixers and I was excited to see the show from the stage. By then Rob changed the mood - right when he grabbed the spray to paint. He was another person, nerves, aggressive, even a tiny lint in his white overall made him curse. And I sunk into my insignificance and resigned myself to do whatever he wanted. The man was painting a three million dollar yacht. It was serious business; if he said I was not worth a penny, I would agree; if he said I was a trash bin, I would let him litter right on me. But I was able to say, "Go Rob, paint, it is going to be superb, you are the best, take it easy." And I started to pray, it was a three hundred thousand dollar service. Being part of that scenario, the only two orders I received as assistant painter was to hold the hose of the air compressor, it should not touch the boat, nothing on earth was more important than that hull and I should control that hose following Rob. The second was to fill the spray can with paint:

"Oh fucking bitch! Demon some of a fucking mother of a cow! This fucking paint finished again! I can't believe! Fuuuuuccccckkkk!" It was the way Rob asked me to fill in the spray can. While coming back running like the cartoon roadrunner, Luis, dressed as an astronaut, was holding that tail of the devil avoiding it touching the most precious object of fetish on earth. And Rob was not able to worry about advising me he was going to change positions or directions; it was my job to guess a fraction of a second earlier.

On that Sunday afternoon we did not resist and went to Mc Conaghy just to contemplate our job after the paint was dry. Ah, it was marvelous, it looked like a mirror. Then I understood all that care of sanding. Then I understood Rob's portfolio and collages. The most tiny details of the warehouse walls reflected on the dark violet hull full of curves. The curves, natural in any yacht, going towards many directions giving the impression that it would gather all in a single point, multiplied by the reflections alternating horizontal and verticals. And the curious deep texture, what a visual, spectacular!

On Monday everyone would let their chin fall and would compliment Rob and his crew, me. But, the first persons to arrive were John Mc Conaghy and Charles, the manager of Morning Glory. When Rob, Helga and I arrived we could not understand the face of frustration on Charles. Rob smiled as if he was used to waiting for compliments but wondered what could possibly be wrong and so we went straight to the greenhouse. There was nothing apparently wrong, however Rob saw Charles snagging lips badly and said out loud, "What?!"

The color was wrong. A micron less in the scale of colors different from what it should be. The violet of the morning erection was a bit off side. Then all the others started to arrive one by one to witness the frustration. It was unbelievable, it was absurd. Three million dollars piled in a warehouse in a unknown place in Australia and a three hundred thousand dollar job was wrong. The schedule was on time, despite that two sanders were killed several times, the result of the painting was superb, a master piece, divine, but there was a micron of color a bit off side. Charles would not take it on it himself to approve the job, or worse, to order it to be redone. Rob started to kick everything he could see and was cursing. I went after him. The huge mistake was not on Rob's account; it was the supplier to blame.

At first, Rob would not accept he would need to paint again, but there was too much money involved.

"But Rob, they did not test the color before sending it to us?"

"Ah Luis, they are a bunch of bitches."

"Calm down, Rob, I am here to help you."

He looked at me and almost laughed, contrary to his mood.

"Rob, you are a professional. Be cool. Negotiate a penalty, a price, some deal and let's paint the thing again once they send the right color."

Dr. Hasso would need to be contacted in Germany, to approve the extra expense, the supplier would fly over to assume the mess, last but not least, the two professional sanders would need to be animated by electroshocks to sand again the now violet monster.

"You see, Rob, equate the situation and you will see it is not the end of the world."

Days later, Rob confessed to me it was my advice which made him not kick the whole world off and leave, and he thanked me. He had lost his crew, he had been pressed by the boatbuilder and went through an ordeal on that job as never before.

"You helped a lot, Luis, thank you, mate."

I just did not consider Helga and I would now be sanding glass. Yes, to sand a surface painted with polyurethane paint is like sanding flat glass. And the same advertisement which brought Helga and I to the job a month and half earlier, brought all sort of candidates hired with out a blink. They were a homeless, a skinhead, two rednecks, a fugitive from Papua New Guinea, and two interesting characters. One, a liveaboard like us, had a wooden box almost sinking, sharing it as a home with three dogs and a lady who like him never took a shower in her life. And James, a South African boat lover but that got me crazy by how much he talked about boats - not even I, a hopelessly boat lover could put up with him after the second day.

Alvidia, my dream coming true as I was going through this episode at Mc Conaghy, was my source of energy to carry on. Zisthzishzitsh... Zitshzitshzitsh... Zitshzitshzitsh... Now the glass sound was even more harsh. Helga was the only worker inside down below the Morning Glory doing a meticulous putty job to cover already invisible holes. Outside I was going crazier with the job plus the South African speaking right in my ears about boats.

In the following weekend the opera would unfold into its second act. The final. The man who sneezes paint with the color of an early morning erection curses while the hunchback ragged one off-stage as a corn stalk under the monster paws stays there, just so he dies with his patron, if the monster wins the battle, otherwise he will improvise a smile he never could have in his humble life. But instead of the doomsday, his patron fights hard and covers the monster again with the color of the universe cloak, transforming him into a bird. "No! You idiot hunchback. It is not a real story, it is just a tale that I am writing to my lover," shouts the patron, while a choir of fifty-one voices imitate a rain of stars. The princess runs in towards the man who takes her in the arms. The hunchback down on his knees grabs the monster's paws and swings the upper body sideways, writhing with pain. He is hurt and bleeds. The monster was real. The hunchback cries. The grand finale is thrilling, making the entire opera house audience stand up. The hunchback caresses the bird with his eyes while the patron takes the princess in his arms and looks to the sky with a dumb faces.

Morning Glory was done. The yacht was taken to an area of the Sydney port where it would be measured by the ocean cruise class authorities before launching. For the launch day I was invited for an extra working day, last minute touch-ups and I eventually met John, an Olympic Gold medalist of the Moscow Games of 1962. He was the authority who measures the ocean class in Australia. I spent the entire afternoon talking with John about boats, saying to myself, "well, it looks like I am already a boating guy, cool!"

...November, no comments.

We were invited for the snacks and drinks for the launching of Morning Glory and better than that to a test sail, which would be the first time in life I would sail as a true sailor. I couldn't contain my happiness and I even thought Alvidia would be jealous. I also thought I could push the South African overboard and stop that torture. However, as we landed at the Sydney Port, actually a side area with the appearance of being abandoned – there was a great surprise. Steve had hauled out the beautiful Nautilus to replace the copper sheets under the hull and to paint it as well. Right in front of the Morning Glory making a contrast of a kind, a classic and a modern, and my body shivered head to toe, creating a rebellion of the heart against the rational side of my brain. I stared at Helga and noticed she also had the same sort of inner rebellion. Our hearts together were stronger than our brains. Thus, instead of walking straight to the Morning Glory launching celebration we made a sudden detour to reprimand our friend Steve. How come he did not call us out for the job of sanding his Nautilus. We owe him that kind of help with great pleasure.

"Mate, I knew you both would be dead after Morning Glory. I wouldn´t do this with friends."

How noble. And so we stayed for the week, sanding Nautilus just for the fun and pleasure of helping a great friend who helped us a few months ago.

When the crew of Morning Glory learned we were helping Steve sanding his wooden 51 foot yacht they all nodded and shouted things out to me like:

"Hey Luis, give a break to your wife!"

"Hey Luis! Let's sail!"

"Hey Luis! You're are out of your mind, mate!"

"Mate, go home, wait for me aboard Alvidia resting and I will visit you in a week or so for a gaucho barbecue." It was Steve, a hundred percent right; I should be doing exactly that. Instead: Ssshssshsssh... Ssshssshsssh... Ssshssshsssh...

My back hurt. Nevertheless, there was always a comfort during the process of building Alvidia - because it was our dream so we were able to overcome the pain. Now we were doing professional work on Nautilus after finishing with Morning Glory. At night, Steve produced a gorgeous dinner and drinks in the beautiful wooden cockpit of that classic yacht. In the following days, John McConaghy approached us, showing respect to us for helping Steve, and it was an honor to be able to introduce them to each other.

"Steve, this is John Mc Conaghy. John, this is Steve Sulis."

John told us he started his boat builder career building wooden boats in his backyard in Sydney. He liked classics. It was good to be able to introduce John to Steve. Mathew and Smithy also came to check out Nautilus. It was the sort of atmosphere Steve liked, plus now he was in touch with Olympic and international race yachtsmen and athletes. When I introduced Mathew to Steve I told him jokingly that Mathew had stolen his Golden watch with the America Cup logo on it, and Steve grabbed my nose with his two fingers as a plier the way he used to do with me.

"Congratulations!" he said. "I know you were recently awarded Athlete of the Year in New Zealand."

Finally, finally, for good, we finished sanding other people´s boats and would now restart on Alvidia. The next step would be to finally paint the interior of our home, with a bit of sanding before.

We decided to leave the Iron Cove Marina and go to the Newport Anchorage nearby; it had more charm, being older, it was almost a run down marina and Maggie, its owner, was a queen. She was in her seventies, abundant in sympathy, and made us feel at home just like family members.

"Do not worry about this sign, just let me know if the Waterways bugs you."

She was referring to a sign at the main pier, highlighting the official rules about limitations to living aboard.

It was a perfect place to accomplish my dreams. There had old wooden poles hosting pelicans. Maggie used to paint the top of them white, and the wooden floor made a perfect subject for a painter to produce a masterpiece of work. The boats along the slips were old and unfinished or wrecked and some even had ropes made out of sisal, giving a strong personality to the whole surroundings. In short, it was a place for professional drifters.

It was good to move into Newport and we could well live forever at Maggie's marina while odd coincidences kept coming up. Our host was a good friend of Hinley, the truck driver who brought Alvidia from Melbourne. She told us funny stories of Hinley. And Peter, who launched his iron Nathan of 50 feet in River Quays, was living there too and was the security guy plus he was the godson of Hinley.

That was a lazy month for we did not make much progress with the last things to be done in Alvidia. We used to wake up late, slacking through the day only to realize it was gone and the next day would be the same. Sometimes Peter called us for a beer or two; when it was in the afternoon we would stretch into a party till late into the night. What we accomplished that month was important from our to do list; it was a variety of items Helga had in mind and dragged me into a shopping center to acquire. A roll of souvenirs from t-shirts to pens and boomerangs, stuffed koalas and such. Gifts to relative's sons and daughters, aunts and cousins, friend's children and neighbors. Helga in her full power. For my part I was able to do the humble job of building

Alvidia´s doghouse, with a canvas spray protector for the sides of the cockpit (it is important for the record to state that the frames for the doghouse were made out of stainless steel tubes that were a gift from the McConaghy crew to Louis, the dusty monster). The canvas cover of the frame was stitched by hand and I felt like an old timer maritime, especially living aboard at Maggie´s marina. The man who sold the canvas to me did not believe I was going to sew by hand. When it was done I received compliments and ominous forecasts that in the first big blow it was going to be torn apart.

Meanwhile, at the marina, expectations about our departure increased including a betting pool among the residents. I could also feel in the questions thrown on me that some of those people did not believe I was going to sail back home crossing oceans aboard a 30 feet yacht. But they all were unanimous about Alvidia – she was so beautiful.

Peter, when he had a moment with us, used to cry on our shoulders about his boat not being finished as ours and that we were going to make to the sea and fear had been holding him for ten years already. It was his dream to reach the Whitsundays few hundred miles up north. He said was not prepared to make to the sea.

"But I can see, Lui, it is your time, I envy you." While secretly, I used to bite my inferior lip asking myself if I was prepared.

During the month of November, we tried to go out several times, for training purposes, but something always got in the way. I wanted to stay overnight out on the ocean to see how it would be but our practice was reduced to a rather reluctant rehearsal. It took one hour just to leave the buoy then we motored around other boats to reach out; we were still in the closed waters but enough to hoist the sails to try a few tacks to port and starboard, scared every time Alvidia healed and I would react on the helm to bring Alvidia back upright. We were trying it out on calm closed waters, reluctant to go out to the heads to the open ocean to test the boat and ourselves. While I kept saying to Helga that we needed to test everything, including maneuvers, like to heave to, for instance, and an overnight on the open waters, she kept saying we needed to finish the boat thoroughly first. And she had a long list of things to do. She was working meticulously on supplies for the passage and three emergency kits, that would be placed strategically in different parts of the boat. Inwardly, I knew it was not Helga holding me to go out on the ocean, it was fear. Or something else.

Around this time our friend Geary arrived at the Newport Anchorage, from Shacola yacht. What nice surprise. We met at River Quays when we were on the hardstand before launching. He came aboard excited and shouting compliments for everything about Alvidia. He even said more than once that it was the boat he would like to own - that Alvidia had a good vibe. He went to the mast and felt the halyards with his hands and looking up to the top he said, "She is so sweet! She will fly out there!"

Geary had just arrived from Noumea. He had to get out of the country due to his Visa expiring and to avoid paying the import fee related to his boat, he said. A passage of fifteen days on the sea to go and fifteen days to come back single-handed - a ride in the park for him. But he showed concern when he learned about our route via New Zealand, Easter Island, and Panama Canal to reach Brazil. He started to talk about mountains of waves between Australia and New Zealand, due to an abyssal difference of depth of the ocean in the area and then the strong winds from east and sudden south fronts. As he was a joker, and with that ironic smile sealed on his face at first I thought he was teasing us but he wanted to warn us for real.

"Man, to New Zealand it will be a tough test already. But then, to Easter Island - anything can happen and often it really does. Look, if you go down to Latitude 40, you get into the variable winds and it is damned cold. If you stay too close to the 30, you run the risk of influences of turmoil from the North currents. And you are going right on the cyclone season that reaches the latitude 27. Don´t go that way, please," he said pleadingly.

"But, Geary, I read Jimmy Cornell and found a narrow street between latitude 30 and 35 that it seems a piece of cake."

Geary would not unplug that funny smile from his face but made an effort to get that crazy route idea off my mind. We went to his boat so he could show me a boating magazine featuring one of his passages. Before we went aboard he placed a small red mattress the size of a napkin on the pier and shouted to someone down below, "Dominique!"

Geary brought a young French girlfriend from Noumea, and when she appeared on deck he became a little puppy - if she had said he should jump into the water he would have; whatever she would say he would do, with that smile on his face.

A flavor of cruising and passages, a life on the ocean blue started to embrace me, mixing an exciting state of mind and a bitter taste in the mouth - so I was between worried and happy. And as we would not be able to work while at Newport due to the social life, we decided to move into Refuge Bay - an inviting place near the exit to the ocean. That was when we received a letter from our friend Lloyd. He thanked us for our offer to help him with painting, including sanding; Tai Hoa was being hauled out of the water for maintenance. He said we should save our energy for our voyage - we would need it. And he also gave us the news that the doctors at the hospital were impressed with the improvement in his health but that he was not taking stunt lessons yet. Attached to the letter were drawings of his own hand of two alternative routes for us to choose via New Zealand, and valuable comments about the prevailing weather conditions, winds, currents, the sea. Details he certainly collected himself along the way in his sea life. They were hand drawings of Easter Island and possible anchorages including hazards we should avoid. Not few. He noted a suggestion that we should hire a helper to come aboard with us since we would sail against the wind most of the time and I would be tired due to the fact that Helga would not steer or navigate. He even added that Alvidia would handle all right but he was not sure I would, even being so young and strong. Before finishing his suggestions he placed in the middle a short "PS" note: "do not take any of the above alternative routes". Then he resumed his true recommendations highlighting that we should hop up the Australian coast, sailing along the coast during the day sleeping each night, lifting the anchor as an early bird and anchoring again at sunset. This way we would enjoy the passage, avoid problems and stress of ourselves and of the boat. He wrote we should not be ashamed of using the engine, why would we? It is normal if we had to cover a certain number of miles in order to reach an anchorage before dark. So he knew a lot about my personality and vanities. He was a senior sailor on top of his eighty years, advising a person almost three times younger and without any sea experience at all.

Thus we were prepared to leave Newport Anchorage when Maggie came to shout at us from the pier saying Geary had phoned us. He was requested to bring a boat from Melbourne and took the time to call us and leave a message similar to Lloyd´s: we should not go via New Zealand and that we should wait to leave after April until the cyclone season up north had ended. I was almost swallowing my upper lip. And I did not know where Helga was. I mean, she was next to me but lost in her thoughts. Would she have a notion where we would be diving? I don´t think so, much later on she confirmed that to me.

...December.

Maggie granted us free parking during the month of December once a week so we could leave the anchorage at Refuge Bay, moor the boat at Newport Marina, fill up the drinking water, shop groceries and things; it was an exceptional privilege provided we gave her a warm hug. Thanks, Maggie.

Refuge Bay became a temple for us. The energy that we gathered while anchored over there, walking in the woods, climbing the rocks and sightseeing from up there among birds, butterflies and strolling back down to take a shower under that waterfall made us feel literally Adam and Eve, including their sin. Not enough; we received a box of goods with letters from Brazil - pictures, a Brazilian flag and this book about the magic manuscript found in Peru. My soul was already now trying to reach out for some piece of the very faraway universe, my prays had been an exercise of breathing, trying to capture from the air a clue about my next move and praying. I started to build a deep retrospective about myself and made private confessions even regarding my childhood going on, I was thinking about the world as a whole, scanning by memory all the people that I knew, from the very close ones to the casual acquaintances, as many people as I could, wishing good upon them all, including those who treated me no too well in the recent past. I was practicing what Bhagavan Das had taught me back in California - that we should love everyone, love each other without restriction and without even the need to let people know we were vibrating love towards them. It should be an exercise free of any pre-concept and repeated as often as we could until we could not anymore go back the way we once were, we were loving the entire world and nothing would be able to hurt us.

"Love is love, Louis!" so he said, laughing at my suffering back then in Mill Valley.

Now I was reading *The Celestine Prophecy* by James Redfield and because I had kept my old habit of reading two or three books all at once in my lap I also had Paulo Coelho´s *The Pilgrimage*, truly magnetized. It did not matter whether the manuscript did exist or not, whether Paulo Coelho was born one thousand years ago for real or not; the ideas from those books seemed to burst out of my own chest as mine and made sense with my crazy reverie with Milton, the Uruguayan in Mill Valley from years ago when we both invented a device able to release particles of light into the universe and to capture them back with a centrifugal force ultra fast, photographing everything throughout space and time, aiming to collect the truth of all. The elements around myself were the most important things to care about along with the love to everyone and finally I was worried about the speed we all move in our lives - way too fast - not taking care of the way we breathe and feed ourselves with not only good food but also good thoughts. I was anchored in one of the most beautiful places on earth, a magic place if I was not entirely insane just yet, and I was obstinate to sail back home, crossing three oceans without the experience of sailing. I interrupted such a challenge to give myself to those two books until I read the two of them twice each. Helga was next to me, following the reverie on a similar pace. And the atmosphere around Alvidia did change. It was good. We could now have a natural intuition about the next minute, hour, day and make a decision without fear or uncertainty trusting everything around us were signals to where to go, what to do, or not. We certainly were self-inducing but it was working. Such was the astral the night we had dinner in the cockpit, lit with a kerosene lamp and the sky full of stars when we heard a knock knock on the hull of Alvidia.

"Larry! Wow, what a fright."

"I saw you guys last week coming to Refuge Bay and figured you would be around still. I am anchored a little up above."

Larry was sad because Michelle left. We drank wine, just the three of us until late that night. Time used to pass by very quick with Larry while we were talking, as if without words, in silence. Larry told us a bit more about his sailing experiences and I am sure it was an excuse to tap into what he really wanted to talk about, "You are going against the stream, Luís. If I was you, I would hop up the coast around the Cape York and towards the Indian Ocean and around Cape Town by then I would be one quick leg away from Rio. This is the way to go."

Geary told us; Lloyd told us again and now Larry too in the middle of the night, as a shooting star. It was a conspiracy of the universe pushing us towards the milk run, the classic route of the old time sailors, the prevailing winds, the horse´s route. And the universe may have had sent angels to convince us.

Our problem was that we could not wait anymore. Missing family, and Helga´s mother was not doing well, so a feeling of guilt was building in my chest. To leave Alvidia in Australia and fly to Brazil - no way. After all we went through, during the factory process, during the construction, then cleaning our souls with acid and recently sanding a monster inside ourselves? To choose the right route we should wait until after April when the cyclone season was going to be gone. So with time to think in Refuge Bay I was able to figure out that philosophical puzzle: if I could draw a picture of what was going on in my head it would be like a spiral figure being on the top of Helga, our families and my dream to built a boat and cross an ocean to anchor at a white sand beach. The next spirals would include an endless scale of values, theories, and principles along with other dreams because a man does not have only one dream; we are always wanting many things, too many. Noticing Helga next to me, supporting me and realizing that picture in my mind was a fair figure I remembered a poem by a Brazilian poet, Vinicius de Moraes when he says: "a woman can be there next to you while you will never know exactly where are her thoughts..." Rarely Helga was standing still, relaxing, enjoying idleness. When she was it was no more than sitting in the cockpit while resting her eyes, far away, beyond the waterfall, beyond the woods, probably beyond the Pacific Ocean, the Indian Ocean, and the Atlantic Ocean, and she looked a bit sad. Maybe she was not able to articulate exactly what was going on in her mind, fearing we would both mix our fears with our doubts if staying in Australia until being able to sail back home or to fly out of that situation immediately and condemn ourselves to remain in prison, away from making our dreams come true. Maybe she was afraid of waking me up from my own dream because I was that happy, very happy living aboard a boat I built with my own hands and this was the point I started my reflections.

About justice: Would it be fair to drag Helga to my adventure?

About freedom: To be free is a form of selfishness or it is a cynical hypothesis as per the philosopher Diogenes?

About happiness: How big is the gap between being free and feeling happy!

About fate: If there is fate, is it right to think each person is a mark, what is mine? Is Helga part of it, am I part of her´s? Who am I in this Stockholm syndrome?

I got tired of dancing around that spiral picture, jumping over my own wreckage and decided that my time was almost done, so hang in there - you will be out of the prison soon, one way or another.

I spoke with Helga and we both got to a point we could just pull the anchor up and leave but that big list of things to do was, in fact, helping us. We were not ready, plain and simple. Thus the four months ahead was a long passage of preparation, finishing little important things and climbing a huge learning curve through the many backs and forward between Refuge Bay and Newport Marina. While around the mooring buoy I started to feel like the owner of the place. Weekend sailors used to ask me if they could grab that certain buoy or anchor at a certain place and such. Some left their stuff for me to take care of. Often I was invited for a lunch or dinner aboard luxury yachts to entertain the hosts with my plans to sail back to Brazil. Helga mastered her cake baked in a pan for our guests. I used to shout to everyone, jet skis, yacht, houseboat, power boat, fishing boats, cats of all sorts. Near New Year´s Eve a group of Australian girls, a female crew of six sailors wearing microscopic bikinis and topless showed up asking Luis to help them anchor and they said people from the Newport Marina recommended Luis for them, so I could not refuse to help and they were so happy that they jumped on the water, right after I set their yacht on a buoy and they shouted, "Hey, Luis, come on to enjoy, show us how deep and neat the waterfall is!"

It was then when Helga thought I should take a break and we went just the two of us to walk in the woods. During the weekend indeed Refuge Bay became unbearable with city habitants.

...January.

The first business day of that year was to visit the Taxation Office to withdraw our income tax return we had never done - a handy six hundred dollars, just in time with the departure atmosphere in the air.

I negotiated with the Royal Prince Alfred Yacht Club to haul Alvidia out for antifouling painting and, with a war plan in mind – war against the clock, must be said –, I could get several other things done while on the hard stand. The Prince Alfred Yacht Club allowed me stay the night on a Friday and over the weekend until the next Monday for the price of a day, so with a meticulous plan many things could be accomplished and it was scheduled for January the 13th. During those two weeks prior to the haul out, Helga wrote in our log book several things such as:

"05/01/96 - Luís was upset because he left our dinghy to knock Alvidia´s hull, making a scratch. Tony (the stiff man, nickname Luis gave to him), an expert in models, came with his kayak to show Luis his model race yacht and Luis played like a five-year-old kid with that toy... "

"10/01/96 - Our first true day of going out for sailing just for sailing. We tied up everything, I placed my seasickness bronze bracelet... It was great! For the first time, I believed sailing can be a therapy..."

So January the 13th knocked on our door and by five o´clock in the morning we jumped out of bed, had breakfast and left Refuge Bay to Newport. By seven o´clock we were in front of the Prince Alfred Yacht Club. Alvidia was hauled out and we washed the hull, making a party like two kids. A mechanic came to inspect our engine and to deliver me spare parts I had ordered. He gave me compliments for the installation of the Yanmar 18HP and said I could motor up to Whitsundays. Fast paced - I took off the rudder that was still too stiff. Dropping all the expensive recommendations from neighbors, I started to paint the antifouling thinking how I would fix the rudder. Within three hours we painted Alvidia, time enough to make up my mind about the rudder. Then I unassembled the propeller, lubricated it well and put back in place, like a pro I thought, that is how much I was proud of myself back then. Who would have known years ago in Copacabana I was doing that in that fashion? And, while I was painting I drafted a plan for the rudder: to use my powerful rasp and solid will, thin out the rudder gasket around the shaft slightly, just enough to make it smooth for the rudder to turn. The ogre crows started to try to scare me; I should do a good job to keep the rubber around the shaft a perfect round cylinder, any minor difference would make the rudder hammer and tend to break during heavy seas. – Ok – I said to myself, deaf to all – so I will concentrate, focus on my job and do it to perfection. While I was engaged in the impossible mission, Helga was asked to pray and just get me water to drink sometimes. I became a rubber, a part of that rudder, nothing else on earth would distract me, I would do a perfect job at rasping gently the rubber, double checking with a pattern I made to make sure I kept the rubber round, and using a powerful torch to light up the soul of that rubber so not to miss a nanosecond of milligram. And to rasp rubber is difficult because it crumbles while its particles are not linked regularly, it means, the same effort you can take that much or that little. My back could not hurt, my eyes should not neglect my wish to see the soul of that rubber, my breath should not get in the way. That rubber was going to be perfectly round and slightly smaller, even all around, and the rudder would turn smoothly. A two hour job. Two hours of torture.

When I finished, happy with the result and ready to try out, my knees were bleeding, my eyes with deep dark circles. The club´s boatyard was already being shut down for the day and only two employees were around. I asked them to help me put back that solid shaft of nine yards of very heavy stainless steel. And I almost cried with happiness. The shaft went through smoothly, the rudder had been fixed, no hammering, no looseness, not tight. My spirit was at its highest and Helga wrote in our log book this:

1/15/01/96 – Scary night. Too much wind. I wake up scared, fearing we could fall from the hardstand. I´m missing the water... "

1/16/01/96 – The rudder job was a success!!! Luís shaved his two weeks beard and left a mustache. Now he is Rodrigues, from Port Rico... An old nice man taught us how to build a manual laundry machine aboard with a plastic bucket. Alvidia went back to her natural habitat, the water..."

Another phrase from Steve was, "Yeshhh you cannn!" when I complained I could not do something. His interjection was an order. And I would embarrass myself if I was to disappoint Steve´s mantra. Later on, I thought if this adventure shall inspire someone that it be that, yes you can.

Joy aboard Alvidia and the captain pays for beer for the boatyard employees; get an extra day on the club´s pier and hire a rigger to inspect our rigging system. All good to go, except a detail that could cost our lives: a chain plate behind a U-bolt on the boom to hold the vang was loose. For those are not from the field, it is like to assemble a tire back on a car without tightening the nuts and bolts. The reason why I guess Alvidia did not want to sail up until then. The angels! And I got a free lesson on how to gauge the halyards. Vroom... Vrooooommmm... Vroommm... We left the Yacht Club happy as two ducks and the rudder very smooth.

Along the way back to Refuge Bay, I gave the tiller to Helga and threw a plastic bottle into the water without warning her. I meant it to be a man overboard drill, by surprise, as it may occur although I knocked on wood three times. What if I fall overboard, how Helga would steer and get me back? Time to try that, so I was that bottle and Helga saved me, I mean, she passed the boat right over me, the bottle, and excited decided to steer up to near the bar when I then took back the tiller. As a reward, Helga got a haircut under the waterfall at Refuge Bay and I acquired one more professional diploma: Hairdresser.

Steve has asked that I should keep in touch. He was worried about us. In one of our touch base, Steve said he had this "rubber duck", the way he called his inflatable dinghy French brand Avon and that he wanted to give it to us.

"No, Steve! This is too much already!"

But the ambassador was hard to convince and after arguing back and forth he agreed to charge me something, and he asked me for two hundred dollars which was only half as much as it would have cost or even less. Goodbye Blue Mystery. And the rubber duck could also be used as a life raft.

Around this time, boats began to be prepared to hop up the coast towards the Whitsundays and many other destinations including New Caledonia, Fiji, and Samoa for when the cyclone season was gone. And so as an ex-adman I made a flashy sign to sell the Blue Mystery and paddled around the anchorage to show off. Interest zero did not get a single inquiry and, in the next time we went to Newport, Maggie bought the Blue Mystery for few bucks. Thanks again and again and forever, dear Maggie.

Once in Newport one more time, I received aboard the last expert I needed. It had been part of my building strategy to do it all by myself and after to call an expert to check it all to make sure I was spot-on or to recommend fixing something. And Bruce Blond, the technician responsible for the Morning Glory electric and electronics, accepted an invitation for a cup of coffee and Helga´s cake as a barter for his expert inspection of my SSB and VHF radios and my ground system. I was amazed; he showed me his schedule commitment, he was booked until the year 2000, five years ahead. Even though, he came aboard with patience, stayed with us a couple of hours talking and admiring our cozy Alvidia, including putting up with my old stock of stupid jokes. When it was time to leave, he asked me to follow him to the parking lot and while I was rowing the rubber duck he was pointing to boats nearby saying the age of that and that other one, who was the owner and such. At his car, he opened the trunk and took something from a toolbox saying it was a gift to me.

What?

"Yes, Louis. As I have said, everything is superb in your boat, but I also suggested those oversized copper wide tapes must be welded. You have ground for three boats the size of yours, and to weld it you will need this iron. With this thing, I paid my first technician course when I married to my wife decades ago. Now is yours. Hey, McConaghy was right, he told me about your beautiful boat, good luck to you and your lovely wife, fair winds, mate."

Embarrassed, speechless and now I knew that John McConaghy, who lived in Pittwater, had been watching Alvidia from his veranda somewhere.

"Hey, Alvidia, you haven´t told us you pumpkin."

I could not wait to go back to Refuge Bay and digest all that just happened. I was afraid to lose any nuance of that good vibe and miss the meaning of all that. I wanted to be in front of the waterfall, watching the contours of those hills which became intimate and reflect with a smile. A happy reflection. As Larry used to do upon the lighthouse. Helga also was eager to go. Her lips and her eyes shining were signs of contentment. Along the way, I stared at her, loving each wrinkle, each vein, each hair out of place, those stained t-shirts, she was so beautiful. We could be two abandoned away from home, lost somewhere in Australia, we could be two bluffs, but we were excited and happy and in love. What else matters?

I wished that all dear people I knew could be there to celebrate with us. It was not a birthday of anybody, it was just a happy day.

Thus, once back to Refuge Bay, we took advantage of that atmosphere, including finding a small hidden waterfall on top of the hill - again like Adam and Eve. We then had a few days of rain and I took the time put to study celestial navigation. I had started to read about the subject thirteen years ago and of course, those theories, never made so much sense as they were doing now. So we went for a sail during the night, although we did not feel confident enough to go out of the bar. It was good news for we discovered at night we had a different perspective – the distances to a landmark for starting acquire a peculiar profile and we discovered our top light on the mast was burned. Next morning I hoisted Helga on a chair and she changed the bulb. My brave Helga, afraid of heights, went up to 12 meters hanging on a rope and trusting on my skills at the winch.

A boat flying a Canadian flag had arrived at Refuge Bay from New Zealand. The cruising pace and flavor was in the air. I had already seen American flags as well as a Belgium and a French flag although we did not have time to make acquaintances with any crew. Just a wave from our cockpit, the anchorage social code. The Canadian captain observed our exercise of changing the mast top light and when I tested to see if it was on he gave me a thumb up from his cockpit. That was a code, we should soon get together. Within half an hour, in fact, we were talking aboard Alvidia. He was making a round-the-world cruise. He left a year ago from Vancouver. He had been on the Pacific Islands from West to East, the way it was supposed to be, going down to New Zealand and now waiting for the fleet to the milk run. His destination once on the top of Australia was to reach Europe via the Mediterranean sea. To talk about those routes was a joy to me. When I told Michael about my sailing plans he thought a bit and very gently assured me that if I was going to make that for real sailing for the first time in my life, I would never want to sail again. He just made the first part of what I was planning to do and downwind contrary of what I was going to face and said, "Please don't go that way! If you really want to leave Australia by the shortest way… wait a bit, I will be back," Michael jumped on his dinghy and ran to his boat leaving a suspense in the air. After eternal few minutes, he came back with charts under the arm. He then showed islands so small that could not have a soccer stadium. He had been in the Marquesas, Polynesia, Tuamotus, Samoa, Fiji, Vanuatu, Noumea. Told me about the characteristic of each, its culture, facilities for cruisers and apparently would not stop to talk to convince me to change my plans.

"Lui! Get these charts and draw a new route for the both of you. A route that you will be able to enjoy, sail wearing a bikini and sunbathing. Jump from an island to another. From Australia to the first row of islands it will be a bit with the wind on the nose but as soon as you approach the Pacific system you will have the wind as your crew aboard and making short trips from one anchorage to the next."

"Michael, we can not take your charts."

Michael was another angel in our way. He insisted and gave us approximately fifty copies of Pacific Islands charts.

"I don´t know what to say, Michael, I am embarrassed. At least get this book about the Australian coast that you like. What else could we possibly give to you or help?"

Of course, we could help him. We should accept his invitation for a dinner aboard his boat. He was waiting for his girlfriend from Canada that afternoon, she would help him cross the Indian Ocean. And we could also watch a movie with him, Apollo 13.

The reception aboard Equity was superb. It was a Hunter 42" with all the stewardships a modern flat could have. Everything was high-tech. Microwave oven, fridge, ice maker, stove and furniture, even plants and his trendy electronics - the same brand as Alvidia. A small interesting detail, Michael apologized but warned us about the toilet, saying men should use it seated as the girls.

Ah? No problem, Michael, my pleasure.

We drank wine; we had dessert and espresso. During the Apollo 13 movie we drank Irish coffee and after the movie, Michael kept pouring coffee and talking. Merida, his girlfriend, was very nice and we could not tell she had just arrived on an airplane, from a law office in Vancouver, had jumped on a bus in Sydney to Pittwater, and made a passage from Newport to Refuge Bay on Michael's rubber duck, and that during the passage they rescued a windsurfer with problems near a rocky area at high tide. So almost four o´clock Helga and I were authorized to go home, but how would we sleep with so much Irish Coffee?

A lot was going on, those hills and that anchorage was going to be in our memories forever; we felt as if we were already cruising without even leaving the buoy. The sailing plans did not matter; it was good already.

By ten o´clock Michael came to see us and pointed his forefinger to his short pants. I could not believe it. We had been talking about lifestyle, life planning, philosophy... He was a conservative kind of person maybe even sober-minded, being a lawyer in his own firm, an expert in real estate and equities. He had clients in the USA, Canada, and China. He had left everything behind, including his marriage, and was there telling two strangers about his ordeal to make up his mind about leaving the city slicker life. It was when I told him about quality of life against a pretending financial solid life, the benefit of the slow consumption, health food for the body and mind and that sort of thing. While we were talking about these things the night before I tried to mix in few stupid jokes; after all, we were on the hook, at Refuge Bay. Alvidia´s bunks turned into psychoanalyst's couches and Michael´s main complaint was that once on shore he missed the cruising life, where he was able to meet up with humans made of flesh and bone and heart; it was when I added "that clap with eyelids showing happiness" and he said he loved the expression. He was divorced, had two daughters. All of the sudden he says hi to a couple anchored twenty miles from Sydney, reachable only by the water; next he went aboard a small homemade yacht to meet up with that couple and gave them fifty Pacific Ocean charts; then the couple had a dinner and spent the whole night with him and now he was opening his life's diary to that couple. Refuge Bay was a magical place.

I told him my rugged path through my personal life and business and up to the building of Alvidia and he interrupted me:

"But you were able to abandon the Italian suit and ties, fancy restaurants and groove life?"

"Look, Michael, don´t even think of comparing yourself with my humble life and my original environment that is Brazil where you area invited to play mind games all the time, where nothing is well done, or most of the things are not finished, which is the same, and there is no pattern for anything; nothing is standard. It's a big mess, you know. Then the government is corrupt from the top down, poverty mixed with corny luxury; in general people are illogical or incoherent. But you know what, I miss Brazil, it is so beautiful but I don´t want to live there. Get me some more Irish coffee, please."

Then I began to tell him about my old dream to have a boat, while I was being paid as an office boy working as major Advertising Accounts Director for the top fourth Ad Agency in Brazil, speaking to college students and writing for business magazines I had this dream to build a boat all by myself and anchor at a place like Refuge Bay. It was then that I realized how healthy it is to make a fool of yourself and laugh about it. Michael and Merida laughed so loud that they stared at each other, a little embarrassed. He stood up and grabbed me by the shoulders shaking me and laughing, when I told him when I was kid I used to watch the TV series Flipper and mimic Bud (Tommy Norden), the youngest boy of the show wearing jeans cut to the knees, swimming with Flipper, I had cut my brand new jeans and during commercial breaks I ran to the washing tank to dive pretending to be in the movie; one day I almost killed myself by drowning.

Two days later Michael invited us for another dinner and I accepted, provided he would not offer Irish coffee again; otherwise I would resume my stupid jokes. Michael told us that the other night I changed his life.

"What?" I said. —

"Yes," he said, "Look!" He showed me again that pair of pants cut short. "Thanks, Luis! You helped to make up my mind. I will continue to liveaboard, finish my cruise and if I go back to Canada I will manage to change my whole life forever - no more conventional habits. Our dinners represented at least a year of psychoanalysis "Luís, you've changed my life! I wrote a letter to my daughters, my ex-wife and my partners."

Instead of making me proud, he worried me - what was our childish conversation capable of? Should I counterbalance a bit with a comment or conservative recommendation, or should I stay quiet? What would I say, encourage him with compliments or just say "Wow?" I said wow and wished him happiness.

Before we said goodbye to each other, Michael gave us another important gift. The book by Larry and Lin Pardey, *The Care And Feeding of an Offshore Crew*. It became Helga´s bible to plan supplies and emergency kits. The farewell party was aboard Alvidia and the chef on duty prepared a gnocchi *al sugo* followed by red wine from a plastic bag package with a tap inside a cardboard box, I learned later that NASA has invented it. For dessert, Helga made brownies which got stuck in our teeth and gums and we could not talk and while laughing we looked like a doped bunch under a kerosene lamp around a dinette table anchored somewhere that no one on earth would care about us.

That same week, we were already leaning to change our cruising route, one more time. Michael did not appear by accident, we said to each other, Helga and I. With all those charts in front of us it was hard not to rethink our plans. Since we have read *The Celestine Prophecy*, we decided to read signs and I even tried to actually see the energy of those hills around the anchorage. And believing the universe can conspire towards your wishes, as said per the *Pilgrimage*, I used to look at the trees around suspecting those charts had been fallen from the sky.

On the last day of January, we sailed as grown-ups in the waters of the Hawkesbury River, "Sunny day, and a little boat sailing away..." as per a famous Brazilian song, and all of the sudden around a corner of the river we saw that astonishingly beautiful boat, Nautilus with all the clothes on, the crew dressed up, spectacular. Aboard Alvidia the maneuvers were already easy, took us to come around Nautilus. It was Steve´s birthday, what a nice surprise! So both boats aimed Pittwater Bay to anchor at the opposite side of Palm Beach, one hook, two white boats, one half the size of the other, what a contrast, a modern built one, yet virgin next to a genuine classic yacht full of stories logged. And there were six of us with Steve, Maureen, Ron, and Inga.

As we set the anchor, Steve established a program for the day. We should go for a walk in the woods, then windsurf lessons to Luis, lunch and spent the whole afternoon working on Alvidia which according to Steve needed few things to get done. How would we not obey the Ambassador? At first, I thought he was kidding but he was not. After hopelessly trying to stand up on a windsurf board, many falls and a bunch of thorns on my feet, we had a gorgeous lunch followed by cold white wine, and Steve set a workshop on the deck of Nautilus. And who would say he should not do that? And he wanted to taper the tiller, to place a bronze cleat for the anchor rod at the bow of Alvidia, to install an extension for our gas system, to improve the mainsail heaving set up, and last but not least give me a condensed course of mechanics – on that Sunday of his birthday while anchored outside Sydney. Ron, with his white beard and a captain hat, had a way to follow Steve's order as if he was in an epic movie. Everything Steve asked he would repeat out loud and run to get it done as if he was on a warship. Stubby, he runs up and down shouting Steve´s orders, throwing himself down below as if he was a trapeze acrobat. While coming back, he would shout the description of a tool in his hand

"Lewis! Your anchor would fall from the crest of ten feet wave without a strong cleat at the bow! It would stick in the hull and fill your floor with water till you sink!"

My life became a nightmare although I was getting a gift on Steve´s birthday. I did not know how to ask Steve to stop because I did not have even time for it. He was already actually doing it all and biting his mustache and had grabbed my nose with his fingers. In less than an hour the tiller was tapered and in fact much prettier. "What?" Steve said to me. "The rudder is so smooth, did you fix it?"

"Yes, Steve, I did it at Prince Alfred."

"Ah! You kidding, does not have looseness?"

"No, Steve, nothing, no vibration but look, you don´t need to do anything else, thanks..." I tried, while Ron turned on an electric circular saw, deafening all of us. I looked at Helga asking her for help but she also could not do a thing. It was already ten o´clock at night when Steve´s platoon called it a day. The sails had been taken off several times, the boom unassembled from the mast twice, the tiller was tapered and in fact, it was great. The bronze cleat at the bow was installed and the gas system improved. Ron played his role as first mate aboard a warship. Steve ate his entire mustache and I hurt my hands. Alvidia was stirred around, undressed in front of guests. Two or three shots of wine, a bite, and we all fell asleep. But truth must be said, those little details from Steve made so much difference. In the morning we made a breakfast in Alvidia's cockpit for everybody. Then Steve "invited" us to follow him to Sydney, sailing; it would be our chance to test ourselves out on the ocean sailing. How would we say no to Steve? Especially that he said it would be a sunny day sailing on a flat sea, which means no or little wind.

I started to make everything wrong, that is to copy Nautilus moves. We maintained contact on VHF radio channel 67 and so I was teleguided by Steve. You don´t do this while sailing. You take information from other vessels, but you need to be in control and make your own decisions. At the crossing of the bar, there was no wind and only those typical swells of the incoming tide. Steve told me over the radio that we should make a wide tack to the other side and then I saw Nautilus awkwardly in a diagonal line towards us cutting halfway through the exit and while any light breeze would make Alvidia move we got out and Steve asked where we were going.

"Sydney, Australia!" I said.

"Well, I have no wind, are you with the engine on? Let´s motor," He said.

I was sailing at five knots without any acrobatics with the sails but I obeyed Steve turning the engine on. I manage to stay next to Nautilus between her and the shore. Steve called asking me to pull the throttle full power he wanted to see the performance of our engine. I was following his orders via the radio. No good. Soon I got to a point when I did not know what to do next, until he ordered us to, or worst if he didn't. Then a stronger breeze came in and I saw Nautilus turn off the engine with no orders via the radio. I purchased the sheets of the sails tight and turned off the engine, choosing a portside tack getting away from near Nautilus so Steve could make a sudden maneuver if he needed. A bit further on the ocean, I got an even stronger breeze and Alvidia was flying already. I could see a lot of activity on the deck of Nautilus. The sails were reduced to a minimum. Steve called me on the radio and told me something about a big blow coming from South, it means we were going against that blow. I did not understand, the wind and waves were making so much noise, the communication became cut. Helga called on the cockpit to point out that they were turning the engine back on. Then I saw Ron running to the bow and folding down the sails, then at the boom putting down the main too. Steve told me on the radio that a strong south front with winds and waves would turn that leg to Sydney a bit too rough and that we should aim to reach Sydney harbor before dark. I paired with him still without engine only the sails up and making great progress already climbing six feet waves and at a halfway to the Port Jackson entrance. The horizon ahead of us became lead-colored it was like a wall coming over us while we were going over the wall. Aboard Nautilus I could see the crew running and I saw Ron losing his captain hat, I called Steve on the radio but did not have a reply, I went back to the cockpit and could see that wall right over embracing us. The sea became confused, I could not tell from where the waves were coming from, it could be from everywhere while Alvidia became like an untamed horse. I was frightened. When I realized just that Alvidia stuck the bow under a wave down a through and stayed there too long and my legs trembled immediately thinking how I would protect Helga at the moment had a dread face and an open mouth holding herself with the two hands on the companionway entrance. The next thing came to my mind was how come I did not have all the leashes on my own hand and let other people take care of my moves. I was a fool. While I was punishing myself a cloud of small fishes swimming out of the water like flying through the spray of the waves. Then I shouted to Helga to hold the tiller right in the middle, no time for the proper terminology on deck and it was enough for us to understand each other. I cranked the engine back on, while on the same token left the headsail sheets off and folded the sail with the furler fast and also got down the main all so fast that I couldn't believe it. Even bare pole Alvidia was leaning – how many times I had read in adventure books about a yacht going forward bare pole and now I realized it was not a situation to be in. Fear took over me. I was trembling and with teeth chattering. The thing is, I have a tendency to hypothermia and the shock of temperature which was hot and became sudden cold and the fear made my body temperature collapse too fast; I was having a thermal shock. Plus, the waves were coming, swiping the deck from the bow all the way to the cockpit, gush after gush. On the sides, the waves were throwing themselves over Alvidia. The world became crazy and was assaulting our little once-upon-a-time cozy nest. I could barely see Nautilus hugging the shore now with a small staysail and a mizzen already approaching the Port Jackson entrance. On the radio no more orders. Our engine stopped right on when Alvidia was thrown up in the air from the crest of a wave and fell making a noise like a cannon. – And now? – I asked myself – what I am going to do? Hoist the sails back on? *The Old Man and the Sea*, by Ernest Hemingway, came to mind, I recollect the memory of my daddy, and my mother in heaven. I looked at Helga next to me and realized I had to maintain my head straight and focus on the solution, or try to take control of the situation. Trembling with cold and fear. It upset me, I hated myself being with so much fear, teleguided, stupid. Shall I go by the book now, as they say, run with the wind, that is in my case to make a U-turn and sail back to Refuge Bay? I could see the entrance of Port Jackson. I also saw a sailboat coming from the opposite direction of us and crossing the entrance almost touching the rocks the other side, maybe he was coming from Tasmania or who knows where. Half of his deck was under the water and aboard I could see only one man apparently calm standing still with the wheel firm under his hands. It was an old boat and could well be portrait by a painter a Nordic picture.

"I'm fucked up, no engine to take us out of this, I have to sail" – when the boat went out of the water the propeller run free and made the engine to stop. Nautilus also got into the Port Jackson behind that other boat and the dark made us be alone in the middle of a would-be tragedy. Helga went down below and grabbed a jacket for me, I was already getting blood concentrated on my fingers tips and lips, next I would collapse paralyzed but Helga had this impulse of massaging my wrists and I decided to breathe fast to warm my airways. Alvidia was doing fine. I could hold the tiller with a leg, thank God the rudder and the tiller were spot on. Then Helga and I saw the Sydney Harbour at the same time and it was a relief, we knew we were going to make it to the inside of the Darling Harbour; we just need to get in the Port Jackson. I should now change tack in order to get in but the sails were stuck, I could not pull or ease the sheets, they were entangled. The waves at the very entrance were confused again. We were like a ping-pong ball. Up and Bummm! The Sydney downtown skyline lighted up made my sight obfuscate while behind me a solid dark. A huge oil ship was coming out of the bay and of course, it had the right of way, so I had to maneuver out the way. "Ok, now this. Dammit!" I said out loud, cursing even more. Since I could not change the tack I jibed, that is, I threw the tiller to the other side and made Alvidia turn almost on its center and then I felt as we started to be pushed over the rocks, right in the middle of the entrance of Port Jackson. Diagonally we made progress of fewer than fifty yards in, and again another big boat was coming out - it was a huge passenger cat, a ferry boat. Another jibe. I was moving in circles and slightly inward into closed and more calm waters but one more time towards the rocks and then it was over a huge buoy with a green light - one of the signs of the entrance channel. I try to aim in Direction of the Opera House but I was unable to sail close-hauled, the sheets were hopelessly entangled. Alvidia insisted to come out of the wind, meaning going backwards while I was working hard on the tiller to drive my dear boat. I asked Helga to help and when Helga puts herself to help you can rely on her. We were fighting our way into the Sydney Harbour. But Helga grabbed a rope and I shouted "No, that one no!" It was too late; it came undone from the cleat and the boom fell over the cabin.

"Bring it back in!" I shouted; we used to communicate between ourselves perfectly even with expressions that did not make sense at all, and even when we did not know what to do. We were a professional clumsy couple.

Ok, the wrong rope stayed entangled in the dark and Helga was apparently reading my thoughts; she climbed the cabin and folded the mainsail around the dead boom. The wind inside the bay was a little weaker now; I jibed again the only way of sailing Alvidia, in circles - and it looked like we were making small progress although getting too close to that green sign that we crossed already three times, and escaped from a third cargo ship so close that I could almost touch its hull in the dark, as if Alvidia's wish was to go back to Sailors Bay. I was tired and let the current push us towards that pleasant place we were once. At this point, Steve called us on the radio.

"Alvidia, Alvidia, Alvidia, this is Nautilus, over."

I asked Helga to answer while I kept playing with Alvidia in circles until I did not know when.

"Helga, answer Steve, tell him we had few little problems but we are fine."

She was dreading but told me we should get out of that by ourselves. Brave Helga.

"Of course, Helga, but answer him."

"But answer what? He will think something happened to you. How do I speak on the radio? No, you answer, I'll get the tiller."

"Helga, you will not keep Alvidia the way I am going, just grab the phone and talk, just like a telephone."

"Ah no, I will not, you will do it."

"Helga, say: Nautilus, Nautilus, this is Alvidia over!"

Then she said, "Nautilus, Nautilus, this is Alvidia, over!"

Steve asked why our mast top light was in a circle right in the middle of the entrance of Port Jackson.

"What do I say?" Helga asked me.

I told her to mention a problem with our engine and the sails and she replied, "I said, now what?"

"Did you push the button, the red light was on?" I asked her.

"No, what button? Ah, I found it and now what I have to say?"

"Over, whatever you say, say over in the end and wait," I told her.

She grabbed the phone and said, "Over!"

"Did you answer, push the red button to talk and say over?" I asked her from the cockpit while she stuck her head from down below through the companionway towards me.

"Ah! No, I am not going to talk on the radio. We will get out of this by ourselves."

"Ok, ok, look; come here and get the tiller. You look to the stern of the ship, stay looking straight to that and when Alvidia approaches that green light over there you push the tiller to the other side. Alvidia will make a U-turn, ok? You can do it. I will calm down Steve."

At the radio I breathed deep and calm, very calm as if nothing had happened, I told him a short story of our ordeal. Steve said that he had serious problems and he was already under the Sydney Bridge but would come back to help us, maybe tow us to River Quays. I told him not to worry; just to say something because I knew he would come anyway. I run back to the cockpit to find Helga a bit scared almost in the middle of the exit of the bar although now our position was better to jibe and make a long run into the Sailors Bay. I could then sit and relax for few minutes. I needed a quick rest and a moment to think about what and how to do it.

The night was so dark that from the bow I could barely see Helga in the cockpit. It was also true that the city lights blinded me. Nautilus came slowly in from the dark and its huge volume gave us a sort of sense of being rescued although we were already in safe waters. I had inspected our ropes on deck and I concluded that if I wished to make that mix up

I would not be so efficient. The whole running rigging system was entangled in a way that it was impossible to know which line was which. As Nautilus approached us by starboard, I could notice Steve was concerned as well with the problems he had while entering Port Jackson and we never spoke about it; he could not stay out there and help me, in fact, there was no reason to even try to help, I should be able to manage my self in with or without experience. While Ron was a mutineer pirate aboard Nautilus and he was discussing it with Maurine.

"Grab that defense, Ron," shouted Maureen.

"And you, Maureen, get me that rope, would you?" he replied, visibly upset.

They had a plan to tow us to River Quays. They wanted to throw me a towing rope so I could tie it around a cleat. Ron was trying to guide Steve, shouting instructions as we approached the two boats, "Fifteen degrees to portside! Thirty degrees to starboard! Maureen! You, now, defenses overboard!"

The hulls were close enough already and Ron hung on the safety lines, stretching his short legs, trying to anticipate and avoid the impact of the two hulls. It was all happening in the dark inside the Darling Harbour. Steve asked him to take it easy while Maureen screamed, "Ron, we will have a collision!"

"I can't do everything! We'll both sink!" shouted Ron.

I whispered to Steve from about five yards in the dark, and gently threw an end of a rope to him from the cockpit, while Alvidia slid back a bit. I tied the rope on the bronze cleat at the bow. There was silence aboard Nautilus and we started to be towed to River Quays. Ron traveled, standing at the stern of Nautilus, staring at us from behind. Helga and I looked at each other and could not resist bursting out in a big laugh, finding everything too funny, from the Refuge Bay with a grand finale near Sailors Bay. After all, it was all funny.

Ron pointed at us nodding several times and shouted out loud, "You two are mad! You could kill yourselves! Look, Steve, they are laughing!"

The next morning we could not believe what we saw. The entanglement of ropes on deck was worse than we saw the night before.

We spent the entire week at River Quays at a berth that was courtesy for old residents. It was a busy week though. Steve took us to his company in the suburbs, driving his truck on those bumpy and busy streets. We were much more scared than from our first storm sailing Alvidia days earlier. Steve decided to help us with the engine, to figure out why the engine stopped. He said it could be because the diesel escaped from the pickup hose system inside the diesel tank while Alvidia was jumping over the waves. So we worked together to assemble a device to make sure the pickup hose inside the diesel tank would not miss the fuel.

Every night there was a little party on the deck of Nautilus, good food, and good wine while Steve worked hard to convince us to stay longer in Australia, to learn how to sail, and get used to the boat out on the ocean. He found a job for Helga in a Greek restaurant and I could help him in his company; he even offered to lend some money to us.

"You are diving in an abyss. Don´t go just now. Wait a bit."

That Saturday early in the morning while it was still dark we left the mooring lines very quietly and sailed away from the River Quays, down the Parramatta River. Sleepily, I made three turns in front of a bridge along the way en route to Birkenhead Point. My eyes threw me a curve so I thought the mast would not pass under that bridge, but as the first sun's rays cleared my sight I saw it was an illusion, there was plenty of room above the mast. And once again we passed in front of Woolwich, under the Sydney Harbour Bridge, in front of the Opera

House and did not resist making a pit stop at Sailors Bay. It would be the last chance to catch up with our friend Lloyd.

We were welcomed as usual with warmth and smiles aboard Tai Hoa. Lloyd was skinny but with the same sense of humor. He told me the doctors did not want to deceive him, although his physical appearance showed he was doing ok, the laboratory and medical exams were terrifying and by the look of the doctors, he would have few days of life. He even had his will made and despite the two smiles in front of us, only the Captain of Tai Hoa had a countenance of joy. I felt a bitter taste in my mouth.

We had sent Lloyd a type of mushroom called kombucha introduced to us by Maureen who was a naturopathy practitioner. According to our readings, the tea made out of that mushroom after a process of fermentation had proprieties enabling remarkable rejuvenation. It had been discovered in an ancient Russian city where the average age of the population reached one hundred years old and the mushroom had been taken to Japan with the same results. Lloyd adopted the mushroom and so did we and together we had said we would beat the doctor's prediction. We talked a bit more about his health and he read fifteen pages of his new book about the history of boating in Australia. In the end, I felt like kissing Lloyd´s forehead and I did. He smiled a thanked me. It was the last smile I spent with Lloyd and the last time I would ever see him. So I kept that as a keepsake, an eighty year old child full of unique life experiences and generous and kind. Before Lloyd answered me any questions he would make a serious face and think a bit, as if looking far way with the same look of my Indian in Arizona, then he would release his opinion with a smile, basically saying "take it for granted or not, as it pleases you," never forcing an opinion.

The leg between Sailors Bay and Refuge Bay was half boring and almost a tragedy. About five miles from Berenjoey Head we were in the cockpit and Helga screamed, "Water inside Alvidia!"

I looked down below and saw the floor splashing, covered by water. I jumped down and felt the water up to my ankles. We were sinking. Immediately I started to search for the source of intake. I looked under the sink, at the drinking water tank under the bunk and then at the engine compartment. It was there. Three major squirts. We panicked and at the same time were trying to survive. "Helga, get the bucket and I will work on the manual bilge pump!"

Instantly Helga started to vomit but she placed one bucket between her knees down on the floor and with another bucket started to bail water out in the sink. Seizures of vomiting at the same speed of the water bucket being dumped in the sink and then two or three buckets of water for each vomiting surge. I saw that for a little while pumping the bilge, seated on the toilet because the bilge pump was placed on that corner. It could well be a good place, such was my dread. I recalled the flyer of the sealant for the engine shaft that said it should be bled every time the boat was hauled out of the water; a very simple operation according to the instructions and I did not do that at Prince Alfred a month ago. So after Alvidia jumped so much going into Port Jackson - yes, it was the reason we were taking water. We were driving powered by the engine because the wind was near nothing and I went back to the cockpit to figure out if we could make the rest of the trip to Pittwater. I looked down below and did the math to figure out if Helga would do it by herself while I would be sailing our way in, and she was winning the squirts, kneeled on the floor and was not vomiting anymore. I would never forget those two delicate shoulders, that beautiful creature, my Helga bailing water out of Alvidia. Sweating and apparently acquiring more and more energy from I never knew where. So I turned off the engine and hoisted the mainsail although the squirts kept coming, three against one bucket and a half, enough to keep Alvidia afloat, provided Helga didn't faint. Within an hour we reached the bar with the lighthouse to our portside, almost touching the rocks, and I feared that with the water turmoil at the entrance the squirts would increase. I thought to call the Coast Guard on the radio. But how much time I would spend on the radio, and even worse, what about our trip back to Brazil? And the expenses to fix the problem? And the psychological outcomes of that? My mind was spinning fast. I drove around the Berenjoey Head asking Alvidia not to jump too much and decided to duck into any pier nearby, at least I would sink in well-known waters and could save us and what would be left of the boat. Sealed to the tiller I went very close to the piers and kept going along the way, passing each one and progressing until we finally reached the Yacht Club, approaching the guest pier as usual, very slowly as if nothing was going on aboard, getting the sails down precisely as we used to do and getting the mooring lines tied one from the stern another from the bow. I took a last look down below to see Helga and was happy to realize she had now dragging the bucket to catch the water so it wasn't above the ankle anymore and I said to her, "Helga, hang in there, I will run to the mechanic and ask for help," I then dashed along the boatyard.

The mechanic was busy and said it looked like a normal although not good thing to happen and that I should be calm; he would go there in an hour or so.

"Have you tried to bleed that seal shaft?" he asked.

Two hours later the mechanic came aboard. I was in the cockpit with a beer can waiting for him and had prayed a lot thanking God to save us. Helga and I had worked to dry up everything down below and to make Alvidia tidy as she liked it to be. I had also followed the mechanic's suggestion and with the memory of the seal shaft flyer I laid down alongside the engine compartment and did the service bleeding. Very simple operation indeed, just a push in like in a bagpipe and a quick clamp back to the original position and the squirt stopped. Not a tear in. Alvidia was dry as a brand new baby diaper. The mechanic had a beer, we talked, and he never knew how desperate we had been and so we moved on with our lives. From then on we included in our daily routine checking the engine compartment and Alvidia became the driest boat on the surface of the earth.

Being so close, we took a chance to visit Maggie, check mail and buy groceries for our next retreat at Refuge Bay.

"Hi, kids! How´s life treating you and Alvidia?"

"All right, Maggie. And yourself, luck with the sale of your flat?"

She used to share her things with us, she loved the flower we gave her and was amazed how strong the flower was, even watering it once a day it was still fresh after three weeks.

"It will live forever, Maggie, it is artificial, plastic!"

We burst out laughing together and she blushed like a chili pepper.

...February again, one year aboard.

It was summer and gusts followed by scattered shower were normal. One afternoon we went for a sail and left the mooring buoy under sails, with no engine. A quick summer storm just passed by, the sun had taken over and everything was shining. Birds were all over, of different sizes and colors, flying apparently with no direction in the sky, some diving to fish, some just trading trees - beautiful natural choreography. I was wearing just short pants, no shirt, was sunbathing and leisurely eating a pear, enjoying the scene. After helping with the mooring line, Helga went down below to grab something and later on I noticed she wrote in the log, "02/13/96 – The sun shining. Two full rainbows we can see their two ends fallen on the water of about hundred yards from the boat. The third insight. We are amazed. Ahead, when we turned our back, the river was Golden. The sun was setting slowly, so beautiful..."

We did not include the waterfall anymore in our descriptions because it became a commonplace. What a luxury. I looked at Helga and remembered each episode in the last week, the last months, the last four years, and since we met. I felt the breeze and breathed it deep into my lungs, looking right into the sun. It was already purple and gold and it was like feeding myself with that good energy. I imagined that energy could well go through my body, down to the earth, around, and faraway reaching all the people I loved, my family and friends. Alvidia was going over the rocks but I slowly pushed the tiller with the leg while Helga left the headsail sheet to go, passed behind me and grabbed the other sheet at starboard. All natural now. No words. We were learning how to sail and we were making progress.

To me, Alvidia was done. My list had only one item to check. A base for the autopilot. But Helga had an infernal list, operational things, a folder with detailed notes and it was too dangerous if I made a simple comment about a bolt or a noise on the boom, it would go to the list. And without checking her list we would not leave Australia. I am a mix of Virgo and Leon, I had been a System Analyst and O&M detailed oriented mind but Helga was many notches above me about details.

I thought of a few things I could get done along the way while going home. Perhaps get a temporary job here and there to pay a third party to get it done for me. Alvidia had been launched unfinished and we were already living a cruising life getting things done; it would not change now. But Helga wanted white curtains and many other things, some important indeed. But we were unanimous on one thing, to leave Australia and go back home. Helga had fear while out on the ocean, but she also missed her mom, the tension was her state of mind, cause and effect alternating order of importance.

Thus, while on the mooring buoy at Refuge Bay, I built the autopilot base with hand tools and aboard our dinghy because Helga would not let me mess up our home. My benchtop was inside the dinghy tied to the stern of Alvidia and the task include cutting, sanding, laminating with West System, bolting down and painting. After three days work, a test and the euphoric approval of the Captain, Helga sponsored a nice dinner. And we decided to baptize the autopilot after our friend Ulysses. Every time then when we got tired of steering we gave the tiller to Ulysses, the autopilot.

From then on, I had to input the coordinates of latitude and longitude of the waypoints we want to reach and Ulysses would do to the hard task of steering. Alvidia did not complain, actually I think she liked because I never made a straight course while holding the tiller and Ulysses was like a metal ruler.

Next week while we went to Church Point for groceries and to fill the water tanks, I noticed another boat from the cockpit while anchored on the hook, with a couple aboard in a pace similar to ours. On the beach, a gentleman was sanding a wooden tiller. I thought to make acquaintances and jumped on the dinghy to row. Helga remained aboard Alvidia. When I got to the beach I shouted to the gentleman that job was mine, that I had post Doctorate in sanding; he was well dressed although in short pants and a linen shirt and shaved. He was preparing, for varnish, a tiller of a classic wooden skiff heritage in the family.

We were starting to engage in a friendly conversation when the couple from the other boat got to the beach as well and after the inevitable introduction, I discovered Ann and Alan were preparing their boat to sail up to Darwin and then Indonesia. They were easily around in their seventies; she reminded me of Jane Fonda and him of Sean

Connery. They asked me where I got my accent from and both said, "Wow! So far away from home! You and your wife must come aboard Lituana before we leave," After a few words back and forward they finished with, "Let's face it. We are mad!"

The couple referred to "us" all, we as cruisers and being included in that community was a hell of a compliment to me already, without ever having left port.

The gentleman stopped his sanding entertainment to follow the cruisers, enchanted. When I invited him to come aboard and replied that I had built the boat all by myself he laughed out loud. "Ok, let´s go, I want to check this out, thanks for the invitation, accepted. Am I with the right dress code?" he joked. And before we boarded the dinghy he ran to the parking lot to store the tiller in his convertible Mercedes' trunk.

I asked if he was preparing himself for the Mediterranean route. He was so elegant; he should take his shoes off and step on the sand to enjoy it more, and we kept joking and laughing. The skiff of that tiller belonged to his father who got it from his grandfather and it barely left the garage and I had been dreaming of a boat for thirteen years.

"What would you like: white or red wine with homemade fried pastry?" I asked him after a gymnastic effort to get him aboard from the dinghy and I showed him two card boxes with taps.

Another big laugh.

"Ok. How about a red?" he said, laughing again while I poured from the tap.

My new, already old, friend had a Real Estate business in Pittwater with three branches in New South Wales. He lived in one of the mansions of Woolwich. He liked to drive his Mercedes to escape from home. His marriage was not going well; he slept in a separate bedroom away from his wife, spoke very little and they did not fight, argue or disagree much on anything - they were just bored and lost interest in each other. Their children were already grown up and had their own lives. Soon he would have a definition for his future life but still, within a lapse of less than an hour I already knew it all. Alvidia was a temple. My turn of revelations started by answering him how must cost my boat. Big laugh again. And he had this cacoethes of making a beak with his lips and wide blue eyes as if he wanted to hear the whole story of anything I was saying. When I showed him pictures of the boat on the hardstand in River Quays a year back he coughed with laughter. By then he answered a phone call from his wife and the issue was which car she could use that afternoon or if he would return home with the Mercedes. Ending the phone call he asked for more wine.

"I did not know this card box wine was ok," he said. "Thank you, Luis."

We kept going until sunset; it was already dark actually when I took him back to the beach after we finished with two liters of an ok red wine. I left him but not before he promised me to help Maggie rent or sell her flat and he confirmed he would take care of it personally, provided I would send him postcards from our trip up north. He also promised me to use the boat, to take it out of the garage and shake the bugs out of it every once in a while.

While going back to Alvidia, I saw an iron-made boat approaching the Anchorage in the dark very slow and anchor as if it was a parking lot. On deck was only one man. Always it was a chance to observe how other boats approached anchorages and set the anchor; it was my way of learning, watching and trying myself. That one was so easy. The anchorage next to Church Point became busy and at night the residents of the Scotland Island ran up and down with their aluminum runabouts. I was afraid one of them would run over my anchor rod and so I tied reflective tape on each yard of the rope. Each initiative of the

Captain aboard Alvidia was a reason for a celebration and a record in the log. As a baby to be born we recorded the first kick; later we recorded the first word and so on.

...March, don´t stress yourself.

Helga showed me our financial report and her list. We had exactly one thousand dollars cash, food aboard for three months but fresh veggies for our passage of fifteen thousand miles, which translated into a year or so and her list of things to do numbered two pages. The list included an awning because I let it fall from my mouth that in my dream I imagined to anchor at a white sand beach and stay in the cockpit "under an awning".

And again, on the beach, while tying our dinghy we met our new neighbor. Willie, from Sagitta II, the iron boat. He had been sailed to Brazil, had been in Rio de Janeiro and sailed around the world, twice already, single-handed. But it was our lives, Helga´s and mine which made another round now when Willie came aboard Alvidia and would later convince us to hop up the coast to the Whitsundays, turn the Cape York, the Torres Strait, cross the Indian ocean down to Africa and then the Atlantic back home. Willie loved Alvidia at first sight. He said the boat had a personality of kind. But found it was funny it had so many electronics. He had a thick German accent and did not behave as per his mid-sixty years. He had this intense brightness from the eyes and a deep young voice. He spoke spinning his head and shrinking his neck. In the end of each phrase, he used to lower his voice as if he was reciting a poetry. We also loved him back.

Willie liked a good book and had a strong preference for philosophy. We did not have time enough to discuss everything, like if the sea was a living creature or not, and what would come first - the material or the soul – but we followed instantaneously the one rule that a mature intelligent conversation must take into consideration, the right meaning of things, especially the words. But apart from this, Willie was also a joker. After each opinion of mine he would say, "Marketing man! – laugh - Strip planking expert! – laugh. - Computer man! – laugh."

When I told Willie about our route he raised his eyebrows, gave me a slanting look and with a hand in the air told me we should speak later about this. He noted that Helga had a German name and did not talk too much and I explained to him that, as a social scientist, Helga was very careful at discussing certain things but had an irresponsible theory about boating men. That we looked like females discussing dresses and hairstyle when reuniting discussing boating including we like to gossip about neighbors. And so we started the session of unfair and stupid jokes.

We had coffee and cake, rice and chicken, ok wine from those card boxes, coffee again and Willie went back home very late after his first visit.

The next day it was raining and Willie rowed to our stern, inviting us for a cup of coffee aboard Sagitta II. "I want to show you something," he said.

He noticed we wanted to travel, not exactly to cruise to enjoy the journey. And right from the first step aboard Sagitta II, we could see that everything was robust and had a precise utility and was very simple. There was not much sense or preoccupation with aesthetic, only functionality. It was a boat of a single-handed sailor who lived aboard for thirty years already. From that drizzle, for instance, a light rain, he had collected two gallons of water in a simple collector system made by himself. I felt as if I was aboard Spray, the boat of Joshua Slocum. There were no electronic instruments, not even a VHF radio. The only gadget he showed us shrinking his neck was a watch made in China glued with chewing gum on a bulkhead and a shortwave radio. He gave us two options: homemade beer or home-roasted coffee. Coffee would be ok at that time of the day and so we saw him roasting in front of us from a manual mechanism. Then he served a nice black coffee with homemade bread stuffed with fruits. During the feast, he opened cabinets to show us glass containers with all sorts of preserved food, from meat to fish, from veggies to eggs. After the tour he asked us, "Can I help you with something?"

I was not expecting that question. "Ah, Willie, tell us how it is like to be out there on the ocean blue. How do we keep the boat on course that sort of things while we cross an ocean? For instance, how do you think Alvidia will behave?"

"No, no! I can see you are with a wrong view of the true sea life and a long passage. You don't do anything, you simply go. The boat will take you to the waypoint you plan. You sail two days and it seems sometimes you did not move. You will be always prepared for a storm and it will come. Most of the time you don't sail five days without getting a bit of rough weather or sea or both."

He did not know from where to start. He knew I was zero. "By the way, do you want to go home or cruise, see places?"

"Go home, Willie."

"Then choose the fastest way. Hop up the Australian coast, around the Cape York, Torres Strait, through the Indian Ocean, Cape Town, and the Atlantic. By Carnival next year you will be in Rio. "

"We need to leave Australia, our Visa has expired."

"No worries. You are leaving already."

Any subject about sailing, seamanship, crossing, and boating in general Willie treated with extreme simplicity. Only about society and life in general he was that German philosopher. With a natural way of speaking as if he was describing a recipe of rice, he told me about the sea and winds around Australia, how to put up with the coral reefs, interact with the coast guard, fuel, and water where and how to get, and many other valuable information and lessons.

When he started to talk about the African coast he raised those thick eyebrows again, shrinking his neck, smiled and poured more coffee for himself.

He worked in South Africa as an engineer. Around my age at the time, he bought his first yacht, a Dutch vessel of thirty feet, gave up a wealthy life of high profile income and started to sail. Before that, his hobby was to pilot his own single-engine airplane. His first sailing experience near Cape Town left him with the impression that he would never learn or adapt to the sailing life.

In Durban, he told us, after going around Madagascar, we would have workshops about how to go around Cape Town, there would have much information and help available and he listed many anchorages and sources for help. I told him I exchanged a book by some charts of the Pacific Ocean.

"Trade man, sailor!" He got up and opened a drawer with a gesture as if he was introducing a queen. His stock of charts were intact, clean, without a single trace of pencil or pen. Charts from all over the world. He was proud of using his chart the Admiral way - that is to have notes on a pad instead of on the actual charts preserving them. His notepad had annotations of the stars and sun dating back 1969, 1973, 1984 - they were the years I could quickly notice. Then he produced to me his sextant. So far I had seen sextants in magazines and my Mark V made of plastic yet in a card box without use. His was a genuine Zeiss.

In the afternoon, Willie had a visit. Another German, Horst, aboard his yacht Empede who was moored tied to Sagitta II. While the two friends drank beer all afternoon, Helga and I were quiet aboard Alividia, staring at each other with hearts beating towards changing our route again. We were making a round the world tour through the four quadrants of the wind rose Westbound. Without leaving port we were making progress.

Willie opened a real perspective to us. A thorough schedule with wind speed, the height of waves, depth of oceans, date of departure, estimated date of arrival. It was hard not to think. On top of that, he woke us up from our bureaucracy nightmare about port authorities, Visas and without telling us he also influenced our budget for food, from now own we would preserve food in glass containers too.

The two little mice were planning crossing oceans, with a calorie feed chart trying to balance protein, minerals, and vitamins when Willie knocked on the hull under a light rain still.

"Luis! "Relga"! Let´s talk. We have a lot to talk about!" He was a joker.

"I am going to Brisbane but I need to change your mind about going eastbound to Brazil, it is westbound my friends," shouted Willie, already coming aboard.

The rain kept washing and now gusts were sweeping. The Lituana nearby seemed to be ready to leave. Funny enough, every day we just waved to each other, Helga and I to Ann and Alan but we never actually got together. Let´s face that, we are mad! Another boat flying a British flag came to the anchorage. There were already seven yachts waiting to leave for the Whitsundays. An atmosphere of cruise embraced us for good as I never felt before. Empede came every day tied to Sagitta II leaving in zig zag after perhaps too many shots of vodka. One day it came straight to tie up next to Alvidia, Willie was aboard as well as a new friend, Dieter, also German, and when Horst asked which anchor we had Willie said no worries, which made me proud.

It was raining when the two Germans invaded our territory. Coffee and cake and jokes were not enough aboard Alvidia so we all went to Empede to drink vodka. Horst was a man full of energy and had made everything in his life. As Willie he also knew Brazil. He lived in

South Africa, Argentina, France and made a round the world sailing. In Australia, he lived with his wife and two children in the Scotland Island. Three times a week was the pilot of the ferry boat. His hobby was flying before it had been sailing and he had pictures to prove it. Three German friends but each with a particular characteristic. Willie like a polemic, Horst only jokes and Dieter with his female small dog in the arms was gay and anything he said would start with an "I" long stretched as his mouth could be open and was a nice guy too.

That night our German friends went to Sydney to check out a pub Dieter had wanted to. Early morning Willie was back alone visibly upset because the club where they took him had only boys. As he was a sort of a cave man he decided to come back to Sagitta II. It got to be in my log diary.

In the middle of the night, I woke scared with a nightmare. It was about my daddy. Helga woke too and we decided to find a public phone to call home. It was around three o´clock am and Larry was right – it gets to a point the civil calendar and watch don´t count anymore when you live aboard a boat. The longing was devouring us.

In the morning we were woken by our German philosopher. Willie came rowing under the rain with a roll of charts to give to me. He was not joking saying he wanted to change my mind about my route. He would leave for Brisbane at any time and wanted to give me last minute inputs.

"Luís, these are charts of a large scale, you will need to buy a smaller scale but with these at least you will know where you are all the time. Get them copied and bring them back to me. We don´t have much time.

I saw how much care he had with his charts and to bring a selection of them to lend to me was something to respect. To bring them under the rain was invaluable. Those charts covered a large area, I could not navigate around corals and shoals and ten miles would be represented as a dot but they were a treasure fallen from heaven. Willie gave me a quick introduction on how to read those charts.

Before leaving for the north, Willie would beach Sagitta II next to a cliff on the low tide to clean and paint the antifouling all alone. That was seamanship. At four o´clock in the morning I heard his anchor going up with the heavy chain and got up to see Sagitta II going away slowly.

By night we figured Willie would already be somewhere between Port Macquarie and Coffs Harbour but we heard a noise of a chain and it was Sagitta II back.

What would have happened? While going out of Barrenjoey Head, a northeast strong gale slashed the coast and did not let any yacht go forward; boats coming from north told Willie to wait and he decided to try again the next day. Willie came aboard and asked for a hot coffee. He brought two sheets of paper and asked me for a potato and I would never forget that. He had taught celestial navigation to a girlfriend and saved some notes about sun and moon sights. After making sure I understood how the stars interact geometrically with Earth, he taught me in five lines how to calculate my position in any part of the planet starting from a given time and place. He asked to turn on my SSB radio and taught me how to calibrate up my watch with Greenwich. He left those two pages so I could copy them by hand and return them to him. As he did not have a radio, he asked if I heard the forecast for the next day. I was proud to be able to help him but it was another catch of my master. Willie said that the forecast for the area we were did not tell much for our sailing ambition, he wanted to know a hundred miles around, before the wind direction and up above to where we want to go.

Willie tried twice to leave and returned; that was how bad the local weather was. He spent two days aboard, we could see his neck only stick out of the companionway and duck back down below. On the third day the weather was still nasty but he disappeared through a curtain of spray.

It was March and we were advised to leave only after Easter. The weather would be better. So we had two weeks to relax and prepare psychologically for the biggest trip of our lives.

Worried about finances, we decided to find a temporary job to bring in extra cash. So off to the industrial area around Mona Vale we checked every warehouse, every boatyard, club and marina, with no luck. Ok, we were feeling good, a bit tired, but as if everything else was in place – the universe was conspiring in our favor. Going back to our anchorage, near Church Point, we caught a bus full of high school students and I was amazed thinking of how weird a mix of Michael Jordan, three different superheroes, elfo and punk, gothic and hip hop and perhaps half a dozen of other styles I would not be able to recognize in an obese young fellow with red hair, blue eyes and Scottish accent. Or was it an Aussie accent? And there were other young boys and girls too with the same kind of style mixing.

Pittwater did not match with those styles. Or was I being too analytical and from a standing point away from the real world, that is an anchorage? Well, they were going to Scotland Island. Then I saw a Quiksilver rubber label and it was clear it was one of ours made in Melbourne. Then I saw a Maui label and a Rip Curl too. I was rambling when a man in the next seat spoke to me, "Excuse me, may I ask, this anchor in your chest, are you aboard a boat somewhere here?"

...April, we left.

Steve was another friend living aboard. When we jumped out of the bus leaving behind a bunch of teenager going nowhere, Steve came about with us talking as if we had known each other a long time. He was born in Australia but wanted to live in another country, sail around the world and choose a place to be. He came from Melbourne and what a great coincidence, he grew up next to the city we had our factory of dreams. His yacht, Alien II, was an adapted spray of Joshua Slocum, he built from scratch in iron. He had sailed to Tasmania twice, tried the route we thought originally, westbound under Australia towards Africa, but had to come back due to problems on the boat. He was a yachtie, a true boating guy and this time when everything was perfect with his boat, he would go. When we told him we were looking for a temporary job he said we could have his. He had earned enough to leave. It was a helper position in a construction site and Helga could also be used for tasks like controlling inventory or gardening; he would talk to his employer.

We invited him for dinner aboard Alvidia and he declined in a unique way. He said he was restricted to certain food and did not drink, but a breakfast he would accept. He also had to pick up backpackers that night; they would come aboard Alien II, and that was the way he had his crew, contracting backpackers for a leg or two along the way, for two years so far. Thirty dollars per day per head and he aimed to hire girls preferably.

"Good morning Steve, how was the interview last night with your guests?" I asked when he came for breakfast.

"It was great, in two days I will have my crew complete," he said with a big smile when he saw down below our boat was strip planking, that is wood. He thought it was fiberglass and listed many compliments for this and that. "I´m sorry, let´s have a quick breakfast, I have to catch a bus to the city, to interview three more girls, if I like them I will be all set to leave."

By sunset, he was back and invited us for a vegetarian dinner, a gorgeous fried recipe mix of mushroom with six types of vegetables, and he had two bottles of Tasman Pale Ale, one for me another for Helga. A piece of boating social code. Interesting man, he had been many things, from a cook in a five-star hotel to a photographer and miner. Once he took his wife up on a river with said veins of gold in the mountains of Victoria, showed us pictures in a magazine and an article we must include in our diary. He developed a rubberized diving suit specifically for gold mining in that river of cold waters. The thing had a hose receiving hot water from a pump aboard a boat and he tested the prototype himself. All was going well when in one trip down to five meters of depth there was a problem and he became a fried shrimp, almost dying.

A few days went by and the job he tried to pass on to us was the building of an evangelical pastor's house. Right in the first conversation the pastor confessed to us he had been a soldier in the Vietnam war, then a drug trafficker and we could see pictures of him on the wall in his platoon, but he confessed that religion rescued him and he became a pastor.

As in a fast movie, many things were passing by in front of us, a true cruise through lives and places without sailing a mile. We thought twice and decided not take the job; for some reason we did not know exactly and while coming back to the anchorage Steve maneuvered Alien II near us just to yell a goodbye. He had five girls aboard, was hanging on the bowsprit with a smile ear to ear.

"Hey, guys, see you up on the coast!" he shouted.

At this point it was easy to believe in what I had read in sea adventure books that it is possible to live sailing around the world, making friends and planning meetups somewhere in the ocean. We had already made at least three friends to meet up with somewhere up on the coast. All the seven yachts of the anchorage had left and we saw each one lifting the anchor. We could imagine the fleet in route up north.

Helga finished the planning of the supplies after mixing inputs from various sources up against our preferences and figuring out enough for nine months. We thought we could reach South Africa in seven months. She patiently collected receipts of supermarkets and knew the price of everything we needed. What a good feeling, we were also almost ready to lift the anchor and go. And we sent a fax to Brazil receiving a reply that was a huge relief of a kind to avoid a premature shipwreck. Helga´s sisters sent extra cash and this should also go to our diary: first a big thank to Sandra and Andreia, second, that Helga asked less than enough because that is how she is. If Helga was an executioner she probably would say to the person with their head on the stump, "Would you please get your neck out of the way?", and if she was that person she would say to the executioner, "Would you like a cup of tea and a napkin before you get the job done?" Ok, what was I complaining about, anyway?

Two months ago I had bought a long U bolt to hold our safety harness and I could not find its nuts. In one of our many trips up and down Pittwater to buy supplies we realized how easy it had become for us to navigate in closed waters, how familiar we were to Alvidia and experienced to approach anchorages, mooring buoy, and piers. But sometimes we used bus, and one day while waiting for a bus in Church Point a bearded man with greased overalls next to us stared at the U bolt in my hand and said out loud the thread type with complete specification. I was going to thank him and ask where to buy it and he had an outbreak of coughing while grabbing the U bolt from my hand. The bus came and he jumped in just saying he had the nuts in Akuna Bay. I thought to jump on the bus with him as we were going to have a celebration of the captain´s wife's birthday – we should celebrate with or without U bolt. My U bolt now away from me.

In wine veritas / Em vinho veritas
Wine swallow with fury / Vinho bebido com fúria

Dumped in a hurry in the throat / Solto às pressas na garganta

Without a formal warning / Sem um aviso formal

Like a coitus trivial / Tal um coito trivial

Harvest the feeling in the unconscious net of the brain /

Amealha os sentidos na rede inconsciente do cérebro

Revealing half truths / revelando meias verdades

Wine sipped with laces / Vinho bebido com rendas

With petals / Com pétalas,

With a ritual of subtleties / com sutileza e ritual

Goes disrupting barriers / Vai rompendo barreiras,

Dissolving lies / dissolvendo mentiras

From the soul freeing / Da alma soltando

Repressed ties / amarras reprimidas"

It was Easter Sunday and we were anchored at the other side of our waterfall, not in the Refuge but in the America Bay, and Wayne passed by with his giant iron boat; he was the editor of our friend Lloyd. And he had not so good news.

Sadness was not what I felt exactly and Helga had the same feeling. We then went to Brian´s houseboat, a weekend frequent flyer of the Refuge Bay, to let them know we would not come over later for a party; instead, we sailed to Sailor Bay to see and hug Suruj. That leg between Sydney and Refuge Bay had given us many lessons and during the three hours sailing there was not a single incident aboard and we went into Port Jackson smoothly and quietly as during the whole trip but always on my mind the mellow and friendly smile of Lloyd. And I understood then his looking forward to trying to find meaning before replying to a question. We picked up an emergency buoy from the Coast Guard and rowed to Tai Hoa one more time, the last, on those waters full of life.

"Suruj, Suruj, Luís and Helga! Are you there?"

We were quiet sailing back to Pittwater, going trough a rough sea but as if it was normal. The tide was unusually too low and we went straight to Newport to say goodbye to Maggie who gave Helga a birthday gift - a bottle of champagne. Larry saw us passing by and came in to invite us for a dinner. Peter welcomed us as well offering the usual beer. The other acquaintances of the Newport Marina and Cove stopped by or shouted from their boats. The butcher, the manager of the convenience store, the clerk at the post office. Hugs and handshake and good wishes. So it was our farewell pace.

With an extra four inches sunk into the water due to the supplies we brought aboard Alvidia, Newport Anchorage was left behind towards Refuge Bay, our true departure line. At the moment we had an interesting entry on the diary: Helga was so efficient with the planning of food that we filled "six" supermarket carts and the cashiers were amazed both by the volume of things and the final bill being so low. When I crossed under the Barrenjoey Head from the inside I looked to the ocean out there, the Tasman Sea, and thought soon I would meet that place but not before I got back and install my U bolt.

Akuna Bay was some ten miles up on the Hawkesbury River, so why not stop by and meet up with the man coughing with greased overalls? It was easy to find his place while it was hard to anchor in eighteen meters of water with a strong stream, too strong. Now I had a decision to make: to leave Helga aboard on watch and jump on the dinghy to row to the other side of the river to see the man, or stay and let Helga deal with the U bolt business? Neither one, we both went after checking that the two anchors were well set and with strong confidence we left. We saw on the rotten wooden jetty our man waving, he certainly recognized us. He had the same outfit and beard and I opened my arms as if to thank heaven. As soon as we walked into his shop he handed me my dearest U bolt and nuts and, coughing, grabbed the phone which was already ringing. He spoke two words and dashed out the door. I meant to pay and he waved as if to say "no worries mate" jumping on a working boat waking through the river. Helga and I stood staring at each other and then came in a boy of around fifteen, also greasy and wearing overalls. I took fifteen dollars and asked if he would give it to the man, if he was his father. He pointed to a busy and dusty workbench saying I should leave the money there and I saw checks under a calculator so I guessed that was the man´s coffer.

"Ok," I said. "He will come back when? Do you know?"

"When he goes up on the river in such a hurry he stays there at least for the night, it is the woman at the hills who calls him, he is my daddy," said the boy with a sad, shy look.

Back to Refuge Bay, impressed with the U bolt story I installed the U bolt right at the entrance of the companionway in the middle of the cockpit. From now on there would have the one rule, a macho rule, a dictatorial order aboard. Helga should not go to the cockpit without hooking up her safety harness on that U bolt while we were underway, anything else she could be in charge or order me to do but that rule she should follow. "Ok, Helga?" Thanks bearded greased man, have fun with the woman of the hills, from now on Helga would not fall overboard.

Finally, Helga finished collecting what was on her lists, including the curtains. They were nice in white made out of a lace cloth, and gave a cozy look to the interior of Alvidia. The next day would be the "D" day, our departure. The forecast was superb and someone who knows little or nothing about boats may have an answer right away if invited to go on a sailing ride, some people though will accept only if it is on a powerboat with comfort, some will say no right away because of fear of the sea or an attachment to land. It is interesting though if you invite people who know a lot about sailing. Willie, for instance, living aboard thirteen years with no frills and alone probably would not accept making passage with a group of people. A couple would be too many already, for someone like Larry, a lonely fellow demanding a lot of space and quietness – boating for them is like their own skin. Steve, who had never made a long passage beyond Sydney limits perhaps would have to touch things up on his loft, and he would rather say he never had time for his loft and once told me he knows people that grew up sailing inside the Darling Harbour and never went out the heads. Lloyd, contrary to others, would dive into old and many memories of sailing and his years in the ship cargo business. Helga and I could not fall precisely into any of the groups above. We did not know enough about sailing an ocean passage but we knew a lot about boating already, more than many people on earth and we had been cruising around the world several times without leaving the hook on a boat we built with our own hands from scratch.

We woke up as it was a normal day. I went out to the cockpit to stretch on deck and look around to realize one more time how beautiful it was. Sun shine, nature, birds, waterfalls – what good vibrations. It was our home and then a question came to my mind: why are we on the move all the time, why didn't we simply stay until it is not good anymore?

We had breakfast, lifted the anchor, and started to leave the anchorage slowly. It was going to be our first cruise, a long passage and we were aiming for Moreton Bay five hundred miles up north in one long shot. I felt an immense emptiness in my chest that I could not explain. Slowly under the engine, we went out the heads, leaving that paradise behind. I had my hand firmly on the tiller as if I was going to take both of us home in one single long run. I started to try to identify points on shore as we set off. The instruments aboard were not on my mind. Helga, next to me, was apparently calm. We wore storm gear and hooked to that U bolt by the safety harness, hoping not for the worst but prepared by the book. Then I pushed the tiller to starboard to head north, placing the lighthouse dead behind my back. The sea that looked to be flat became bumpy and Alvidia dunk the bow too deep for my nerves and raised the bow to the sky and again dunked, and kept repeating that gallop while I felt the wind too strong to be only 25 knots, according to the forecast. The radio report the night before mentioned waves of five feet and those in front of me looked twice as big. I read once that the ocean can lift monumental waves and the wind can reach unbearable proportions and I did not have parameters to figure out what monumental and unbearable reality that could be. Instantaneously I started to feel fear. I felt for the first time how big the sea was and how blind I had been all these years imagining only a boat anchored on a white sand beach on the other side of an ocean. We were being shaken in such a manner we could not handle in the middle of an environment completely unknown to us and the coastline was just a shadow already. We were well about ten or more miles away. On the radio, we started to hear a transmission about the weather for the next six hours – things like winds around 35 knots and gusts of 40 and 45 knots at times. Fear aboard, too much fear to write in the diary. We made a U-turn and after two hours we were again on the same buoy and I was devastated without telling Helga half of what I was feeling. I just said, "Let´s check with the Coast Guard and perhaps tomorrow will be better."

Before we got to that point to actually leave, months before, of course, we had thought of alternatives. To bring someone to help us cross oceans. To leave Alvidia in Australia and fly to Brazil to come back later perhaps with a friend or two to take on Alvidia. To send Alvidia on a cargo ship to Brazil. And a few other alternatives – all of them included separating us from the dream. No way.

The next day after our failed departure the sea was still rough, but the sun was shining and we understood that if we did not leave we would never do and so I hoisted the sails and dove into the Tasman Sea. The mainsail was reefed to the third point and the headsail rolled half way. Three hours later Barrenjoey Head was not just yet dead behind my back and so I changed course from 31 degrees to 61 of the compass and our destiny now if I carry it on a straight line would be Patagonia. At some point, I would need to go back to the northeast. I gave the tiller to Ulysses – the autopilot – after punching a waypoint and dove into my own thoughts, alternating between moments of great peace and fear. The shore soon was out of sight and the ocean seemed to be increasing gradually, each time wider and wider, its magnitude threatening. Looking at a chart given by Willie we were in a small corner of Australia that nobody knew. I remembered the story of a couple, husband and wife, escaping from Africa after building a small yacht without electronics and comfort, and also without sailing experience. They sailed to Brazil then to the Caribbean searching for freedom. They had a strong reason and I could compare to their story only in one tiny part – we both were aiming to have our dreams come true. I also remembered that I prayed several times as I was used to doing to calm down. Amazed by the functionality of the instruments I started to go to the cabin down below and back to the cockpit every fifteen minutes checking our position and wind and depth and everything.

Helga was feeling seasick, lying on the main cabin bunk, but after a while she came to the cockpit to join me. I was looking to the boom and mainsail system and suddenly a window opened accidentally with the wind; the boom came lose from the traveler.

"Shit!" I shouted and jumped to the cabin top in an impulse.

It was a pin come undone from the shackle which holds the mainsheet system and lucky me the pin did not fall overboard and I was able to grab it quickly and replace it. That was scary and was enough to make Helga throw up. Poor Helga for she realized how fragile and vulnerable we both were in the middle of the ocean and then I understood Steve saying I was diving into an abyss. My second thought was that while I had strength I was going to fight and the fight was against myself.

Alone in the cockpit and already getting dark I decided to change course to 350 degrees. To see the lights of shore even in the faraway distance would make me feel better but the reading of our position on the chart making the math with the GPS records and time spent out there told me we were pushing against a strong current making little progress like we were being pushed backward. The situation for our first leg of the passage of our lives was not good. Sailing close-hauled with wind moving from northeast to east and sudden gusts of northeast again. The sea grew up and the temperature went down a few degrees. Feeling bad to approach the shore during the night, after an hour and a half I changed the course again to Patagonia. Looking over the dog house made by hand in Newport I bowed every time Alividia dove into a trough and I could see the crest of the wave washing the deck end to end. I realized Alvidia had been jumping up and down the whole day and all was ok with the boat although I was so tired, stiff-muscled and my back hurt - it was then I noticed the noise of the waves against the hull of Alvidia and the buzz of the wind on the shrouds. I went down below and saw Helga almost fainting holding a rosary in one hand and a bucket in another lying on a bunk. That was shocking and I also felt seasick and threw up in the garbage bin under the sink.

The operator of the Sydney station on the radio kept going in his monotonous tone reporting forecasts of winds above twenty and thirty knots, gusts of thirty-five and forty to forty-five knots, waves of six to eight feet between Coolangatta and New Castle. We were going against an iron horse. Each station along the coast I switched to were confirming the local situation as the same forecast of the Sydney report.

"I am fine, Helga, ok? And the boat is fine too; we will go through this weather and tomorrow will be better, I will think of something, ok?" I kept saying to her.

Alvidia was heeling fifteen to twenty degrees at times. Helga had her eyes fixed to the hatches holding the cross and closing her eyes every time a wave bashed over Alvidia making a big noise down below like a drum.

I got back up to the cockpit to get fresh air and think. Inside, down below the boat, it felt safe but the soft light and humidity and the smell of vomit did make the place not as pleasant as it used to be. I had to do something. Could I? Our first night out on the ocean not blue but completely black now, I could barely see the bow from the cockpit. The waves were only silhouettes of bumps coming over way above my height and then under the hull some bashing hard against the hull side washing the deck and only then I could feel it was water, a lot of water. When those bumps went under the hull they seemed solid black monsters and I could see their long tails. I stood a moment just watching. It scared me more when two monsters bumped hard against each other near the side and a curtain of water fell over the cockpit. I looked at each part of the boat on the deck and tried to feel how strong each was. It seemed clear to me that they were not paying attention to that harsh environment as I was; they seemed pretty strong. "Yes, Alvidia is ok, it is me who needs to stand up, to fight, to resist, to overcome," so I said to myself while the wind seemed to increase. "Shall I heave to?" I never tried that maneuver, to get the sails, main and headsail, counteracting against each other with the help of the rudder in a way that the boat would be heading an angle with the wind and waves standing still or sort of submitted to the combination of those flows, current, and air. God, it is so complicated, in theory, it is so logical but it is dark, I couldn't see a thing, what if while I try to change the position of the sail Alvidia goes alongside a wave and rolls over, capsizes? These were the thoughts flowing out of my mind. All the manuals and books were open in my mind and I also knew each boat reacted differently to a heave to maneuver. I did not know how Alvidia would. Uncertain, I went back down below to the ICU checking how Helga was, I drank a bit of water and told her I was going to heave to so we would be more comfortable and jumped back to the cockpit, the new interrogation now was: Would I be able to heave to? It came to my mind again *The Old Man and Sea,* Jean Baptiste Grenouille from *Perfume,* Gilliatt from *The Toilers of the Sea* by Victor Hugo and damn it, what a time to think about books! Fear, fear, fear, I must overcome fear. But again, everything, anything I could use to help me I would. I needed to be clear-headed. I took a long, deep breath and disconnected the autopilot, grabbing the tiller with confidence. I steered for around little more than half hour feeling that Alvidia and I were one, I started to learn and foresee the impact of the waves or the interaction of Alvidia with those bumps. Then it wasn't so scary to me because I was also interacting with them. I decided to go over the maneuver in my mind several times, step by step. I would do it now. I released the headsail sheet from the winch while pushed gently the tiller not enough to make the mainsail to change tack and I saw the sails as two fingers crossed, and Alvidia stood right, facing the flow of the waves and the wind in a way that indeed it seemed the storm had been eased down. What a joy! For a second I did not believe it – then I did and felt pride. I did it! Alvidia was just gently galloping over the bumps, now not so abrupt. I went down below and told Helga. "Thank God, Helga, we heave to and it is better now we can sleep until the morning."

I ate two bananas with water, feeling a taste of paint with vinegar that was like my own vomit tasted but even that was like something to overcome and I did, how good those two bananas were. Then, while lying on the bunk next to Helga´s bunk I heard on the radio reports about river mouths situation, heavy rain, flood, entire trees been snapped and floating onshore, cargo ships with problems, warning of containers lost overboard and the same number about wind and wave repeatedly adjusted one or two knots on the same monotonous tone. And I heard for the first time in my already old-time sea life a "Sécurité" call for all the ships. I reached out for Helga´s hand and we prayed together whispering until we both fell asleep.

At five o´clock in the morning, Helga woke and shook me. We must have slept three hours straight. She heard her dad calling her, she said. Oh, Helga had a good nightmare, I thought, dreaming of her dad helping us, but I felt something in the air and intuitively went to the stairs of the companionway out to the cockpit and I could not believe what I saw. Near, very near, about two hundred yards a huge monster made of iron, it was like waking up in front of a tall iron wall. Alvidia was floating like a small duck right next to the stern of a cargo ship. The morning cold slashed my face and I woke up.

Without thinking too much I tried to figure which direction the wind was coming from; it was not automatic to me yet. I grabbed the tiller and pulled the headsail sheet fast round the winch and almost simultaneously the main sheet too and Alvidia spun around on her keel in a violent jibing going over that giant iron wall and kept turning, started to run away from it, already sailing before the wind. While doing all this it crossed my mind to call the ship on the radio, but what for? The entire crew aboard must have seen me all the time. Or not? Helga was on the companionway stairs with half her body out watching it all with a scared face but we both felt relief when we realized Alvidia was out of a collision route.

I sat, steering, and looking back and could not believe what I saw. Of about five miles I counted a line of eleven ships. Later on, I learned it was New Castle coast – a sort of hall for cargo ships before the entrance to Port Jackson. Those giant boats would be patiently waiting to one-by-one be authorized to approach Sydney and twenty or thirty miles for them was nothing. The one we just escaped from hitting probably was coming from Sydney instead. I actually must have been a little dot to be avoided the entire night. I took my binoculars and double checked eleven ships. Thanks to Helga´s radar we were advised just in time to get out of there until those ships got tired of detouring around the dot.

I then turned the autopilot back on and decided to put things together tidy in the boat to improve the captain´s wife's life aboard. Much better indeed and I also decided to take a shower. I dumped over myself a bucket of sea water. How stupid. The salt water made me itch the whole day on. Ok, now breakfast while Alvidia and Ulysses had a nice morning sail along the coast. Helga and I were physically devastated but the morale aboard improved a lot. We survived. And checking out our position since our goal was to reach Moreton Bay in five days – anyone with good sense would not try such a long run at least as a debut sail. Thus after a baptism the night before and mostly thinking to spare Helga for five or more similar nights on the row, I started to wonder if I could tuck in somewhere nearby. I did not have local charts but I remembered Steve mentioned we could make a passage to Port Stephens as training, it would be sixty miles from Pittwater. I heard all the aspiring sailors from Sydney made that a trial by fire. Steve showed me a picture of the Dalbora Marina, an aerial shot showing the entrance of the bay and I had that clear in my memory. So I told Helga I was going to get in

Port Stephens for the Dalbora Marina, without a local chart. Excitement aboard.

I set my eyes on the direction of Port Stephens for the entire afternoon. I could already see what I thought was the entrance of the bay and decided to turn on the engine to make sure we would approach and get in during daylight and at the same time I saw a school of dolphins coming along Alvidia very close, swimming, jumping out of the water as if they wanted to grab the bow. I called Helga to the cockpit. It was the first time I had seen dolphins so close. I could almost touch them. I felt safe, I felt really good. What a good vibration. I got really emotional. I felt guilty turning the engine on but had to do it and thought they would forgive me.

By five o´clock we approached the very entrance. Now, what and how to get in? What were the local hazards, shoal, rocks, reefs, marks, I did not know. A catamaran had been crossing very close to shore for a while I had been watching but it certainly draws less than Alvidia's fin keel so I could not approach that close to the beach. Then I saw a fishing boat coming out of the bay from behind what looked like a small cape which in fact I later saw was a small inner island. I headed right over to the fishing boat; perhaps while passing by them I could shout and ask how to get in. But as soon as we approached the fishing vessel I could see the entire bay with two other isolated masses of land, two small islands standing as a guard. It was getting dark and afraid of wasting time while asking the fishermen I decided to get in their wake left behind as a guide to me and it worked. Pushed full throttle ahead and soon I saw two more fishing boats coming out and I also felt the strong tide stream on the tiller and my heart beat out loud. When I reached the second island I saw a glare over it and beyond I could also see a red billboard reading Dalbora Marina. What a relief. In closed waters I had acquired just recently my master degree so I breathed, and thanked God, asked Helga a bottle of water, reduced the engine to a minimum and whispered to Alvidia I would take care of us now, very slow to approach the marina. It was dark already but who cared, I had done that so many times in Pittwater and Sydney. I had heard about sandbanks in the area and all the care would not be enough so I concentrated as much as I could but I was very confidant and asked Helga to keep reading out loud the depth and so we started to approach that great huge red Billboard. Helga cried with joy, holding the cross still. With one hand on the tiller, I embraced Helga, looking to all those pieces of equipment and things on the deck. I cried of joy too. We were safe.

We stayed two weeks in Port Stephens – out against the wind no more. "Gentlemen don't sail dose hauled," they say so better follow the old-timers.

We were so nicely welcomed. As we arrived at night we could stay for free in the guest pier and moving around on those protected waters was so natural to me. As if I was at home. I tied up the mooring line very slow, touching Alvidia´s hull as if I was tapping a puppy or a child. Helga stayed aboard while I walked to the security booth and as I did not have money to pay, the nice guard suggested that the next day we anchor up above and watch for the low tide of the sandbanks.

Very quickly we incorporated ourselves into the local atmosphere. The marina was full of boats waiting for good weather to carry it on up north, actually all the boats we saw in Church Point and had left earlier. A man reminding of John Wayne was coming from Melbourne on a beautiful 42" yacht, the Liberté. He carried so many fancy types of equipment that his boat could have come with no skipper aboard. To hoist the mainsail he needed just to push a button. Nevil was his name, and we liked each other at first sight. While we were introducing ourselves he was touching the halyards, shrouds, safety lines, pushpit, pull pit, anchor of Alvidia and just muttering "huumm". He asked about our brown sails and "huummm". And, without saying goodbye or goodnight he said would be waiting for us for a dinner aboard his boat. Ok, we have a social occasion. We just got here, coming from the worst nightmare of our lives and we will dress up for a private reception, I thought and in fact, Helga and I thought together we should not talk about what just happened to us in the last 24 hours, to say the least.

Nevil was waiting for a friend flying in from Melbourne to help him sail up to Southport, Queensland. His wife traveled by car with a little female dog, Monty, and his wife would take over the management of the boat while at the pier so they were cruising more or less together, for the third time already that same route.

The dinner was a mix of oysters, lobsters, and shrimp followed by a gorgeous green salad with edible flowers and cold white wine. What a life! To finish off with, Nevil loved Sylvester Stallone and we were invited to stay a little longer to watch *The Specialist* on his widescreen TV. So the anesthesia was thorough and very different from our private library of exoteric and boating books.

Going back home, that night, as if we were walking over the water, we decided to leave that straight route to Moreton Bay in one go as Willie and hop along the coast as every other human being was doing.

With a good night sleep, a gorgeous a prolonged breakfast, not talking too much, we left the marina for a corner of the bay called Cave. I liked the place full of ocean drifters, like us. We mentioned it only once – whether to stop or to carry on the cruise back home – but to either leave Alvidia alone or to be apart of each other, Helga and I, it was not an option. And now we had many other boaters to learn options from.

In the second day anchored in the Cave, we agreed that Helga should sail the boat all by herself to be prepared for an undesirable emergency, just in case. I would stay lying on a bunk down below and she would hoist the sails and move around the bay for an hour or so. There was a light breeze; a sunny day, perfect trial war zone. It is true that it was a bit of a mistake because of the movable sandbanks everyone advised us about, but as a saying in Brazil, "children and the drunk, the angels protect". Helga had an induction class, because of theory I was a master and in the end, I was proud of my first mate. I noticed from down below she made several different tacks to portside, to starboard and even a full jibe all by herself and when I decided to take over I was amazed how organized all the sheets and ropes were in the cockpit and over the cabin, I was impressed.

Going back to our Anchorage we saw Liberté stranded on a sandbank and he would be there until sunset waiting for the high tide.

A week of easy life and I started to worry about our calendar. When would we leave? The forecast kept saying strong winds coming from the quadrant north. Trees kept floating out of the river´s mouth. Containers falling overboard from cargo ships. We even heard about fishing boats wrecked and loss of human lives. We moved to a place with public moorings near where we could make a short trip with the dinghy and visit a green market and to see a bit of civilization. It was good to be on those walk sides of Port Stephens among ordinary tourists as if we were one of them although we liked it better to walk in the woods along the coast.

By then I was embedded as a local worm around the marina, joking with new acquaintances, exchanging tips for this and that, helping newcomers with mooring lines at the visitors pier; Luis was back.

So popular I became that I was invited for a happy hour aboard the Pacific Explorer – that catamaran we saw rubbing the coast. Keith, the Captain, built himself the boat and lived in Coffs Harbour, two hundred miles ahead and according to Nevil, our next stop.

...May, God bless you always.

My club now listed noble members such as Nevil, his wife and dog, their friend yet to arrive, Keith, and his catamaran crew formed by David and Patrick. David had made his third trip between Port Stephens and Coffs Harbour with Keith and it was his entire sea experience. Patrick was almost seven feet in height and had a huge diameter, red beard and a vast chin; no sailing experience but he was a fisherman by trade. Keith complained about his age going on the fast lane for him; he liked beers and used his cat as a charter boat. Lastly was the Coast Guard boat and crew.

The club´s veranda was Keith´s Pacific Explorer where every day we had a meeting to know who was better informed about the weather for the next few days. Nevil knew exactly what time to go, how many knots the wind would be blowing and how high every single wave would be. Just looking up the sky, Keith claimed enough experience to pick a better day to leave, earlier than Nevil. Reading inputs on the radio and talking to the Coast Guard, I was tempted to shoot towards Nevil but not so precise about wind and waves. Keith moved his Pacific Explorer next to the Coast Guard boat. Luis was invited and we all had a party. Twice I went to the Pacific Explorer to check out the forecast and the beer session was on the neighboring boat, the Coast Guard.

Meanwhile, with the discretion of the security personnel, the Alvidia crew sneaked under the door of Marina´s bathroom, which would require a key otherwise. A good hot shower, while you are cruising, is like gold. There was a chapter of the world circuit of triathlon and Nevil´s daughter was one of the top seed. Nice atmosphere. And the occasion went to the diary because we won an important gift when the competition was over. A plastic container of twenty liters with a tap for drinking water used by the competitors. An extra toy for Alvidia.

Keith invited me to leave on Tuesday. Nevil would leave on Thursday at six o´clock am sharp. I kept watching my wind vane moving the wind to the South with my eyes. At ten, Keith passed by Alvidia and invited us for a quick ride to Coffs Harbour. Next day we would arrive with the sunset. It was an irresistible appeal and also a big mistake to let him influence my decision.

They left an hour ahead of us. I could see their maneuver and that they were going fast and rubbing the coast, escaping from the strong current between two and three knots going south against us. Without charts and even with a local friend's boat in front of us I decided to fight the current instead of being too close to the beach so I stayed ten miles into the sea. I asked Nevil to show me his charts and plotter and knew there were many rocks, shoals, reefs, wrecked ships and a few other things to avoid along the way.

By mid-afternoon, Helga grabbed the bucket. By night I turned the engine on and I could not see anymore the lights of the Pacific Explorer. I was scanning the horizon for anything that would not be water and kept the radio on listening to the forecast, eating bananas, sandwiches, drinking water, juice, relaxing for five to ten minutes and back on watch while Ulysses was steering. The wind was from a good direction, south, and southeast, but it was increasing and I did not like to see the same movie again, the one I saw while leaving Refuge Bay. In the morning I called Keith on the radio but could not hear him well due to the engine noise but I understood they were flying over the water and would make it to Coffs Harbour by three o´clock or close to it. I was at least three hours behind him and much away from the shore because during the night we were pushed even further by the current. I saw a few sharks around and imagined they came for the content of our buckets. By five o´clock I could see the contours of Coffs Harbour but the sea was like it was falling on our heads. It became dark all of the sudden and next started to pour a deluge. I heard on the radio a boat crew asking the harbor master instruction on how to get in Coffs Harbour and I paid attention to every single instruction noting that they were coming from the opposite direction of ours, from the north.

They should pass a jetty, sight the middle of the entrance, aim for an old pier, navigate rubbing the rocks straight to that old pier and then turn to starboard and once again to starboard as if coming back and they would be inside the marina. When they finished, I called the harbor master on the radio.

"Harbormaster, harbormaster, harbormaster, this is Alvidia, Alvidia, Alvidia. Víctor-Hotel-November-6377, Over!"

"Alvidia, Alvidia, this is Harbor master, go to 67. Over!"

"Alvidia going up to 67. Over!"

"We are not seeing you, Alvidia! – said the harbormaster – when you get closer call again, so I can not see you, Over!"

Closer? How come? Only if I get to your shoulders, I thought upset. I told him I did not have a local chart, that I would like to have instructions to get in and make a reservation of a berth, that I was about only five or max eight miles from the entrance, and I did not say we had been throwing up for almost 24 hours already. It was dark and the entire world was falling over our heads. Water, wind, waves. To talk about fear on that day, considering the recent experience coming from Refuge Bay, well, it comes at a time when you don´t really know if you are still alive or you are at the purgatory or being buried alive and watching zombies coming toward you. Your heart won´t stop but the time goes by and nothing changes; only your fear increases. You don´t feel your arms and legs anymore and in my case, a tiny part of my brain was still working and Alvidia was responding greatly, taking us away from that coffin. Coffs Harbour is a place full of rocks slightly above the surface of the water, small islands, reefs, wrecked boats; I don't think it was missing any other type of hazard. It was a perfect collection. The engine was running ok and I changed my course to Patagonia without seeing more than fifteen meters ahead; such was the darkness. And now I was against a strong east wind. I turned on the autopilot and lay down next to Helga. The same movie.

Within intervals of half an hour, I put my storm jacket on, went to the cockpit to watch the horizon for ships or anything that could scare me more than those waves and wind. I checked our position and would come back to my contrition position. When we were well off Coffs, I figured more than 15 miles, I turned the engine off and hove to again, now it was the second time, and I did the same exercise I used before, to repeat in thoughts first while breathing as if I was in labor, which somehow it helped me to relax and keep focus. I knew I should keep my mind clear. It was working. By morning, the balance was twenty miles back and away from the coast so in total to get in Coffs Harbour we needed now to navigate nearly fifty miles, with luck we would get to the same spot the day before by mid-afternoon. So I cranked the engine again and headed to Coffs on a straight line. The sea was a little bumpy but nothing compared to the night before. The wind came down from forty knots to fifteen and from the southeast. Nevil, you were right!

The whole day under power and with the main up to balance up and help a little but when we reached the same position we were the previous afternoon, we ran out of diesel. I did not bother to call the harbormaster and just pulled from memory the same instructions he gave to the other boat. The dolphins were following us and we would succeed, I told to myself. At the entrance of the bar, a manmade breakwater left an opening of no more than hundred meters. The waves were breaking on the rocks on both sides and over the outcome tide coming from the inside of the artificial bay. Very boisterous entrance. Before I challenged that washing machine, I saw the old rundown pier at the very end. Standing in the cockpit I was able to picture the whole area and figured I should keep Alvidia well on the center of the entrance where should have a channel, it was logical. But to approach that turmoil I went as close as my heart allowed me to the rocks on the north side, aiming that the current would pull me back and then I steered in a diagonal to actually get in and it was like a roller coaster. Almost reaching the south side rocks I pushed the tiller to portside and Alvidia went nicely to starboard without changing tack and then we surfed the last wave on a nest of foam and that was it, we were inside the little manmade basin. What a great boat. *But now, Alvidia, who will take our hands?* We don´t have the engine, no fuel. We will need to make under sail four turns and keep in the middle of the channel once inside the marina. How? And with the segment, we were too fast. I tried to steer. Alvidia was responding well. But we were way too fast and I asked Helga to get the mainsail down.

The brave Helga stood on top of the companionway and worked on the main which got stuck, but Helga forced with her guts and folded it down the way she could. Alvidia kept moving fast with the segment, the afternoon breeze, and tide stream, we did not have breaks; how were we to stop, or slow down? We turned once, turned twice, turned the third time and reached the main channel. Piers on both sides. The outer pier was completely empty, no boats, and something told me not to go there. Aboard a huge power boat a group of people waved to us, raised their glasses welcoming us, they did not know aboard Alvidia was a potential disaster. We carried it on and now Alvidia at least was slowing down almost stopping and we reached the end of the inner channel between piers. I worked gently on the tiller and Alvidia pointed her bow to a single empty berth to that side opposite to the row of empty berths. A single empty slip was waiting for us, thank God. I looked as if the bow of Alvidia was the aim of a gun to a mooring cleat on the pier and thought the hit might damage the pier or Alvidia or both but we would be safe. Alvidia was going very slow, good girl, and I anticipated a minor hit but then I saw a vast volume of a human being, Patrick came from three slips behind were the Pacific Explorer´s crew was soaking in beers.

"Patrick!" I shouted, while his hand was already grabbing Alvidia´s pulpit.

The crew already had seen us and they all raised beers cans. Helga meant to jump and I said, "No", too late and she hurt her ankle. "Oh, my Helga, how bad it is, are you ok?" and we hugged each other, and Keith, David, and Patrick started to take care of the mooring lines. What a joy! What a relief! Helga went back aboard and seated on the deck with her hands on her face and stayed there quietly for a moment. A can of beer was placed in my hand, hugs, and claps on my back and shoulder, friendly curses towards me like, "You bastard have made it, thank God", and finally Helga opened her eyes and smiled. Now I was entirely happy.

We stayed two weeks in Coffs Harbour. Geographically speaking, what an unheard-of place. There is a headland prominent to the sea. From its outer end was built a breakwater of about twelve feet above the sea level longitudinal to the coastline to a point where it was left a gate of about two hundred yards although I thought was half of it between a small mass of isolated land called Muttonbird Island. Between the other side of the island and the beach, another breakwater was built leaving a basin hosting the Marina. It is a fishermen's nest with the sea breaking around and Coffs Harbour, apart from being noticed by this geographical peculiarity, is also known as the land of the giant banana and they claim to have samples of the fruit within three feet.

The first action I took, after a couple of beers with Keith, David, and Patrick was to visit the office of the marina and asked the harbor master if I was close enough by then. Keith stopped by the office and shouted to the people that I was a friend. Patrick came abreast and said at night we should resume the beer session with seafood at the local club.

The second action was to visit the Coastal Patrol and apply as volunteer to rescue a couple we heard on the radio reporting a boom problem with their yacht – the wife was steering with no fuel and the husband injured with a broken rib. The Coastal Patrol had already activated its emergency voluntary system already in place and there was no need of extra hands on deck but it was a nice way to start up acquaintances. At night, in the club, the Coastal Patrol officer came to our table and asked if I would like to report a complaint about not being helped the night before so they heard about my first try to get in Coffs Harbour. Of course I did not want to as we were now among friends and being well treated with a tray of seafood and free drinks.

When fell into our bed our bones seemed to dissolve. The euphoric arrival and rescue with warm welcome made us follow the flow but looking at each other intimately we knew all we wanted was to be left alone together in our own nest, Alvidia, and thank God we were safe and able to sleep for days.

The following day, I counted more than twenty boats with damage, from broken masts to torn sails recently coming from the sea. We met Gene and Kay, Americans from the yacht Moku Nani II, each late in their sixties years. They were sailing for fifteen years, aiming to get to Australia and had just arrived. Gene made a point to us that he became the laziest man on earth, after retirement from the construction business. He bought Moku Nani II in California, met Kay who agreed to follow him at the same pace and had been jumping from island to island along the Pacific Ocean. In Pago Pago, Samoa, for instance, he saw three seasons of cruisers coming and go. He said stopped at Pago Pago because he wanted to find a public phone and stayed there for three years. Laughing out loud it was the way he told us his stories – like this one of a Mexican friend, met in Pago Pago, who won a prize in a TV show to choose a place on earth to get a free ride with all the works included. Live on air, the Mexican man was introduced to a world map, his eyes bumped onto this small island and accidentally he read "Pago Pago" so the TV production gave him a ticket to the island. He liked it and was living there forever. Kay also used to laugh out loud so with Helga and I, we looked like four children together. We went to eat a baked chicken aboard and had a ball. Gene gave me a tour of the boat confirming Helga´s theory that two men talking about boats remind two school girls talking about makeup. I was fascinated by the way Gene took care of his boat, his ropes, rigging, anchoring arrangements and things like the sails with the corners reinforced with leather sewn by hand. On top of the boom, there was a strange thing at first sight. He said built that stuff hoping to never use it, and a few days before we arrived he actually used the thing for the first time. It was a storm anchor developed by the American Navy. A mesh in the format of a Christmas tree with cones of a reinforced synthetic fabric and ropes of two inches diameter. Gene used that storm anchor coming from New Zealand flying bare pole so he needed to slow down the boat.

But our lazy friend did not like to talk about tragedies; he introduced us to the beer storage down below Moku Nani II and offered us the meal of the night starting to strip the chicken meat, stopped and said, "Excuse me for a second." He went to the cockpit, made a noise in the water like an open tap and came back drying out his hands on his shorts to resume working on the chicken to fill in our plates. Kay was more exposed, while she was telling us a funny story, she carried it own then sudden also said, "Excuse me for a second," and one step from the dining table she seated on the toilet with the door open and continued to tell us her story and laughing, after also making a similar noise just lifted back her panties and came back to the table. Helga and I were also almost peeing with laughter. Kay told us that one night they were sailing on the full moon stream, she was doing yoga on deck and started to groan out loud and louder. Gene was sleeping, woke up and went to see what happened, only to witness a bunch of flying small fishes coming all over Kay while she was naked and groaning, Gene meant to get the fishes away but Kay shouted "No" because it was good, so good, she told us it was almost like an orgasm.

On the fourth day at Coffs Harbour, I had sad news. Helga told me she could not handle nor even half of the cruise along the Australian coast, so how could she possibly handle the Indian, Cape Town, and Atlantic passage? We had a serious and open conversation and I knew from the beginning she helped me a lot; without her I wouldn't have come that far, and she also knew I never forced her in any way to follow me. On one hand there was a part of myself I fought to have, a dream of mine I nourished for more than a decade. On the other hand, there was a half part of my own being, a person who I need to have at my sight all the time otherwise I would feel unprotected, alone, incomplete, and unhappy. But Helga was also part of Alvidia. Big dilemma.

The weather forecast was not encouraging for the next few days. The wind and waves were out of the ordinary pattern for the area and time of the year. Two days before we arrived, a fishing boat sunk inside the marina; it was in one of the empty berths Alvidia did not want to get in. The waves were so high that came over the breakwater making a waterfall on the inner side. The atmosphere developed by those just arriving from the sea was frightening. I thought it was insane and Gene had agreed with me while we were peeing in the marinas restroom. Right there we shook hands saying we would not talk about wind and waves. We needed a break.

Aboard Alvidia, however, the conversation needed not to be kidding. Helga needed to spell out all her concerns and feelings and I needed to listen. She had made up her mind a while ago but could not tell me, fearing she would disappoint me, destroy my dream in the progress. She did not want to just give up although she was sure she would not stand up to the hardship of such challenge. We hugged each other and stayed in silence for a moment and I knew I had to support Helga´s decision. Coffs Harbour was the end. I kept that idea in my mind spreading all over my body and went out for a walk to think, to experiment that decision, realizing how far I was. The wind was buzzing beating on the halyards of the many boats in the marina making a dreading symphony with the crash of the waves. I went to the top of the breakwater to watch and could not believe what I saw. What an infernal place.

And all these people - I thought and actually said out loud to myself – *how come they can do it and I can not?* Almost every single one has a problem with their boats and is just waiting to carry it on. Alvidia did not suffer a minor single scratch... And I was thinking all that biting my lips while a huge wave came over the breakwater and smashed itself right over my head. I trembled instantaneously and the first thought was that the sea wanted to claim me. I cried but it was a cry of happiness so that I realized I was able to let it go, accept that I failed, or that I had to give up for a good reason that was to support Helga´s decision. I went straight back to Alvidia and said to Helga we were going to sell the boat and go back to Brazil, that she should not feel guilty or anything, that she should leave me alone suffering a bit and soon it would be gone. It was intense between us, me trying to convince Helga we were ok, and she trying to undo her previous decision.

The next day, I was organizing ropes on deck as if saying goodbye to Alvidia, joking with everyone passing by disguising the pain in my chest and realized how integrated to my boat I was. I learned fast, I was sailing on the ocean blue as a grown up and I mastered abilities in closed waters. The fear was something everyone has or at least should have in order to show some respect to the power of the elements. I was able to walk blindly on Alvidia´s deck and down below. Meanwhile, Helga was busy taking things out to dry. A couple dressed up as ordinary earthlings approached us and asked if we did not remember them. No, I could not. They reminded us we had met in Refuge Bay. They bought a day sailing yacht in Sydney. Yes, I started to remember, they had a dinghy with an intriguing design.

"Of course, now I remember, how are you Steve, what are you two doing here?"

Steve lives in Coffs and was the pastor of the Presbyterian Church. He liked boats, recognized Alvidia and came to invite us for a lunch in his house next day.

"Wow! Steve. What a surprise, we would love to get together, thanks, but right now come over for a coffee and cake."

Refuge Bay came to our minds and brought all the good memories. Stephen and Marilyn, his wife, bought a thirty foot sloop in Sydney, sailed to Port Stephens and tried to bring the boat home but at the very entrance of Port Stephens they hit a rock and got stranded almost sinking going through the most terrible moments of their lives. They left the boat there to be sold. Decided to build a small vessel and when to retire soon would settle down in Port Stephens where Steve was born. He wrote in our book: God bless you always!

On the same afternoon, we met Dal and Cath from the yacht Aries, they were going to the Whitsundays. They were around late twenty years old and had very little sailing experience. Cath wanted to talk to Helga to learn how she put up with storms at night, to learn tricks and such. Dal asked me to help him to convince Cath not to give up in Coffs Harbour a thing they already discussed. I told him I knew a pastor who would help him better. It was a strong sign that Lui was alive and well, making his stupid jokes as usual. To my great surprise, Helga was encouraging Cath with her best tricks for seasickness. Dal was so grateful that he gave me a gift. We had this intense discussion about the scope of the anchoring rod. He said I should have more chain than I had and went to his boat bringing me extra ten meters of brand new chain and I should not say a word. Learning about their individual stories and hearing them saying how fresh they were about sailing, according to their own words, I told them ours and they laughed out loud thinking I was joking. Cath had been in a Sydney-Hobart race aboard a boat with ten people, other than that she used to sail with her dad in the Darling Harbour. Dal ran three Brisbane-Sydney races and sailed Hobie Cat in Pittwater. They were challenging the open sea for the first time of their lives more or less alone. When they learned we were Brazilians and friends of Gen and Kay they plugged the idea that we were sea wolves.

The lunch with the pastor and his wife was superb. Steve and Marilyn were lovely. To be again in a normal house, eating at a normal table made us feel good and we went back to Alvidia staring at each other as two unruly children sure that we would resume our plans to keep cruising back home. Steve and Marilyn did not know we had given up our cruise idea and spent the whole time together trying to convince us not to dive into an abyss. Again, another Steve said the same thing. Steve kept repeating for us not to challenge the power of the elements. He was a nice man but every single phrase of his we read backward. Each time we agreed with Steve, pretending to be polite, we looked at each other agreeing on the opposite. We left the pastor's house with a childish smile on our faces. I could not hold how happy I was feeling with the idea of dismantling that sad conversation and decision we made together, Helga and I, two days earlier when the crazy wave tried to swallow me. How could we give up because we do not respect the power of the elements, the sea had been so gentle with us, we just respected so much the sea, the wind, the whole nature, birds, dolphins, everything, we had a direct link with the universe itself. The real danger was living inside ourselves, the danger of not being honest enough to face our wish, to face our fear of failure, to give up just because of fear. Alvidia was going to take us home. We built her with love, we had our souls blended into it and when you build things with true love there is nothing to fear and you only give your dream up for reasons external to your own fears. Thank you, Steve. We even had a little shame to have thought to give up. In Coffs? No way.

We had a busy social life afterward. Dinner at Keith girlfriend´s house, dinner with Nevil, and a breakfast with a cruiser from all over in a Swedish boat. And we started to prepare ourselves to leave. I was the happiest human being on earth and Helga without a trace of regret was still feeling that itch of fear from the storm and seasick threatening her, but her heart was winning.

Nevil arrived four days after us. His crew member could not talk for two days. They made the worst passage of their lives. Nevil even stopped in an alternative anchorage along the way and regretted it because his anchor slipped, it was a nightmare to avoid end up on the beach and he was so upset that he wanted to sue Neptune. Mad or not, Nevil invited us for a round of lobster aboard Liberté.

"Lui, here is the money. Go to the Market and get a nice portion of lobster for us."

Nevil arrived and hired me back as his servant stunt of a special guest.

The breakfast with international cruisers was aboard Albatroz. A beautiful fiberglass European boat, crewed by a Swedish family, two couples, a father, mother, son, and daughter. They had been sailing for fourteen years already. The mother was a photographer and writer, had published a book about their adventures, the father was the captain, and the children learned everything they knew so far aboard, how to read, math, science, history, everything. Lin, the photographer, wanted to have a picture of Lui and Gene, interview us for a possible article, and it was impossible to have a serious conversation with Gene because Erik, the Captain of Albatroz, wanted to compare storms and ordeals we all had. He described his sail torn apart several times all many terrible episodes speaking in English with a funny accent even for Latin ears. Two days later, when they left they came back on the same day with the mainsail torn apart and I suspected he used a knife to get the job done blaming the wind.

A fax printout with the daily weather forecast was placed on the window of the marina office and always you could find at least one Captain interpreting the report, and making recommendations on when and how to lift the hook and leave.

The rain stopped; the level of the river started to lower, and soon whoever wanted to leave would be able to go. Dal was the first brave seaman. He tried to persuade me to go so he could follow me. Imagine that!

From the top of the Muttonbird Island I saw them exit the bar and followed them with binoculars, praying for them to have fair winds and I remembered our neighbor in Church Point who said, "Let´s face that, we are mad!"

I waited four hours and contacted the Coastal Patrol to ask about Aries. No entry, no logged call from them. I asked the Coastal Patrol to check two stations up north. Still no sign of them. From our own radio I contacted all the station up to Brisbane, nothing. That night we had reports of winds around fifty knots. In the morning I received a callback and learned that Aries had made contact. Thank God. Dal and Cath were ok and went straight to Brisbane without stopping.

The tail of the last south front passed by Coffs and boats started to leave. I had said goodbye to Gene, Kay, Nevil, Keith and all the people I knew in Coffs Harbour, and I notified the Marina. I was holding a cup of coffee in my hand looking through the main hatch and saw the sheets of the mainsail moving, with the gentle balance of the boat, a chain plate holding the traveler system. I did not like that. That chain plate was not strong enough to me. "Helga!" I shouted. "We will abort leaving today. I will change that chain plate." Helga had been so active lately, so determined and when Helga shows determination I feel even more encouraged. She asked if I wasn´t being too fussy with that chain plate and it was a good sign; now it was I wishing to slow down.

I took off the piece and found a welder. I wanted a similar plate in stainless steel but thicker with two holes for one-quarter of an inch for two bolts. The next time I looked that chain plate I wanted to feel confident about it. We would then leave in the next day and I was feeling like I started to learn how to level up with the elements, as Lloyd tried to teach me. That night, aboard Moku Nani, Gene gave me seamanship lessons. He told me that when I learned how to get my boat in the groove, that is with the optimum angle to the wind particular to my boat, that each boat behaves differently, I was going to jump on deck like a happy child, the boat would sail so smoothly. His philosophy of sailing while cruising was that you never should demand from the boat all it can handle, never sacrifice parts of the boat, like shrouds, rigging, gears, ropes. That way I would have boat forever and would be alive aboard. I saved that for a grant, I actually adopted that as my philosophy too.

We decided to leave quietly early the next morning but, as soon as we turned the engine on, Kay ran to hug us one more time. We started to leave slowly through the corridors of piers and saw heads coming out of boats and hands waving for us. We were just a branch of an enormous tree of dreamers. Each one with peculiar convictions. I felt a knot in my throat. Kay ran to the tip of the last pier and took a picture of us. What a farewell.

I turned the engine off before we got to the gate, the bar. With the sails reefed to a minimum, we started to get out slowly. According to the forecast, there would have waves of three feet but there was no time and need to measure them up. The wind was coming from the right direction and was the last tip of the south front tail with twenty knots and gusts of thirty. I had all the local waypoints input into the GPS and autopilot, set to go around all the chartered hazards. I still didn´t have local charts, and those waypoints were copied from other sailors, but I invested forty dollars on a cruising guide by Alan Lucas, with a detailed description of the entire West Australian Coast, made for sailors, provided you don´t follow the instructions as law.

In a stretch of ten miles wide by thirty miles long north of Coffs Harbor all we read on the sailing instructions were: island, islet, breaking waters, shoal, wrecked boats under surface, coral reefs and extra care for fishing nets and lost large objects from cargo ships – I think nothing was forgotten. They should prohibit winds above fifteen knots and unforeseen events. As soon as we got into that stretch of hazardous waters, the line from the furler came undone out of the drum, a mistake of mine not to had made well past that line. The headsail opened entirely and without control. I ended up crawling over the narrow bow bouncing up and down trying to fix the furler system while the line got entangled by bashing so much and it was even harder to undo a crazy knot done spontaneously. While I was trying to undo the knot the line and the loose sail slapped my face several times and I felt the taste of blood on my tongue. Alvidia was answering well to the autopilot and I could read the dread of Helga holding herself with two hands on the companionway and hooked on the safety harness to the U-bolt on the entrance. She could not do anything else but pray and she said with her eyes "the knot will be undone". And from the top of the Muttonbird Island people were watching and were unable to help.

With so much preparation, praying, lessons, decisions, confessions and now I was stuck in a situation. But finally, I managed to get the knot undone, learning the hard way with many lessons. After all, we both felt so energized; we had passed another situation together and had a sunshine day ahead of us with the favorable wind pushing us ahead. It was then that Helga asked what would happen if I took down all the sails with so much wind?

"Of course, Helga, I think Alvidia will keep making good progress in bare pole."

South Port, the next stopover, according to Nevil and Alan Lucas, is in the so-called Gold Coast, right on the border of New South Wales and Queensland. A tourism-oriented region reminding me of Florida in the USA. With casinos, parks, the MGM and international hotels, nice streets, fast food chain stores – the whole nine yards for fun. But for me, first I had to overcome all the obstacles and I was already getting tired of watching so many danger points. Looking around I saw foams, waves breaking out of nowhere and all of the sudden the wind was increasing. Helga was not feeling good but was handling it ok and stayed with me on watch. The psychological positive injection was that after passing by the North Solitary Island, the fifth island or islet or rock with the word solitary in the name, we would rest. The true danger was sixty miles ahead, named exactly that, Point Danger, right on the border with the two states and making an elbow of the land into the sea. I was down below recapping our position when suddenly my eyes got confused with so many solitary islands, I thought to have passed all of them, I went down below to double check and there was the last one still.

"Helga, we are going over a reef!" I shouted, running to the cockpit.

Alvidia's stern pointed to the sky, we were fallen down in a free dive after going on top of the crest of a wave over that charted reef. I could see a dark shade through the water and also mixed with the foam a rainbow. Helga and I were petrified. A divine hand took care of us for sure. I kept my eyes on that point looking back and saw all the waves breaking right there. I was speechless.

On that day we logged a true speed of eleven knots without sails, bare pole. I would not believe it if the math reasoning of the distance versus time were not so exact. Helga was seasick and Alvidia, despite the bare pole, kept flying. As if I was driving a car downhill without breaks. The night came fast and I had great news. Helga came to the cockpit to split watches with me. We took fifteen minutes turns sleeping, and I learned how to sleep for fifteen minutes and wake up for my turn. It made a great difference to sleep, unworried I was going to shut down too long and to be awake by Helga and vice versa.

When we reached Point Danger, all the tension experienced on those thirty miles behind near Coffs Harbour we had again for two hours to go around a headland. Afterward, beyond that point we were in calm waters, we could see people on the beach, children, civilization, and it was hard to believe we had been through such an ordeal. All the vessels coming in must make contact with the control tower and it was the first time I was doing that and feeling good about it. So, as usual, I went in slowly, waving for the boats nearby, and searching for recommendations taken from Alan Lucas 'guide, like a marina with the first night stay for free. *Thank you, Alvidia! Just help me now with the captain's wife, her mood is not so good.*

Nevil was there. He arrived a day earlier with the fleet. He hauled out the Liberté for a coat of antifouling. He would make a break flying to Melbourne because Mounty was missing her boyfriend. Dog's wish. South Port has a vacation leisure atmosphere. Helga had a great good shower and her mood improved a lot. We went out for a sandwich and theater and her good mood flourished back up as a blooming sunflower.

The next day we left the free pier for an anchorage for four days of deserved rest and sightseeing on foot. The first wine bottle we opened was to celebrate great marks. We had passed a few of the most difficult points of sailing in atypical weather conditions and we reached Queensland which seemed to us so far away. Apart from that, we logged electronically 2.000 miles on our instruments. A zigzag that started on the Parramatta River. I was proud of myself but looking at the Indian Ocean chart it was nothing and so I kept biting my upper lip.

We had committed ourselves to a very tight schedule. The Coral Reef Barrier was just around the corner, the most sought destination for eco-tourists, divers, and cruisers and we would pass by in a snapshot aiming to reach the top of Australia in time for preparing ourselves to cross the Indian Ocean, Cape Town and the Atlantic. Then our pockets had been assaulted by the two last unpredicted stopovers, in Port Stephens and Coffs Harbour. My mind was full of monkeys discussing and arguing about everything.

Once close to Brisbane, I decided to phone our German philosopher friend Willie. We were anchored in Moreton Bay which is, in fact, a small basin from waters coming from the north and designing the coastal land into many waterways in a stretch of one hundred miles building two huge elongated islands. The Moreton Island and the North Stradbroke Island. We had two options from South Port. Through the sand channels of the inner side of that area, if we wanted to reach Brisbane by the shortest way, or by the outer side straight to Cape Moreton, the very corner of the Australia where its coastal starts to point vertically to the true north. Willie was already in Cairns, answered his friend on the phone so we skipped Brisbane. The Alan Lucas guide advises well about the need of negotiating with tide currents through the many channels and we did not have local charts so I made the decision to go around by the outer side and anchor in a place I read about that was a cemetery of ships and fishing boats.

Fortunately, as Lloyd advised, we had built parameters but this leg of the cruise was terrifying; it is for anyone in any circumstance. And now we had the real flavor of a cruising life, listening to the radio transmission from a variety of stations along the coast. From Sydney, from Brisbane and even from Townsville up north. Alvidia was in good shape so we made the passage of eighty miles in twelve hours following a Germanic routine of watches like the old timer sailors. I was rubbing the coast keeping my eye on the depth instrument and escaping from the counter current. Of all the arrivals, this one Helga found the most nervous, danger and horrifying. For a start, I could not see well because I don´t have good night vision and refused to believe there were two lighthouses instead of only one on the Cape Moreton headland. On the chart with large-scale copied from Willie´s, I could not see the two lighthouses. Helga´s radar and good falcon eyes insisted she was seeing two lighthouses and I kept theorizing to her that in the dark the eyes do get confused with sparks of lights and we can have double vision. Helga kept saying "no, no, no, I can see clear, there are two lighthouses."

Thank God and Helga. I was entirely wrong with my clumsy theory. When you pass the first lighthouse you actually head to the north and there is a lighthouse for those coming southbound and for the theoretical ones going north. But the tension aboard was so much that I kept trying to see the two lighthouses until I gave up and lost the bet. Meanwhile, there were waves breaking all over near us and I could see the shades of huge rocks nearby. And all would be easier if a yacht anchored right there was with its lights on; I would call him on the radio and ask for tips. It was Koala, an iron boat on the hook around the rocks. In the morning the captain called me on the radio and apologized because he turned off his mast light fearing I could be a pirate boat. At 8:00 am we had our breakfast done, had said goodbye to our neighbor, listened to the weather forecast and left Cape Moreton heading to Mooloolaba.

In my wishing basket, there were places in Australia that I wanted to be able to say "I was here" and Mooloolaba was one of them. I'd read about in sailing adventure books, plus Bundaberg, Townsville, Middle Pierce Island, on this one had a solitary gentleman, Mr. Andy, and I wanted to shake his hand.

...June, what a gorgeous sailing day.

We arrived at Mooloolaba after a day passage without any event out of the ordinary. The sky was overcast, the sea bumpy with a light breeze. Helga had her regular seasickness and sadness, asking herself if she would ever sail without being seasick. And every time she was sad it was because she was missing her mother, especially with her deteriorating health.

The approach to Mooloolaba was easy, following Alan Lucas' recommendations but at the very entrance I trusted my hand more on the tiller, our instrument of depth, and Helga´s eyes. When she was working on deck her mood changed substantially to a great one. Slowly, as usual, we strolled into calm, sheltered waters. I found out that the arrivals are one of the best things of cruising. You proceed slowly making a reconnaissance of the local as a conqueror must have done in the far past. Afterward, I used to read about the place I had been and it was once again a joy to rediscover highlights of the area and facts.

Alvidia attracted attention because of her white hull and modern lines, dressed up in a classic style with brown sails. But at the end of the main pier of the Yacht Club of Mooloolaba a person was smiling, making a connection to us.

"Helga, who is that? I don't recognize him," I said while waiving to a smiling gentleman.

We went straight to the showers of the club. On the way, we met the owner of that welcome smile, John Deegan. He said knew us from Refuge Bay.

"Our boat also has brown sails and a white hull, we always wanted to meet you guys, but no time – he was referring to himself and his wife, De Deegan."

What a reception! John and De were hopping up the coast aiming for South Africa; from over there they would cross to the United States. John knew all that was going on lately from Sydney to Fraser Island, our next stopover. I told him if we could buy a larger bucket we would try to cross the India Ocean and he went straight to the point asking how Helga was holding on. At a shy reply, he said very nicely, "From here onward you will sail in calm waters, always with good wind. You will sleep at night anchored in beautiful places, come to our boat and I will show you each mile of the coast and the ocean until Salvador, Bahia, and you," he said, to me, "Let's build a spinnaker pole so you will be able to sail wing on wing with stern wind, your boat will sail with more comfort for you both."

Fifteen minutes took the first encounter and changed our spirit completely. Helga was excited. John and De worked for the Wooden Boat School in the United States. In the last few years, they had been splitting seasons in the US and Australasia and they had a house near Refuge Bay. They just had Sotalia delivered to them, a custom built classic wooden boat. They came from Bundaberg to fix a problem with the engine. By our account, we liked to believe they came back to help us. Two angels on our list. After we had a good shower and got the bureaucracy with the club out of the way we went back to Alvidia to find John on our deck taking measurements. He was really serious about helping me to build a spinnaker pole. Although the original plans of Alvidia included the piece, I did not have money to build one, nor experience to use it afterward anyway... Gene had suggested I build one; he actually insisted saying it would be fundamental to sail with the trade winds. Now John echoed Steve Sulis when I said I could not afford it, "Yeesh you cannn!"

He dragged me to a corner of second hand stuff in a boating store at the marina, and on the way there he said "we" should install a wind vane next to the spinnaker pole, if I was serious about crossing the India Ocean, as it would not be enough to rely only on the autopilot (which could fail).

We found a spinnaker pole larger than I needed and John said I could make it shorter; he even said that piece was there waiting for me. I went back to Alvidia and did not know what to tell Helga, I was speechless. We had just arrived! Feeling like pebbles rolling in a river, we made dinner and sat quietly to eat, thinking probably much the same things but in different order. Amazed with all the recent events recently in Sydney, Refuge Bay, Coffs Harbour, South Port; thinking about Helga's mother, my dad, my sister, and about our budget – ruined after too much extra expending – also how happy I was enjoying the cruising atmosphere, getting more and more acquainted with Alvidia, learning how to sail in the fast lane after being taught by master like Steve, Larry, Geary, Lloyd, Willie and Gene.

We both certainly were thinking about these things when we heard a knock knock on the hull. John came to introduce De, his wife. An energetic young lady, fit, jovial, sharp and willing to help us even before we met. One of the first things she recommended to us was to move into a public anchorage, to save money. *Did they have a hidden camera and recorder on our boat?* We went to bed thanking God out loud together.

In Mooloolaba we saw Albatroz again – the Swedish boat –, and Koala, the one from Cape Moreton that came after us. Listening on the radio we knew about all the other boats, but as for Sagita II, Alien, and Equity respectively of Willie, Steven and Michael – we lost contact with them entirely. Up to Mooloolaba, I never used the SSB/HF (long range radio) which I was able to install all by myself following the manual, and the Bruce in Pittwater had approved it, recommending only to weld the grounding bronze tape. *But guess what, Luis* – John is a kind of Public Relations manager of the cruisers all around Australasia and gave the Alvidia Captain a complete intensive course on how to operate the SSB/HF, that weird black box hanging over my head next to my bed. Listening to John demonstrating real conversations with other cruisers on my SSB/HF it seemed so easy. All about boating coming from John came as natural as to ride in a park.

"Luis, with these tools no, Luis!" It was John, when I started to work on the spinnaker pole following his instructions. He saw my tools, shook his head and went to his boat to bring back a box of professional tools I could use. We finished the job in time, just before our free 24 hours at the marina expired and we moved to the public, and busy, anchorage.

Strolling on the sidewalk of the town, along the beach, something happened, interesting enough to be logged into our diary. I passed by Liza Curry, an Olympic medalist, with 15 gold medals plus many silver and bronze medals under her belt. I gave her a smile and probably she thought I recognized her as the famous athlete and I said to Helga, "This lady does not know who just smiled at her."

We never actually met, so Liza could not have recognized the creator of her logo and rubber badge for one of her bikini collections. She also did not know how concerned I had been about the invoices and that we had spoken on the phone several times. She was always so nervous about rush orders.

The weather did not improve and we were anxious; wishing not staying in Mooloolaba for another week. John and De were ready to go and said we could follow their wake up until South Africa; that our next leg would be through the Whitsundays islands and coral reefs, like a paradise, anchoring in calm waters at sunset and sailing with light breezes during the day. Finally, our next stop would be at Wide Bay Bar inside the Great Sand Strait, a must-see place. Seductive. But again, I would be following a boat, and although John and De were sailing instructors I did not feel good having someone worried about us.

"Eeny, meeny, miny, moe, catch a tiger by the toe..."

"Let´s go?" I suggested to Helga, she said yes, and I was crazy about testing the spinnaker pole.

It was another overcast day and we sailed about two hundred yards from Sotalia, sometimes we could not see each other – such was the depth of the trough, the vertical space between waves crests. As soon as we set a north course I went to the mast and worked to set the spinnaker pole, following John´s instructions by memory. What a joy; I did it and seriously, those old-timers were damn right! Alvidia became a gentle lady, sailing with no healing at all, nicely, smoothly and even faster, wing on wing. I also used a rope as a preventer for the first time – a simple mechanism with knots, and used the bow cleat to avoid causing the boom to collapse. The autopilot became less stressed too; what progress. Alvidia was sailing as Willie liked, as Gene advised me, and as John had taught me. Lloyd up in heaven must have been clapping and smiling, Steve would not believe. Or he would. Aboard Alvidia a child replaced the Captain, and Helga could believe was sailing without seasick. What a gorgeous sailing day on the ocean blue – seven hours on the same course, without changing tack or touching the tiller. This is what Willie was talking about.

On the radio John called and asked, playing with me, "Hey, Luis – how does it feel to be without a home like a complete unknown?"

"Beautiful, beautiful, boy. Thanks for holding my hand to cross street, John," I replied.

The approach of Wide Bay Bar had to be negotiated very carefully and lucky me there was a frequent traveler towing me into the area. I took off the spinnaker pole, rolled in the headsail and with the main only and my firm hand on the tiller I tried to follow my angel guide. Coming from the sea you don´t believe it is that tricky to get in, the sea seems too flat, and you don´t see the breaks. All of the sudden Sotalia started to bounce sideways. "Wow!" I said out loud and tried to copy Sotalia´s wake, and soon I saw a kind of ladder of waves in front of me and Alvidia started to bounce and jump as well. We surpass the breaks and were now sailing in the Great Sandy Strait, the largest sandbar in the world – a vast shallow area between Fraser Island and the rest of the Australian continent, full of mangroves and birds of all kinds.

We both anchored near the entrance for a night's sleep and to get out the next morning with the help of the tide. John rowed his dinghy to join us in the cockpit and we stayed until dark talking frugally; De came only to measure hour hatches and went back to Sotalia saying there would be a surprise. One hour later she came back with covers for those two hatches to protect us from the mosquitos, which are said to be able to eat a live horse in Australia. In Melbourne, I saw flies holding elephants in the air so I was willing to believe about the mosquitos. *How would I thank her?* Helga invited the couple for a dinner but they declined saying we were expected to follow them aboard Sotalia instead, for a chicken parmigiana with shredded fried potato and peas, red wine and a dessert of meringue with chocolate on top. During the dinner, we had a private presentation by John on our possibilities along the Australian coast. He made a list of anchorages, sketches by hand of each one with the distance between them, depth and assorted useful information, while we listened to a CD of mellow jazz. From outside we could hear the gentle swash of the tide stream passing by Sotalia´s hull.

When it was time to go to bed, I thought John would go with us to kiss us goodnight and to cover us with the blanket, shutting off the light, but it was not that. John needed to take us back with his outboard power dinghy because the tide stream was so strong no one would be able to row and of course I did not know about that.

Early the next day we left the anchorage, synchronized at the same time and I stayed behind Sotalia about three hundred meters and made the same turns to starboard and portside, amazed at how often and sudden we had to change courses. The moveable sandbanks were our enemies. I noticed De traveling at the bow of Sotalia with the binoculars at work and occasionally going to the cockpit to talk to John steering the boat. What an intricate place to navigate. There were signs of a would-be channel but the depth instrument said it was not deep enough so we had to go around. At times we had nine feet of water under the keel, then only three or even less. Around us was a vast body of water. All of the sudden: Bummm! We hit a sandbank. Alvidia lifted its stern with the impact. Silent, a glimpse of panic and action. This became our pattern for such situations. I ran to reach the throttle but passed in my mind by crank the reverse gear I would throw sand right on the keel and bury it, although it was too late, I did reverse strongly. Alvidia spun around eighty degrees and stayed at the same place. Fearing I would damage the rudder, I cranked forward. Nothing. We were officially stranded.

The next six hours ahead were consumed with self-punishment digging out a ditch with a shovel. John could not help this time, he was too far and could not come back; he carried on and called me on the radio with the comfort that I was not the only one who had been stranded in the Great Sand Strait. He did it once; everybody does.

Not me, John, not me, I am perfect man! I kept slashing myself on the back, bleeding my soul. "How come I did that?" I kept saying, beating my myself helplessly. I feared that the four tons of Alvidia over its rudder would damage the critical piece of equipment. So once again with all the seamanship manuals opened in my mind, I decided to shift all the weight from the stern to the bow. Backup anchors, tools, bags of souvenirs – anything that weighed more than a feather. The tide was on the low flow with a spectacular speed. Alvidia started to kneel slowly like a camel and I feared it would get to a point of collapsing abruptly. From the mental seamanship manuals, I read a title "how a stupid sailor avoids his boat from collapsing while stranded" and decided to use a halyard from the top of the mast with an anchor to the other end thrown to the opposite side of the said collapsing tragedy.

Within two hours we were sitting on the mud which in boating terms means in a completely dry and Alvidia kneeled as an elegant princess. Feeling we were definitely bogged, I went down below to find out what happened to Helga. To my surprise – Helga always surprises me – she was calmly drying out the water of our drinking water tank that tipped and had two sandwiches ready for lunch. No signs of seasickness – no signs of fear. I guessed she was feeling safe not moving and curiously, apparently it did not bother her that our lives were upside down. As Alvidia was laying sideways, what would be the walls were now the floor, the ceiling was the walls and the floor the ceiling- synonymous of all that could well be chaos. Thus I decided to do something while waiting for the high tide to lift our Alvidia back up, our lives. To inspect Alvidia, the hull, the rudder, the transducer of the instruments. Splash! I sunk my legs above the knees in the mud. All was fine with Alvidia, I was the one damaged. But I decided to do something extra. I grabbed my main anchor and walked fifty yards forward and left the anchor where there was a fine blade of few inches of water. Then, along the anchor chain and rope, I started to dig a ditch so when the high tide came it would help to speed up our way out of that embarrassing situation.

But I would not step aboard Alvidia covered with mud. Helga would not let me. So I had to improvise a shower hanging out of the stern to get permission to go aboard. When I finally got in I could not believe it – Helga was sitting in the lotus position calmly sewing a pair of pants. I would never understand completely the vast universe of Helga´s being.

As I was a too obvious fellow, I went once more to the mud territory to clean Alvidia´s hull and after another improvised shower, I waited for the tide. When it started to show signs of change I assumed a position on the winch and as the water started to fill in my ditch I pulled the anchor rope little by little. I needed that feeling that I was helping myself and it worked. At five o´clock the water-filled under Alvidia and soon we were again floating and sailing away. Happiness aboard! Party! A half bottle of wine and a good night's sleep anchored near up above toward where John was, still inside the sand strait. At around four o´clock in the morning we determined Larry was right – we didn´t care about the civil calendar. We started to sail and soon we reached Sotalia and received compliments for one of our first baptisms. Yes, in the boating life one needs to be baptized more than once. Overall, the sensation aboard was "what a beautiful place the Great Sand Strait is", no signs of regret, and a feeling that one day, who knows, we would come back.

Our next stopover was going to be Bundaberg.

For some reason, or because of things I had read, I don´t know, my idea of Bundaberg was a kind of old western cowboy town and I refused to learn more about the place before getting there. I wanted to rediscover the place. Bundaberg for me was a hidden place for ocean drifters and I wanted to be there. When we started to approach the entrance of a river, John called me on the radio and asked if I could go ahead because his chart of the area was with me, he thought he left it in Alvidia.

"No, John! It is not."

Ok, we were both with no directions to follow and it was already solid dark. John and De carried on slowly between two lines of green and red lights and Helga and I stayed way behind, unable to see an inch in front of us. I could feel already that we were in a river flow, completely different from the sea and a strong contrary current as well as contrary to our route was coming a huge monster full of lights making a strange noise. It was a floating ship manufacturer of canned sardines. It sounded to me like billions of cockroaches being smashed.

Wow! We passed too close to that ship. The feeling was to be nearly sucked up underneath.

Suddenly I was betrayed by my own eyes, and got confused with the running lights of Sotalia and lost it out of sight. Helga was shouting the depth read from the instrument and I was at the tiller, touching inch by inch in the dark and noticing what seemed to be a bunch of yachts anchored. I steered towards them very slowly, and threw our anchor. From his cockpit distant of two boats apart from Alvidia, John shouted at me asking if it was true that I did not have his chart, just joking because he found it.

"Helga! We anchored next to Sotalia!" I shouted.

Before we went to bed, John gave us a bad news. For some reason, he could not pass Bundaberg. His engine was leaking oil, he would need to go up on the river and discuss the serious issue with someone. We could carry it on and wait for them in Pancake Creek, the next anchorage of the list.

We decided to stay one day in Bundaberg to fill in water and fuel, and buying some fresh veggies for a nice dinner for our two great friends, instructors, and angels, but again there was some not-so-good news – they would have to wait a part from Sydney and stay up the river away from where we were.

In Bundaberg, I checked one item off my wish list - to use my membership ID from the Drummoyne Sailing Club and be granted a stay at the local yacht club. Within sheltered waters, it was once again Luis comfortably playing like a kid with everyone. I gave away keyrings, made in our factory in Melbourne, and made acquaintances with people at the fuel pump, at the supermarket, and at the newsstand. To finish off, the captain and his wife had a good shower at the club and the next morning we left for Pancake Creek.

In Bundaberg, we also met Barry and Paola, a couple from the yacht Salesi, a replica of the Spray, the famous boat of Joshua Slocum. They were traveling with their children – two boys.

Going to Pancake, Salesi was following us, copying every tack on our same course. Alvidia was steady, between six and seven knots for speed, although the sails were set on the second reef. Salesi was with all the clothes up and with the engine on I don´t know how they could to that. Right before approaching Pancake, my eyes told me the Middle Rock was the Outer Rock and that the headland to me was the Inner Rock. Those were three rocks I charted, notes taken from somebody else´s chart. I should go through between the Inner and the headland. Helga, with her eagle eyes, told me I was wrong, that "the Inner that you are saying is actually the Middle Rock, the outer is way out there, look". She pointed her finger to dead starboard to where I'd never been looking. We were so close to the headland that we could feel the breaking waves, sailing to portside tack. Alvidia was gliding. I took the tiller from Ulysses's hand and pulled it tight to portside, giving the beam to the southeast wind and Alvidia made a sprint on a straight line in front of the headland towards the inner rock, bringing water on deck while heeling to her maximum capacity. It was like sailing on a windsurf. Meanwhile, I looked behind and saw Salesi going straight to the same trap. There was no time to call them on the radio and I waved, trying to say they should get out of there. Salesi became like a crazy chicken out of control and lucky for them the engine was on. All safe, thanks to Helga´s eyes.

As we moved away from Sydney, we noticed the contact with the rest of the world became a little tricky, to say the least, now that we were in the Whitsundays it was a surprise if we could get a Sea Phone contact, a landline to VHF radio service, so the most reliable sources of connection still VHF to VHF or SSB/HF. So no contact with John and De that must have been somewhere inland. While in Pancake Creek, we saw the arrival of another future friend, a couple, and then there were the three boats, Alvidia, Salesi and Delicado from Bill and Marguerite who came aboard for the famous coffee and cake by Helga. It was then that I convinced myself that the sea is not only the last resource for food, being the origin of the food chain, but the ultimate source of water, being the start and end of any drop of water on Earth; the sea is also a place of angels where one can only make friends, and wickedness does not flourish so easy.

Bill and Marguerite were retired grandparents. Bill had been a radio operator and worked in many stations along the northeast coast of Australia, his last post was on Thursday Island, Torres Strait, on the border zone with Papua New Guinea – the passageway of all leisure and commercial ships from the Pacific Ocean to the Indian Ocean. We learned a lot chatting casually with Bill and Marguerite, not only because of his trade, dropping valuable tips here and there, but through their life experiences. The Delicado was their second boat, the first one was lost in New Castle, right there where we had to heave to at night among monsters made of iron. Many years ago, Bill and Marguerite were trying to escape from a severe storm and were shipwrecked. They had to swim to shore and were hurt a lot on the rocks. They were helped by locals with clothes and pocket cash. All they had was aboard the first Delicado; they had to restart their lives. They were finished raising their children and built the second Delicado. Now they were on their third passage of their dreams, sailing around Australia. What could I tell them that was as interesting from our own experiences? I apologized to Bill and Marguerite for disliking Australians during our first months in the country and told them that I regret that feeling and now once again I was ashamed.

"Well, Lois, if you didn't tell me I would never have known," he replied laughing out loud showing his only tooth.

On that same afternoon, Bill rowed his dinghy to Alvidia when we had aboard Barry and Paola from Salesi. Bill brought a hand drawing of few extracts from charts, he said they would be a must up north.

"Wow! Bill, what brutal work!" I said and he once again laughed. Marguerite explained that he was worried about us approaching Cape Capricorn, Port Clinton and Great Keppel without charts; he would not sleep.

Barry, from the Salesi, just introduced to Bill and Marguerite immediately offered one of his charts to us. Barry was a musician, turning fifty years old and that was also his cruising dream – to reach the Whitsundays playing his songs for a living. He was born in South Africa and raised in Australia, played guitar as a cover of James Taylor from whom he was a look-a-like. His wife was the great-granddaughter of a

Samoan king and sung the blues. They had two boys, we planned to meet up again in Airlie Beach and Barry promised never to follow me again.

Before we left Pancake Creek, with the tricks learned from Bill I was able to make contact with John Deegan and he told me his problem was as big as eight thousand dollars. I offered him my laptop he could sell and make some cash because I was saving that piece of equipment for an emergency, although beyond money John would need to wait until who knows when to get the part to fix the engine. Big problem. That same day I carved a wooden sign for Sotalia from a scrap left from the work Steve made on my tiller to make it thinner and one day I would give the plaque to John and De.

From there we headed to Great Keppel Island. The largest of eighteen islands in the Keppel Group much sought after by Australians and foreign tourists with comfortable accommodations and fun, an atmosphere of a group tour. Since we had all we needed aboard, our dinghy stayed tied down on deck and we did not row ashore. At night, Delicado and Salesi also arrived. The next morning we discovered that Dal and Cath from Aries were there too. They made it! And it was funny to see Cath in charge, the Captain aboard Aries and Dal a mere second-class sailor.

What a joy, they came aboard Alvidia as old friends. They told us that they had stayed five days out on the ocean being sent back and forward by storms that changed from North to South and the strong currents against their desired course and the ginger recipe Helga gave to Cath was amazing – doing a great job aboard. Cath was a lawyer and confessed to us that when we met in Coffs she had lost her direction, did not know where to head to in life.

"You two came across our path right in the moment we needed someone to be inspired from. Thank you. Dal, go to Aries and bring some wine!" Cath told us and shouted an order to the second class sailor.

"We have wine in stock, Cath," I told her, "but tell Dal instead to do the dishes, would you?" I joked and we laughed out loud for hours. The more I kept saying she should not feel inspired by us the more I feel it would be useless, after all, what happened, in fact, was that they simply realized they could do it and they did it. What else is important – who inspired who?

Next day, with a light rain we left in the French leaving way, there is without saying goodbye. We sailed to Rosslyn Bay, following John´s list – a fishermen's stopover but it was too busy and we decided to carry it on to Port Clinton before dark – whose approach included going around reefs, rocks, tide current, sandbanks, and turbulence. Without Bill´s hand drawings, only Alan Lucas would not be enough for us to get in there.

The weather deteriorated and the contacts with John became almost impossible. I had to use a contact bridge – pass on messages to other boats and receive John´s reply the same way, also via the Sydney station to where John used to report daily of his position. This way I was practicing all the futures and possibilities of my VHF and SSB/HF radios.

Our next anchorage was going to be Island Head Creek, a headland and last touch with the continent before our route through unimaginable beautiful islands and coral reefs under our keel. We stayed two days anchored in Port Clinton, one of the best sunset horizons we have seen and that would compete with so many ahead of us. Good food aboard, wine, good coffee, home baked bread, homemade sweets, light rain making a nice noise on deck, what would you do? I had an old sail found in the garbage in Pittwater and after feeling guilty at such laziness, I cut that old sail into an emergency staysail, stitching it by hand as I had done the dog house and spray protection. Happy with the result, it was my turn to record our log:

"June 06, 1996 (...) Today I remember important things happened in the last two years... Helga saying "the boat is coming along"; Helga under the tarpaulin

in River Quays holding it under the rain while I was working on the boat; Helga holding my face with her two soft hands in Birkenhead, encouraging me while I freaked out; Helga with shopping bags full of veggies coming from her job at the Market in Woolwich; Helga rolling up her sleeves for the interview with Rob when we got the job at McConaghy; Helga in Refuge Bay trying to accomplish tasks that would finish the boat according to her list; Helga keeping Alvidia as a cozy cottage; Helga when we got stranded; we did not step on land for seven days by now (...)."

While writing the notes above and thinking, I realized all the young monkeys in my loft were getting mature and the old ones less stressed. I also realized the bumpy seas and gusts over 40 knots did not scare me so much. Alvidia was a part of my body and soul so was Helga too. I stared at all the trees and elements surrounding me with special care and respect and satisfaction. Those crystal waters that we could see colored coral down to more than thirty feet deep, and the dolphins always at sight, what a life. I thought about all these things and did not reach any conclusion other than to wear the look of my Indian from Arizona. As a backdrop the astonishing sunset now that the rain has stopped. In the Alan Lucas book, we read "We are facing the most breathtaking sunset on the Australian coast."

We had a very good night sleep and at four o'clock I was woken up by the GPS featuring the anchorage alarm. I could not believe it but went on the cockpit to check it up. It was the first time I used that feature. To the stern, I could still see the two lights of the two boats I used as a reference as well as the top of a hill nearby. The GPS got to be wrong but the feeling aboard told me otherwise. I stayed a moment watching the instrument and noticed the coordinates were changing as a digital watch increasing steadily. It would happen only if we were moving towards the same direction not spinning around the anchor as normally you do while on the hook. So I wore the storm gear and went up on deck to look around. Still very dark and the wind was at twenty knots. It was true that the points of reference were on the same angle in relation to Alvidia but when I turned my head to a forty-five degree I saw a tree passing by and another and another and it was too fast and I realized what was happening. The wind and current were pushing Alvidia into the creek maintaining the same points of reference. No more time for geometry experiments. We must have been dragged three hundred yards at a minimum, what a place to be, John said that could happen and Bill warned me too and without his hand-drawing I would be helplessly stranded again or worst, wrecked. I turned the engine on in a snap and called Helga on deck, she would stay on the tiller responding to my signs while I was going to be on the bow trying to pull the anchor up on deck. The anchor rope had been passed around and under the bow of Alvidia as a horse halter. Alvidia was being dragged and it was hard for Helga to manage the tiller in such conditions so I run to steer Alvidia to make a complete circle around the anchor carefully not to get the rudder entangled with the chain. I then gave the tiller back to Helga and run to the bow asking my Helga to keep the course whatever she could understand what our course was at that time of the early dark morning in the middle of nowhere. We became a pro in awkward situations; our communication was perfect, no shout, no scream, no appearance of panic, no appearance, only the invisible real thing.

Praying for Helga to figure out what to do, to push forward or to back up as per my signals from the bow, I grabbed the anchor rope from under the stem and pulled it with all my strength, all my guts, all my unimaginable energy. Seeing my effort, Helga pushed hard and slowly forward, seeing that I rested a bit she would back up slowly, she was doing a great job, just feeling sorry for my muscular effort and translating that into the tiller motion. I had to dig out the anchor from the mud, pull it on deck. I was almost there losing strength already but I gave a last breath and gave all my strength once more – the anchor came out and could feel it hanging out of the mud, then I pulled it on deck and almost fainted from so much effort.

"Helga, check the depth."

"Three meters!"

"Good. Stay on the tiller, slowly making a circle right here while I rest a couple of minutes," I said and gave her a thumbs up, sitting completely soaked with my own sweat. The strong cold morning breeze was a good help, I pointed to Helga to steer to a direction, gradually I started to recover myself and asked Helga to give the tiller back to me and it was her turn to rest. Taking that for granted we carried it on and left Port Clinton heading toward Island Head Creek. We spent the day chocked with the morning adventure. Not exactly for what happened but what would happen if we did not act timely and if we did not have that extra chain Dal gave to us. And from then on I would take all the anchorages even more seriously, warning all the monkeys of my loft even while on an anchor lunch for a couple of hours in daylight.

The day sailing was tranquil. With winds of fifteen to twenty knots and as soon as we got out of Port Clinton I set a tack and the sails reefed to the first reefing point. Just in case and with the autopilot in charge I did not change the tack until the very anchorage. We were like an express train. On the way, we saw strange creatures, a huge yellow snake, organisms floating on the surface of the water and dolphins with whom I almost jumped in the water to play with. From the galley, Helga produced baked bread, coffee, orange juice, and bananas, and we could well say our home was the entire sea. What a backyard. To approach Island Head Creek we had to negotiate with the same things as in other places and it would be a routine from now on. Shoals, sandbanks, tide stream, rocks. And once again the recommendations from John, Bill, and Alan Lucas were fundamental.

We anchored in a mangrove available to get in and out only at high tide. I had an updated tide chart and excelled myself in the calculation picking up a place to throw the hook where it would have less than three feet of water under the keel at the lowest tide. Here we were also advised by John not to miss the giant turtles. A private show of nice and friendly ladies; we could touch their shells from the deck and we kept watching them, placing names on them after our families members. Two of them were our own faces, according to Helga.

At night we were invaded by a cloud of tiny small mosquitos that did not bite but covered the interior of Alvidia in black. In the morning they simply were gone with the wind. Nature.

The day was overcast when we left Island Head heading to Piercy Group with the same wind we had in the last days. Alvidia was gliding nicely and I was so used to the spinnaker pole to set up the headsail and mainsail wing to wing that Helga down below would not even notice I was working on deck. So with the autopilot engaged the entire day I spent great moments sitting on the pulpit at the bow just watching the dolphins following the Alvidia´s wake. I saw birds fishing so close that I could see their eyes shine. I felt like I was one of those creatures and recollected memories of my dad who taught me to be in the nature and to like nature.

We reached South Piercy and from more or fewer ten miles we noticed it was busy and as our goal was Middle Piercy, the largest and most beautiful of the group, we skipped the South Piercy, although knowing that according to Alan Lucas, Middle Piercy has an abominable swell disturbance for anchoring. Later on, I learned that beyond the truth about the swells, there was a feud between the author of the cruising guide and the single permanent resident of the island, Mr. Andrew Martin. Matter of gossip. Human thing.

To go around South Piercy we faced a tide stream of three and a half knots holding Alvidia. We felt like a bird against the wind and our speed went down to two knots. I invented a better tack and got an extra knot although I would not reach Middle Piercy with daylight so I had to turn the engine on against my wish and a bit ashamed for disturbing the nature. On the same token, afraid of a mutiny aboard Alvidia. The humor of the Captain´s wife was not very good and I never knew exactly the reason why whether due to my maneuvers or because I was with the beard to be made already for two weeks and saving water on very quick wash-ups I must be also smelly. Probably all of that and something else was upsetting the first mate aboard.

"Helga! We are going to meet Andy! One item off my list. And the island has a lot of fresh water," I was persuading Helga to smile when something happened even more abominable than the swells. Middle Piercy has a beach with white sands and the color of the water is unspeakable; I was admiring the place, approaching slowly to a point to throw the hook. There were three boats anchored there at a good distance from each other so Alvidia would be close to one of them. As I walked to the bow I saw the boat nearby starting to move and while I was about to wave a hello as I used to do when approaching or passing by another yacht I heard an angry shout towards me. "Hey! Do not anchor there! I´m moving my boat to that spot! Get the fuck out of there!"

It was like a knockdown, a straight right on the chin. I got disoriented, perplexed and feeling like a bird being attacked. I flew immediately to the other side. The only lucid reaction I had was to open both arms to the man saying, "But here in this Paradise, brother?" I could send Helga after the man – poor guy if I did so – and the disturbance of the swells was indeed terrible, probably the reason why that human being was so stressed, but even Helga forgot any would-be problem. We fell in love with the island at the sunset.

Despite the dazzle, we slept very little. While Helga tasted all the corners of Alvidia trying to sleep, I played tumbler toy as the swells lifted Alvidia – I was thrown and dove with the boat on the way down. Alan Lucas was generous about the swells. To make it worst, Helga had a dream about her mom being sick. In the morning, however, it was a spectacle, worth any sacrifice to be there.

We had a gorgeous breakfast in the cockpit, ecstatic at such beauty and jumped on the dinghy to explore the island. There were in the line of sight two huts. One of them right on the beach as an entry hall, a community place for sailors, chalet format full of plaques, a variety of objects, from leg prosthesis to tools and paintings and even chamber-pots – yes, good question, who would take a chamber-pot on a cruise, or to an island? On an improvised table, a guestbook with many interesting records, including poetry, notes from one sailor to another, protests and next to it, an intelligent counter for trading. Merchandises displayed and no sales person. Some with a price tag, some at the criterion of the buyer. They were sweet jam, honey, homemade liquors, tooling, souvenirs. I liked to believe that as you arrive you try to figure out how that retail store works, then whatever it is your own idea, you trade by yourself. My idea of trading at Andy´s hut store was that you like an item, leave another item as a barter or leave some cash on the counter. Perfect. One thing, the owner did not have issues with the labor department of State in Australia.

The bar of the island was also unique. Self-service coconut. As a bartender, a small ax. Help your self, dude! And walk around on your knees, this is a sanctuary.

With few local rules to abide by, displayed on a pole, the visitor could enjoy the island – the traffic orientation was made up of few signs as you go up to the top of the hill, guiding to the very house of Andy. At the start of the trail, the second rustic hut was available for visitors, with a bed, a mirror, a table, stove and, believe me, curtains. It was visible that once upon the time very long ago someone cleaned that place, but also it was clear that many enjoyed it thoroughly. I saw plastic pipes on the surface of the ground coming down from the hill and I told Helga, "Shower!"

But no luck, no water out of the tap. There was also a kind of kraal that I thought was meant to be a restroom. So after we explored the beach, collected some coconuts recently fallen from the trees and drunk their water we decided to walk and visit the famous Andy. According to the information I had gathered, Andy lived there by himself and bartered fresh food with visitors, for money or any other things of value. We were not interested in shopping, only to meet him. The way up was unforgettable and I recollected how much my father liked to walk in the woods, and how familiar the environment would be for him. We passed by cliffs, creeks, stones the size of a house, a bog and after an hour and a half the first sign of civilization was manure, and it was the first time we saw kangaroos free out in the open. Before we reached Andy´s house, we had a break and Helga sat on the roots of a huge tree. It was like seeing a painting come alive – around the tree there were whitish stones, contrasting the dark green of the tree. It did not need to have that background to make me get emotional. We could see the beach with white sand down there and Alvidia anchored on turquoise, pale green, light translucent blue waters as if she was floating on the clouds and we could see the seabed. Those tears rolling on my face were pure gold, true life melting away.

A breeze came in and I smelled homemade food and wood burning. There was a third hut that I learned, later on, was where a couple lived and helped Andy, who was on the fast lane of aging already. Finally, we arrived. Loose hens, a dog scratching its groin, a rundown shed, a small tractor next to corroded wheels among high weeds, and finally a wooden staircase to the very Andy's house, a mix of accidental architecture with a veranda, many windows, many doors and a mix of construction material too.

"Hello! Anybody home? We arrived!" I shouted.

"Come up here!" we heard back.

Mr. Andrew Martin in person welcomed us behind a huge table full of books; he was wearing a pair of heavy glasses and sporting a nice smile.

"Mr. and Mrs. Da Silva, we made a reservation and our luggage are down the beach," I said and Andy presented a good sense of humor taking my silly joke, igniting a frenzy of conversation for two hours non-stop. As soon as I saw three Bibles on the table and recited a versicle Andy asked if I read the Bible and as I answered that my mom abandoned a convent where she was going to be a nun to marry my dad and that I studied ten years in the same nun's school, he seemed upset, trying to find a way to settle down in his chair. He took off two sweaters, and coughing started to tell me about his job. He was writing a book about "*the chosen people by God*." In his theory, the English spoken people, well, when he said that we battled in such way that Andy took off his other two sweaters and looked like he was preaching in the middle of a busy avenue in some major city of any Central American country. At a certain point, he apologized for not offering us any drink and stood up with difficulty, probably due to advanced aging bones. Only then we could believe he was on top of eighty years. We looked around and guessed from those kitchenware in the sink and stove would not come up any eatable or drinkable substance.

"No worries, Andy, we will accept a glass of water just show us where to get it, please."

He then grabbed two glasses that once upon the time were transparent and poured a turbid liquid from a jar. At least it was cold. He had a generator and an eolian system. We drunk that thing staring at each other. Helga actually swallowed it all at once while I was going little by little. We kept talking about his work and I noticed his bibliography spread on the table and piled on a chair rich with classic titles from philosophy to history, religious art to anthropology and Jewish titles. I made a comment about that and counteracting he showed me a huge volume of Darwin waving it above his head and got mad throwing it through the window hitting the hens down there. He stood up again, dragging himself, and brought out a box of documents and pamphlets.

"You are Latin, will not accept, but look at this!" he said, showing me pictures, notes, and booklets.

The intellectual battle was great, proving all is relative indeed. I had just arrived from the sea, I was a bird a few hours before, I was playing like a kid in the woods and making poetry watching Helga taking a break, I had been sailing with dolphins to check off an item on my wishing basket, Andy, so ok, Mr., spill all out whatever you say after being so long without contact with civilization, yes, let´s have fun, after all, we are on an island. What he showed me was a facsimile of a picture of the holy stone where Jacob would have rested his head when he dreamed of a staircase from earth to heaven. Andy said his research proved that the stone was the same stone nowadays under the throne of the United Kingdom's Queen and that in the early days every time a king was crowned he had to put his right hand on that very stone to be blessed. Today, this sublime reverence is veiled, leaving its revelation only between a closed core of the court. I counter attacked him citing Victor Hugo and he decided to go back to a friendship terms.

"In thirty years living on this island, you are the first one that arrived here and did not speak of boating and cruising."

He said this to disarm me by touching my vanities, son of a gun. And as the wind had turned to amenities I told him I was half Jewish. When it was already time to go back to the boat and Andy stood up asking me two favors: first, if I accept a few books as a gift, second if I would take his letters to the first Post Office on shore?

There were no fresh veggies on the island due to obeying the mitsvá of shmitá when in the seventh year cycle the land must rest, no sow, no prune, no crop, no harvesting. But Andy offered us a treat, opening a freezer from where came a smell of morgue and he lifted a thing that looked like a leg. I looked to Helga, my supply manager and she said with her eyes that we were ok with legs in our inventory.

"No, no, Andy, thanks."

"Ok, you wouldn´t like anyway, it is for my dogs," he said laughing.

We said goodbye, we hugged each other, and we promised to resume our philosophical discussion by letters. Another item checked from my list – I had met Andy.

On the beach, we met a couple from the yacht Capela II with news from John. He needed to change bearings and parts of his engine, very complicated and expensive. They also gave us a nice freshly caught mackerel; we had another round of coconut water and pulp with our new friends, then we cleaned the dinghy and there was nothing else to do. Stay for the night in that heaven and carry on with our cruise the next morning.

With the postal service bag to deliver at Airlie Beach, we headed first to Digby island then we would stop over at Scawfell island and Shaw Island to complete a month without stepping on the continent.

To Digby, just a gathering of rocks in the middle of the Coral Sea, it was a nice ride. Winds from the southeast, fifteen knots over the shoulder, the same tack from lifting the anchor to throw it at sunset using the autopilot all the way. What do you do out on the ocean blue the entire day with no meetings, no phone calls, no errands to run? Especially when all your monkeys in the loft are also with nothing to do? And this is my idea of cruising, sailing, after all, just flowing with the wind nicely. And it was approaching Digby island where I met the fishes that assaulted Kay. We were sailing into the sunset almost touching the water; it was all silver and gold to my eyes and from those rocks along the way a turbulence of water due to the strong low tide current, it was like an inverted rain, from the water to the air, of small fishes. This show was not in the program. I threw the anchor on a natural swimming pool of clear water five meters deep. Following Bill´s recommendation, I should not choose the lowest part because it would be full of corral reefs and boomies, giant sticks of corals pointing to the sky. We would lose our anchor on those piles.

We had dinner and emptied a full bottle of wine, slept tight and left that piece of paradise early to Scawfell island. I almost stopped at Penrith halfway, an island in the format of a mushroom that I heard on the radio was sheltering a brotherhood of ocean drifters but thought twice and carried on with my humble cruising life. Helga, Alvidia and I were already a good bunch. And we were now sailing in the area of the bullets, according to John, Bill, Alan Lucas and anyone who knows the area. They are hidden winds coming from behind headlands with gusts up to twenty percent of extra power in relation to the local wind. You are attacked by surprise as soon you reach the line of the headland dead beam. You can capsize if you're not aware. So I warmed up my brain batteries which were too lazy lately; woke up all my monkeys and brought them to deck, reefed the sails one notch and waited with my hand on the tiller. What a joy to steer Alvidia in that environment. That smooth and light tiller and rudder. At one point before any sign of headland nearby I left the tiller just to see Alvidia on her own. She went straight for few minutes. Helga warned me that I should not kidding and she was right but I was proud to realize how perfect that rudder system was with the sails in the groove. The anchorage at Scawfell was busy. Power boats, fishing boats, local yachts, the pace was one that we did not miss at all but as it was going to be only one night, I chose to anchor next to a fishing vessel that worked the whole night.

Once again, we lifted the anchor very early after a quick breakfast and set course to Shaw Island, in front of which was the Club Méditerranée. Here we saw boats of all kinds coming and going in all directions and one in particular, a catamaran, was in a such a route that if he did not change course he would hit us right on the cheek. Our tack put us on the right way to carry on and I noticed the crew of two men aboard the cat making a maneuver and setting two sails wing on wing – in a cat you must use two spinnaker poles. The way I was spread in the cockpit holding the tiller I waved to the two sailors and saw that they had white beards and were flying an Irish flag. Alvidia was approximately a hundred yards or less ahead of the cat and I noticed they were working hard to pass us by portside, which would give them the right way but Alvidia kept steady at seven knots and gradually moved away from them. Then they would change tack and gain a few yards, approaching us again with their tack close to our stern, and once again losing ground while Alvidia, without moving a line of hair carried on at the same pace, getting away from the cat. We were racing, although I was doing nothing but watching the race. Close to the place I was going to anchor, I stood up and pulled the tiller to portside, and because Alvidia left a wide area for the cat to come in I made a symbolic gentleman's gesture of welcome to the line of arrival. Smiles, acquaintances, shout, salute! When cruising you make friends even before actually meeting someone. And it was so good that day that I anchored without using the engine; I just retrieved the sails, and let Alvidia stroll in. I threw the anchor and let the stream and the anchor rod do the rest of the job.

Meanwhile, Helga was baking her famous muffins for the afternoon coffee. I was organizing the sheets on deck and saw the Irish sailors jumping in their tender, actually a canoe, and started to row towards us. When they got close I shouted that the second place award was coffee and muffins and that they should come aboard to receive their prize. It burst a hullabaloo from the canoe and once aboard they confessed they had been doing all they could to outpace Alvidia. They were smelly, but other than that Michael and Des were added to our gallery of friends and soon as angels too. They signed the guestbook and told us stories of their lives. The sea is full of life, nothing dies on the sea – if it perishes it immediately becomes another living thing or being.

They were sailing on Pangur Bán, a homemade catamaran by Michael, a boat I was going to come to know much later. The sea also has its own timing; there are things that happen only when the sea decides it's time. Michael said his boat was overly heavy. He built Pangur Bán to make an around-the-world cruise, his old dream. He left Ireland and headed for the Caribbean, crossed the Panama Canal, went across the Pacific islands to New Zealand, where he met Des, also Irish, and from there they sailed to California to visit his granddaughter who had been recently born. Then went to Alaska and came back to the Pacific Ocean and finally Australia via the Barrier Reef.

When we woke up with the first light of day, there was no sign of Pangur Bán; they had left early, headed to Cairns where this time it was Des' turn to see his grandson.

As we had the postal bag to deliver in Arlie Beach, it was our due course; we were without charts but had Alan Lucas' guide. The boat traffic was heavy and we had been deceived that the place was the "Copacabana" of the Whitsundays. Used to Rio de Janeiro, we found too few boats anchored, only one yacht club without a pier, a launching ramp and the town with a single main avenue with few hotels and backpackers strolling around. Many pubs, though. It was a nice place, we could live there with no complaint.

We already knew John and De would never catch up with us and we were able to make a Sea phone contact to receive congratulations for having reached the famous Whitsundays. Many Australians have it as a dream of their lives.

The next day the Salesi and Aries arrived together. I could see from far away the leash around Dal's neck and Cath giving orders. He was happy, he was sailing and they had reached the Whitsundays, so who cares who was in charge?

I found near the club a park with free public grills out in the open and I made an authentic "churrasco" gaucho, big chunks of selected meat baked to perfection on a skewer over charcoal with raw salt. After a gorgeous banquet, Helga and I were taking a nap, spread out on the grass and we were awake by Paola inviting us for a session of beers aboard Salesi. What a hard life; we couldn't sleep anymore – it was time to go.

The weather forecast warned of a kind of quick time out of the trade winds, with gusts from the quadrant north and the anchorage would be a bit messy. We heard that nobody would be able to sleep aboard. And it seemed true, from Salesi drinking beers with Paola, Berry and a couple of other guests we could see Alvidia jumping up and down like a crazy mare.

We had our minds set to leave the anchorage, after all, we were moving ahead, but when the other guests left Salesi, Barry and Paola started to play and sing for us. It seemed we had things in common when they told us money was their constant headache. They were raising their two boys and the musician caravan was not producing enough income at that time. We said goodbye to each other and while I was rowing back to Alvidia, Helga asked if I, or we, could not do anything to help them. It was hard to row our rubber dinghy but the sea life was our common place and it did not matter so we continued to discuss the Salesi issue while bouncing up and down on the waves. Helga reminded me that I had proven to be a good salesperson and I could at least try to sell Berry and Paola to the local pubs. It was then that I made a U-turn and rowed back to Salesi to ask for material for my sales pitching efforts. It was so good to see their happiness and for their embarrassment I said, "No worries, Berry, no strings attached, no commission involved, no contract to sign, we just will set you guys on an Airlie Beach gig. Tell me how much you charge, what do you need and pray for my success."

At around two o´clock the following afternoon, I had knocked on almost every pub´s door of Airlie Beach to offer James Taylor and "Clara Nunes" because Paola reminded us a very famous Brazilian singer. They were hired for daily gigs during the week in one of the busiest pubs in the town. Mission accomplished – we headed to Gran Bay. We did not stay to see them play because we had our private show.

...July, salt water in the veins.

This was the narrowest passage through the Great Barrier Reef and we had only Alan Lucas as a guide and a chart with a small scale – useful for strategic course planning only. Once it gets narrower, the channel approaches all its hazardous ingredients. Commercial ships, coral reefs, low tide stream, bommies, bullets and so all the monkeys from my loft came to the cockpit, adding to that a custom small plane used to fly over our heads – it called us on the radio to report our identity, port of origin and destination. From that point on up to the extreme north, that plane would come religiously on a daily basis to ask the same questions on the radio. I tried not to reply once and it came almost to land on our deck so I found it was best to answer them right way – as Bill had recommended.

"White sloop with brown sails... this is customs, over!"

"Customs, customs, this Alvidia, Alvidia, Victor Hotel November 6377, over!"

We anchored in Gran Bay, not too far from Airlie Beach and very early the next morning we left for Bowling Bay. During this passage, we went around Cape Upstart where I saw the giant smooth stones that, according to the aboriginal people, are sacred.

Approaching Bowling Bay at sunset, Helga surprised me by asking not to anchor, to carry it on to the next anchorage, but I was tired of steering through corals and bommies and watching ships and we decided to stay few hours for sleep. It was tough to anchor in Bowling Bay as it was in Moreton Bay and this time not even Helga´s eyes could help. We simply could not see the sandbar that, according to Alan Lucas, hosted a bay behind. For us it was all land and water, we could not distinguish the said sandbar. The only reference was a tall tree more or less two miles from the very tip of the hidden sandbar would be position. How would we go around? Worried that the sun was setting too fast I noticed there was a line of ripples on the water perpendicular to that tall tree and I figured it could be the damn sandbank. Thus I asked Helga to keep telling me the depth from the instrument and went over where Alvidia had two or three feet of water under the keel; slowly motoring I ran parallel to the ripple until Helga started to shout deeper waters then I turned to portside ahead a few yards and went back parallel again next to low water so I was at the opposite side of the sandbar from where I was before. The method I applied reminded when I was a kid and played with ants placing small sticks on their way to see them discovering the way around the sticks, they touched and backed up, touched and backed up, going forward until the end of the sticks. Perhaps it is also the method of a blind person. My hat went off to them.

While I was making that risky maneuver, I saw the light of a mast behind what should be a sand bar. Next morning during the low tide I saw that we had anchored perfectly behind the sand bar. The boat nearby had a German flag. We did not meet the occupants until much later on and again the sea never told us why.

From there we headed to Townsville, still inside the Barrier Reef and, for a change, negotiating with the depth almost touching the sea bed at the low tide. There was nothing waiting for us in the town, so we just jumped on the dinghy to reach the local marina and discharged our selected bags of waste and filled our tanks with fresh water. As our boat was our home, we washed Alvidia, cleaned her deck from the salt water, washed our clothes, cooked, and we drank wine, our routine, and of course slept like angels.

The next stopover was Orpheus Island, a sleeping point only because our major interest was in Cairns, and it was going to be especially important being the last city of Queensland for us and where we would start to climb the very north tip of Australia, Cape York, turning west towards Brazil on the other side of the ocean over the Africa continent. It was psychologically important.

As we approached Orpheus Island, a huge modern yacht flying an American flag arrived. It looked like a racing yacht with its deck flush and clean. At the bow a man with very dark skin and Aztec traces and I challenged my self with my poor Spanish which deserved a severe reprimand from Helga, "No moleste los corales, hermano."

He was throwing his anchor over a sanctuary of corals and I could see it because of the transparency of the water.

"Qué paso?" he replied, inferring about what would happening.

I made a signal that he could anchor next to us with the sand seabed, better protected from the south wind. He became another friend on our list. Kal Ikal the name of the boat, Victor the name of the

Captain. In the morning we left together, Alvidia just a little ahead but I noticed Kal Ikal came with the whole lot while the wind was light, slightly under fifteen knots, and Alvidia could well make six knots with any wind about ten knots from the right direction, which was the case.

After one hour sailing ahead of Kal Ikal, Victor set his spinnaker but had to open up his course a bit and lost half mile from us. I chose a tack close to the continent and he went out to the middle of the shipping lane. When the small custom plane came to check us up I learned that Victor was going to Dunk Island, our next anchorage too. We arrived together at Dunk Island and to me, it was a victory, sorry Victor, because of my handicap. The place was so beautiful that Helga and I decided to throw the dinghy in the water to explore and to our surprise there was a free shower for cruisers on the island, as well as an airstrip landing for private jets, golf field, birds in cages, greenhouses for orchids – despite of all that Dunk island had that summer atmosphere where you just let your arms down and give yourself in. Victor and Karen, his wife, had the same indulgence; he was Mexican and was curious to know where we were from and he could not believe Alvidia was a wooden homemade yacht. I told him that the brown sails were to win Mexicans and of course the mood was one of a kind. Karen was a nice American lady from Colorado, USA. They lived in Cancun, Mexico, crossed the Panama Canal towards the Pacific to New Zealand and while coming to Australia almost capsized twice. Victor was an architect with an office in Cancun with two partners to whom he sold his shares and embarked on his dream. He also sold his beautiful house, left some money in the bank and there were the two of them going around the world.

Is not a good idea to drink too much tequila the night before you go sailing; we confirmed that to ourselves while leaving early the next morning to Marilyn Harbour and the silence aboard Alvidia was also due to bad news we heard on the radio of a terrible accident with vessels in the vicinities. And repeating the other approaches to creeks, islands, and bays, Marilyn was done very slowly due to our absence of charts and the need to negotiate with the tide. When we left the anchorage the next morning we could see Kal Ikal rubbing the coast. We made contact on the radio and discussed the racing rules of the day and Victor took it seriously changing tack to the other side of the channel, crossing the path of a ship coming from the north but as I was looking back to watch his moves I saw another ship coming from the South. Kal Ikal did not change tack; it just retrieved the spinnaker and disappeared between the two ships passing by each other honking their horns, and then Kal Ikal appeared clear again, raising his spinnaker. Cool view! But he was still behind Alvidia. The breeze increased a bit to twelve knots and Kal Ikal was going to pair with us on the same tack while we were approaching Fitzroy Island, then a big question arose aboard Alvidia. The wife of the Captain needed to choose between staying on overnight in Fitzroy or carrying on until Cairns. We were at the extreme south of the island, the approach to the anchorage with the bullets at the beam should be around the north tip. When we reached almost to the point of turning or not Helga decided to stay, and it was just in time to get the bullet wind on the nose.

From Fitzroy to Cairns, now used to the bullets, it was a pleasant sunshine sailing day. This time of the year, Cairns is one of the most sought after places of the Whitsundays from where many charters go to the islands, dumping divers and avid tourists of all parts of the world. As we were out of the mainstream long ago it impacted us to see townies attracted and amused by things that where part of our daily routine.

The anchorage of Cairns was a jam of power boats and yachts and despite the popularity of the place the first thing that caught our eye was that it reminded us of Newport marina in Pittwater with its old wooden piers and poles, the river mouth with turbid waters and a bit messy with a Shopping Center as a business card right on the docks. We threw the dinghy on the water without blinking, eager to pick up our letters at the Post Office because we had redirected them while in Sydney. We almost lost the dinghy because of the tide current due to it being a full moon phase. Helga asked if I was going to be able to row across the river with such busy traffic and a strong stream. There was only one way to know and using the technique of a puppy swimming, fast short strokes, I reached the other side with one foot of tongue hanging out of my mouth. At the pier for tenders, there was a bedlam, a bunch arguing and cursing at each other about something related to "...damaged my outboard, asshole." Sailors of all kinds, from those ragged like us to stylish weekend boaters, nothing against anyone of them but they were too loud. And, already standing on that pier, to avoid an invitation for the party, I thought a bit and stripped off my clothes leaving on only my underwear, then I jumped back on the dinghy, rowed to the opposite jetty to tie it out there. From there I waved to Helga, who was gaping at me, and walked back with the water to my chest – it was that shallow. Once on the pier, I shook my body like a mutt dog, wore my clothes back, and, to my surprise, I received a round of applause.

On the way to the Post Office we saw Erik, the Swedish man we met in Mooloolaba, giving an interview to Japanese tourists.

"Hi Erik!"

"Hey, Luis!"

Another surprise, the automation of the Australian Postal Service. You have an ATM where you input your name and check if you have letters and parcels waiting for you. Joy! Our names were on the display! But! We needed to write the code on a paper and hand it to the counter clerk. Fine, it was a bundle that we gobbled up, sitting on the curb in front of that branch mixing laughs and tears.

Among family letters, from Brazilian, American and Australian friends one gave us a little push to handle the next leg of our cruise. Larry wrote that we were brothers in souls, as writers and sailors and pointed out, "You are now a seasoned couple, with salt water in the blood."

It was like flipping a chapter of a book, once baptized in Cairns with three thousand miles under our belt so far. And the fours days staying in Cairns were full of events. After a long first day, rowing back to Alvidia already in the dark I saw someone with a flashlight on our deck. While I was getting closer a man with the flashlight shouted a question asking if that boat was mine. Perceiving a situation, I whispered to Helga to stay on the dinghy and stepped on our stern platform replying to the man, "Pretty boat, isn´t?"

The man dropped a rope he was already playing with and stepped towards me while I stepped into the cockpit, assessing the situation, and once we were close enough I put my hand on his shoulder and said almost whispering but with all my possible adrenaline gushing out of my pores and rage I thought I had left in Melbourne, "You liked my boat, my friend?" He seemed frightened and I added, "But I don´t remember inviting you aboard."

I was about to push the fellow hard off the boat when he said trembling with eyes of awe, "Your boat is too close to mine and if it hits my boat who will pay the damage?"

His boat was an iron armor-plated vessel; it was Alvidia at a disadvantage and I had calculated with measuring tape my anchor rod, the possible swing around with the tide change and had checked all the rules of my manual of how to anchor a boat in a crowded anchorage. Anyway, the man was pushed off Alvidia´s deck and that day I am sure I exaggerated in all my manners and vocabulary of bad words. It took me too many minutes to calm down afterward and I accepted Helga´s advice to move Alvidia up the river and, the way we left, deserved an entry in our diary. Helga stayed at the tiller while I lifted the heavy CQR anchor. When Alvidia was free, I made a signal for Helga to push the throttle of the engine gently but I noticed the tide current was too strong and was pulling Alvidia over to the armor-plated scared neighbor. I signaled Helga to pull hard on the throttle, running to switch places with her, but she was efficient enough and in the middle of the darkness with the light of the marina and shopping center lights I only had the chance to watch the performance of Hegla and Alvidia, which sunk her stern in the water, jumping forward like a speed powerboat. We were going over the wooden poles. In my mind I envisioned the two and a half tons of Alvidia smashing the poles and the damage to our hull, and the financial disaster and all the outcomes. I made a signal to Helga to push the throttle to idle and tilt the tiller to portside, turning the bow of Alvidia to starboard and we passed with a hairline between us and the poles, and we went up in the river. Now I was with the tiller and Helga sat in the cockpit with her hands on her face.

Up the river, we anchored among local boats. We crashed like stones and in the morning I got tired just imagining rowing in that river, but as we needed to shake our legs we faced the river and created a bigger problem – to decline the beer with the "mates", the fishermen whose pier they were at that I had asked to leave our dinghy. However, while drinking with them we met the marina manager who granted us a free slip for two days in the busy marina, provided we would not tell anybody, to fill up water, fuel, and stock fresh food. From then on we could go straight to Darwin if we wanted.

That day at the marina we met the Belgium couple, Robert and Nicole, from the yacht Orphée. They had been in Brazil and had two good Franco-Brazilian friends who happen to be there next to us, who we did not know until then, Bia, Brazilian, and Bernard, French, sailing on their 51 foot yacht Gwenaskel.

Again, the sea and its timing.

A fortunate coincidence and they wrote in our guestbook: What an enjoyable surprise to meet a Brazilian couple in Australia, looking forward to seeing you in Rio. Kisses.

On that extra day ashore, we took the time to see a movie at the local theater and realized how hard it would be for us to go back to city life. Definitely, we were not the same anymore, forever changed maybe.

When the free-bee ended, we returned to the anchorage. Kal Ikal and few other boats we saw along the way from Coffs Harbor were there. On the radio we were advised not to stay in Darwin due to the international racing Darwin to Indonesia and that many cruisers aiming for Bali subscribe to the race to go around the customs bureaucracy. With too much of that chatting I decided to turn the radio off and sleep, to prepare for the next leg and I was just doing that when Michael and Des arrived and invited us for dinner aboard Pangur Bán. They went to the shopping center to buy some meat to bake, we were just waiting for them to pass by on the way back when a noisy dinghy approached us. Alejandro and Cristina, he an Argentine, she a Brazilian. They arrived from Nouméa and were told about a Brazilian couple aboard a white hull yacht with the Australian flag and brown sails and came to invite us to celebrate Cristina´s birthday, with spaghetti, cake, samba, rum, vodka, beer, wine and a bit of cachaça, the famous sugar cane Brazilian liquor. Their boat was named Bio, short for biodegradable. So our Latin soul made us make an unforgiven sin, failing to attend Michael´s dinner. And probably we also disturbed his night sleep playing samba drums and screaming pretending to be singing. That night also marked the day I almost died laughing at myself. A couple was invited to the party and I engaged in an intense anthropological discussion with the lady and thinking she was a French I spoke English because my French is not that good to convince anyone about my theories. On the other hand she thought I was French too, and spoke back to me in her limited French which I did not notice was precarious, of course. Well, after hours of feverish discussion, Cristina cleared the puzzle because no one at the table had a clue what we were talking about. What a blast. The lady was actually an Uruguayan and spoke very sharp Portuguese along with her *Castelhano*, well known to me as I was born near the border with Uruguay.

We left Cairns sweating alcohol that morning and it was the worst hangover I ever had in my entire life, but insane enough before lifting the anchor we had a breakfast with Bia and Bernard. No wonder why the mainsail did not want to be hoisted, the anchor slammed the hull of Alvidia on its way up, we almost hit a boat next to us and almost stranded on a sandbank. At least now Helga had a good reason to be seasick. Port Douglas was our next stop, ashamed still we decided to stay quiet, sleep early and wake up early next morning to put Alvidia tidy and cozy as she used to be, to make a maintenance cleaning of the winches, organize sheets and ropes and practice meditation. And as Larry said, when cruising you don´t need to pay attention to the civil calendar. I created my own saying: to get closer to the nature we need to get away from the Gregorian calendar. So we left Port Douglas around three AM as energized as we were in Refuge Bay, back on track.

It was so good to be sailing again that Helga asked to carry on when night came. We spent the whole day on the same tack; I adjusted course and went through the second night sailing along a busy shipping lane, with a light breeze, full moon, and with peace of mind.

Lizard Island, 155 miles from Cairns, considered by many the most beautiful of all Whitsundays islands and historically famous due to Captain Cook's Lookout, a place where he climbed to search by eye the exit of the dangerous unchartered Barrier Reef in the early days. So much for fame;

Cookstown was left behind because we wanted to reach Cape York, the very tip of the Australian territory and turn to the west.

We decided to sleep in Ninian Bay, having sailed through two nights and two days approximately two hundred miles, and in this calm desert small bay I decided to dive to clean the propeller because I heard a strange noise underneath, but as soon as I jumped into the water and sunk I went back aboard even faster than I dove. I saw strange critters glued to our keel and I think they did not like to see a naked human being. They were, I learned later, fish with suction vents on their back used to stick on sharks and travel as well as get fed as hitchhikers.

From Ninian Bay, we sailed to the Flinders Group fighting a current of four knots through the Fly Channel. Alvidia had its sails full of a good eighteen knots wind, although we simply stayed almost in the same place moving ahead very slowly. That day was the first time the depth instrument gave us the alarm of only two feet under our keel. Still, we did not have charts but the transparency of the water was such that I could see the seabed.

At Flinders I realized I messed with John´s list and recommendations so from there I had to create my own anchorage alternatives for overnight. My heart was telling me to follow Willie´s suggestion, to carry on up to Thursday Island, TI for the intimate ones and on my wish list. But Helga asked me in such a convincing warm manner to keep ping-ponging on the islands and my doubt now was Hanna island, Night Island or Portland Road. I stopped on each one, just in case.

At the last daylight, we reached Hanna and anchored. From there we headed to Night Island, just a rock in the middle of the Coral Sea. On Helga´s ticket and despite the swells it was good to plan and face the next passage.

There were only two alternatives to reach Thursday Island. One by the outside of Albany island in the extreme north of Australia, too long and without a place to tuck in if needed, and through the coral reef on watch every second not to hit the bommies, the cargo ships. The second, a challenge, the Albany Passage. A narrow channel between the island and the continent, according to Alan Lucas, with current up to ten knots. Phenomenal.

After a lot of thoughts, I decided to try Portland Road, before approaching Albany Passage, where I heard a mother-ship was going to nurse, meaning a boat which fuels fishing boats. I made contact via VHF and got a treat, a deal for diesel and fresh water. I was told to meet the mother-ship within a day and a half at the anchorage. Doing the same strategic exercise was a French yacht, Fleur de Lys, where from we met an ocean hitchhiker who asked permission to come aboard Alvidia and possibly get fresh bread.

At midnight, the mother-ship arrived with a noisy crew, each man sporting in one hand a can of beer, and in the other a lady dressed in a bikini or mini skirt and lots of makeup. So the mother-ship did not provide only milk, but also honey. I counted a dozen heads aboard. And I was told I could approach for fuel in the morning. After two hours listening to the scream of the ladies and an exaggerated burst of laughs of the mates, it was impossible to sleep in such an inviting atmosphere, so I pulled the anchor and approached the mother-ship, tied my mooring lines to its huge cleats and started to ask for IDs from everyone that came close to me. I said that underage was not allowed to drink, that I wanted to run an alcohol test, that also a tattoo on the buttocks was not permitted. They liked the jokes and to make this episode short, it was a big mistake of mine, pure stupidity.

Everyone wanted to fuel Alvidia. I was feeling like the new bitch in town. I was told to put the large gauge hose into my hole, I mean my fuel pick up on deck, and shout when the tank was full. While the man in charge of the fuel pump turned the thing on I said I wanted only thirty liters of diesel and heard a big "What?!"

"Thirty! Three zero!" while Helga shouted from down below that we had diesel all over the floor.

That mother-ship was used to filling a minimum of one thousand liters at a time. The pressure of the pump and the size of the hose made close to sixty liters to flow in a blink of an eye, overloading my tank and turning my next four hours in a nightmare. My entire fault, not the mates, not the ladies. They tried to help with absorbents reminding me of giant tampons, tips, and a special powder. Punishment, what I needed was punishment and it was what I did to myself while cleaning Alvidia. It was before four o´clock in the morning, I set a course out to the sea slowly under the mainsail and started to clean Alvidia, after stripping off her floor bed, her cushions, everything I could out to the deck. Helga tried to diminish my disappointment with myself saying loving words, but the fact is that our lives became as chaotic as it can be. During the ordeal, the Australian Customs plane almost landed on us to run the same questionnaire and I had to keep watching a ship too close to our route parallel to the shipping lane.

Before arriving at Cape Grenville, an alternative anchorage, all the diesel spilled had been collected into plastic containers used for emergency water and now we needed to discharge them properly and move on.

From Cape Grenville, we sailed to Scape River, and our mood aboard was back to happiness and a relaxed mode, nothing like a good sailing day to forget about any setbacks. Such was this under eight knots of speed that while passing by a towing ship, pulling behind a huge iron floating structure, I made contact on the VHF radio with the Captain and offered him a tow. Captain Jordan, with a good sense of humor, thanked and honked three horns, two shorts and one long as a "goodbye, the portside is yours." Hundreds of miles ahead we would meet and have a beer together as old friends. The sea life.

Scape River, honoring the name made us tuck it in and wait, as four other yachts after us also did. One of them was Fleur de Lys and as soon as it anchored the hitchhiker fellow came to us again. This time he asked a ride up to Gove or any other stopover. Mike, his name, well-spoken honestly said he was having an issue with the captain of Fleur de Lys. I had a strong feeling that I should talk to Claude, the captain, and went there to make acquaintance only to learn right when I called him from my dinghy that he could not put up with Mike aboard his boat anymore. He was at the top of seventy years of age, had been sailing for thirty years mostly single-handedly and only brought Mike because he had eye surgery in Brisbane and thought a help could be good; it had proved to him it was not.

"After all, Luis," Claude said to me, "This boy is too big."

I liked to think I was helping Claude and after a meeting with Helga we tended to accept Mike aboard but we also agreed to experiment with that idea in our minds for one or two extra steps in our journey before actually bring him in. That night, we saw Mike going to hunt with local hunters firing guns in the woods after pigs. During our breakfast, he came about once again for a quick chat and to say, "See you soon."

It was the tip of Australia and we were able to feel the full power of its wild vastness, isolated hundreds of miles from the civilization.

The fleet left the anchorage, one by one. Three boats. The first was Claude, the second a gay couple sailing naked in the cockpit and embracing each other, being Alvidia the third.

My strategy of approaching the Albany Passage was to take a far-out route and head straight into it as possible as I could see the whole channel in a straight line in order to negotiate better with the said strong current. Doing so I was able to watch how good sailors were the gay couple and of course they had good charts of the area. I was amazed how they approached the strait and changed tack disappearing like they had turned a corner street.

It was thrilling to sail those four or five miles on a gush of water at 11 knots of speed, such was the tide stream, feeling the power of nature, woods, rocks, water, birds and obviously fish playing a role altogether. The wind was a light breeze from the southeast and it increased a little as soon as we got in the channel. Alvidia was wing on wing. We went through gliding too fast to me through one of the most beautiful landscapes of Australia. And we took off our hats to the gay couple. That is what I can call "machos" if it does exist in the real world. They anchored in the middle of the Albany passage, with that current, they had an anchor thrown to the inside and a rope tied to a tree ashore. I don´t know how the did that, surely one of them swam, and they were there naked enjoying themselves to make me jealous.

Possession Island seems to be an island only by chance. It is on top of the country and since the horizon from there to the rest of the world, to the entire Asia, India, Africa and Europe is so huge I did not pay attention to the island. After the Albany Passage, we sailed around Cape York in front of the Captain Cook Monument and we made a toast, not to the famous sailor, but because our course from then on was going to be West, home, to Brazil.

It was an afternoon of floating on transparent protected waters behind a rock slab formation and our French Captain Claude arrived visibly ready to fire his guest Mike off his boat. So we felt compelled to attend to a demand the sea posed on us and accepted a guest aboard for the first time. Mike was a mechanical engineer, a recent graduate and he immediately volunteered to check our propeller. Mike also like to dive apnea. Mike like to do many things. Just listening to him I got tired. At least he had physical size; he looked like a rugby league defense player.

He was so long submerged that I thought he had sunk forever. When he emerged, he brought a bunch of nylon lines entangled with a lead weight and fishing hooks. It was our fishing line.

Back between Cairns and Lizard, I asked Helga if she retrieved our fishing line and she said, "Hurrummm!" But she did not say it was a short line without a fishing hook. I probably had forgotten the line was thrown over the stern and while anchoring and engaged backward the propeller took the thing in and around.

Our agreement with Mike was to take him to Thursday Island and from there he would find a bigger boat since his destination was Indonesia anyway. The next morning we lifted the anchor, I mean, Mike lifted it and we headed to Horn Island midway to TI. When Mike saw our charts like a world map he put both hands on his head. He was as big as his ability to be scared I found out soon. He then grabbed the binoculars and sat at the bow shouting about every single particle he was seeing floating or under the surface of the water. When we approached Horn island I called Mike to the cockpit and asked him to be very economical with the warnings and alarms, he should only answer my calls and questions, I did not want to be influenced or misled by storming reactions, that I knew the area was full of comb-like bommies and I would calmly divert from them and, ultimately, that I and him were not important aboard. The only thing I cared about was to keep Helga safe and if he did not agree with that he should dive and swim ashore, ok Mary? I called him Mary half-smiling half-serious and I think he never knew if I was kidding or serious about it. I then asked Helga to increase attention but relax, the water was clear, the wind was good, we had time enough to get to TI with daylight; let's enjoy the ride. So we started to touch inch by inch. At some point I had to almost go back and around a row of reefs. It was not easy though and I asked Mike to fold down the sails and I engaged the engine to make easier maneuvers. Helga sat at the entrance of the companionway with an eye on the depth instrument shouting to me any figure under four feet and there were places that we had two feet only and then sudden twenty feet and finally, we arrived at Horn island. Mike ran to his backpack and brought a bottle of Port wine. Classy backpacker. We liked Mike.

Horn Island is at the very tip of Cape York and its atmosphere to me was of a wild cowboy western town and I liked that. As soon as we anchored I saw the tug of Captain Jordan and instead of rowing the dinghy a few yards to the mud beach nearby where I thought I saw a dark tree trunk to tie the dinghy to, I aimed the pier for the promised beer. At the pier, Captain Jordan was waiting for us with a six pack ready to go and it was a quick encounter but enough to learn a few interesting things about the region, including of the salties, a critter cataloged in the science books as salt water Crocodylus, the largest riverine predator in the world. They usually walk up to five mile inland, while out in the sea they used to bite the outboard motors of runabouts, Captain Jordan said, sometimes of illegal immigrants or smugglers of all kinds. That thing I thought was a tree trunk was, in fact, a specimen of a saltie measuring fifteen feet. Lucky me, Captain Jordan said, it might have been sleeping and not hungry, otherwise, my dinghy could have been his target. "No shit!" I had to say that.

On the way back it was Mike´s turn to row, so he was really fast and to encourage him even more, I kept saying, "Faster, Mary, faster!"

At night I spoke on the radio with Victor and Karen. Kallkal was a hundred miles off Thursday Island going straight to Bali. Bon voyage!

In the morning we headed to TI, a few steps from Papua New-Guinea, and I had an introduction by Captain Jordan as one of the two bases for the Torres Straits Pilots, hosting a cooperative of Master Mariners who pilot ships through the Straits and down to Cairns, a necessary service because navigation through the area is tricky due to the reef systems. I can attest to that.

While Helga and I went to buy fresh veggies and to the Post Office, Mike sought a new lift to get on but had no luck and came back asking us to take him to Gove, our next stopover. We agreed to take him on the next leg provided he take a good shower because due to his massive area it was not enough with one bucket of water every other day aboard Alvidia so he was unbearably smelly as well as were the other two members of the crew. And for every joke I made, he used to stare seriously at me for a second and only then smile. He also should buy us a round of drinks and at one of the four pubs of TI, where I negotiated a shower for the three of us. The manager chatted with us like an old friend telling us that drug traffic started to become a problem apparently due to TI being in a strategic position as a hub between Asia and Australia and a corridor between the Pacific Rim and Indian Ocean including the backdoor of the Mediterranean. What a geopolitical analysis, I thought, so after our showers and beers we left TI.

Since Alan Lucas abandoned us at Cape York, I bought a chart for the Carpentaria Gulf and again it has a small scale, meaning it covered a large area, not good to approach specific places.

This passage was the longest of all so far, three hundred miles, with luck three days. Leaving TI with a light breeze, as soon as we lost sight of land the wind also disappeared. All of the sudden we were in the middle of the Carpentaria Gulf as if we were in a bowl of warm kitchen oil. Nothing moved, even a sparse flight of a bird was monotonous. The sunset melted down and an opaque moon reflected its poor light on our greasy skins, adding to the discomfort Alvidia was overcrowded.

It is curious how a minor movement of a newcomer, a guest per say, in a thirty foot yacht on such a passage can impact the rest of the crew. Between me and Helga we knew what we were doing if we suddenly got up and went down below from the cockpit. And it wouldn't matter what we would do anyway. But with that huge baby boy it was different. The first time I got up from the stern and stepped towards the bow, Mike said suspiciously, "What?"

The first time he left the cockpit and went down below, I raised my eyebrows behind my glasses and stopped reading a book. Cannibalism was a matter of time. The most insignificant comments like, "I will have a bit of water," became breaking news aboard. And it did not take too much time for suggestions for alternative routes and navigation decisions to arise. I would stay in the bowl of warm oil until the breeze comes back, after all, we were not crossing the Sahara desert. But after spending the whole night in such a tense environment, in the morning I decided to turn on the engine for a couple of hours, but saving fuel was mandatory. I was hoping the wind could come back and so I spent the whole day alternating two hours of engine and two or three waiting for the wind, getting excited with a minor buff, feeling we were moving few miles and again back in the bow of still warm kitchen oil.

Fortunately, from our true kitchen, good dishes used to come up on the deck near the end of the day and we would finish up with Port wine at sunset. There was a firm intention of diplomacy aboard. On the third day, the horizon became diffuse, next it was dense gray and suddenly the darkness took over while I gave the order aboard to reef the sails to the highest outhaul. Soon a big blow would come all over us. On the radio, a weather forecast was talking about thirty-five to forty-five knots of winds along the shipping lane more to the north of where we were. According to the coordinates of low and high pressure, I figured we were on the edges of the big blow. I had a chart that included half of Australia, Japan, and India, so I drew the two physical masses of forces down to earth but only as an exercise of navigation because the wind could be felt already on our skin, chilly and increasing right on our noses. And any wind on your nose while cruising is not good.

Even with the Carpentaria Gulf sea being shallow, the storm lifted waves of three meters breaking on our hull. I could run with the wind, but going back to TI? No way. To escape more to the south I would be too close to shoals without a detailed chart in the dark. The decision was the only one to make, to carry on because Alvidia was doing good. I split watches with Mike and we went through the night all right. In the morning the wind eased a bit and we discovered how messy Alvidia was down below. On the fourth day, we sailed with relative tranquility and prepared again for another storm at night. I had then a feeling and an insight – I think it was a drop of divine wisdom – it was sudden and filled me with a solid consciousness. While waiting for the next storm, I looked at Helga and remembered the last night and many others, the vigor and determination she had stepping aboard, the stairs, on the dinghy, on the watch alone during the nights and boring afternoons while I was sleeping, she had been watching the horizon for ships and hazards probably not knowing exactly what she was watching for but there, present and on guard, overcoming her fears while in the middle of a vastness ignoring its content. Perhaps ashamed of our guest, she did not get seasick, or due to being too busy, but her mood was not good and she was too quiet lately. I started to imagine the crossing of the Indian Ocean, the passage around Cape Town then the crossing of the Atlantic. Would Helga endure all that? Would it be fair to drag her along? Many other questions arose.

While we were down below, Mike was in the cockpit on his watch, I sat in front of Helga, and it was my turn to grab her cheeks with my two hands and my love and tell her, "I will stop, ok? We will stop and go home."

It was all I said and she understood. I saw a shine in her eyes I had not seen for a long time. But I also saw her discomfort knowing that it was not my self will, it was for her. We hugged each other, not saying a word and cried softly, mixing our tears. Mike appeared in the galley for a glass of water, noticed something was going on between me and Helga, he went to his backpack to fiddle with things and went back to the cockpit. He actually went fishing. Contrary to my rules, he dove and within a few minutes brought in a ten kg gorgeous mackerel already well cleaned on our stern platform. It was a great incentive to lift the morale aboard.

After we ate, Mike told us if something, anything, happened to us on the sea we would have the whole official emergency apparatus of the Australian at our disposal.

"How so, Mike?" I asked.

His dad was responsible for the training program of the rescue crews of the Coastal Patrol. At the moment he was in Indonesia setting up a pilot program for the government. In TI Mike phoned Canberra and passed on our position and route, a description of our yacht and crew aboard. He had been doing this since he left Brisbane with Claude, oriented by his father.

I did not know if I should tie and gag him, or push him overboard with a weight tied to his ankle, or thank him. How come he did that without asking me? I decided to throw him a Mona Lisa look, a look that does not authorize, does not disagree, does not show excitement or sadness. On one token we had been surveilled all the time, on another we were also protected. Now we had angels with Ids taking care of us.

The wind increased a lot as expected for the night. The sea went huge again. As the hull of Alvidia crashed against the bumps, it was causing a crashing of waves over the cabin, making a waterfall in the middle of the saloon.

Wow! What is that? The main hatch is closed. Is it breaking apart?" were my words and I jumped to check it out. It would be a calamity, Alvidia would be breaking. Helga twice got a shower of salt water and she was lying on the starboard bunk. Big as he was, Mike passed through twice from the galley to his cabin in the bow and the floor of Alvidia down below was full of water while Alvidia kept sailing through the storm. Adding to the picture, the spinnaker pole was coming loose on the deck, banging, making noise, surely damaging Alvidia. Mike volunteered to hold the spinnaker pole and I told him to wear the harness and hook it on the U bolt at the entrance of the companionway.

"Roger that!" he shouted and ran to the deck, as if in an action movie.

It was three o´clock; he stripped off his t-shirt and with a small rope between his teeth crawled on deck to the bow where the spinnaker pole was banging. A huge wave washed him over and he screamed very loud, "AAAAHHHH!" while tying up the spinnaker pole then came back to the cockpit and shouted loudly from only a foot away from me, "Luís! A container is coming loose too, I will fix it!"

"No need, Mike!" I said too late.

He was already creeping like a soldier and did it again, "AAAHHHH!"

In the morning, close to our destination, there were two surprises aboard. First I discovered the cause of the shower – it was not a hatching breaking apart, it was a rope Mike left when he shut it down and so there was an opening letting water and wind in. The second was to find out what Mike was reading. I had to reach the bow cabin and saw his backpack half open with a large book titled, *Challenges and Adventures*; a collectanea of sea stories, extreme skiing expeditions, ultimate mountains climbing and the like. Rambo would be too soft compared to that.

Enjoying the plotting exercise on the chart I bought in TI, we approached and arrived at the Gove Yacht Club. Claude on his Fleur de Lys was there already. Next morning Michael and Des arrived from

Pangur Bán. On the third day Bia and Bernard, from Gwanaskell arrived. And one by one many other boats we had seen along the way appeared. It was a true cruisers' atmosphere. The Gove club was so receptive that we would not have a problem living there forever. Bureaucracy tending to zero, facilities opened to use as we will – yet even better, a true hub of cruising information for whoever adventuring around Cape York to Darwin and anywhere south of Asia. Right when we stepped ashore, Mike went to the local radio station and announced that he arrived with Alvidia and was after a lift to Thailand.

"Wow, Mike! How come you put us on the radio?" I said to him, showing a bit of disappointment but no sign of being upset at all. How could I be annoyed in such pleasant place as the Gove Yacht Club?

The decision had been made, I would stop, go home, I simply did not know how I would develop the next immediate steps. Meanwhile, our mood, Helga´s and mine, were so good that we decided to make a typical gaucho barbecue at the sunset on the front yard of the club, inviting our own club formed by Michael, Des, Claude, Bia, and Bernard. Each guest should bring meat, sausage, salad, bread and of course drinks. I meant to make it up to Michael and the idea unfolded into a great party. Claude was bragging, with all rights to do so, that he brought a French sweet made with pears and white wine. Des brought a stock of funny stories. The others contributed with so much food that they needed to take much of it back afterwards. The energy around a fire I made to bake the meats was such that, despite everyone having a little or white hair or beard, except myself, we all sounded like we were from kindergarten.

Learning about our decision to give up cruising back to Brazil, Michael offered to take Helga on his boat, and have Des with me on Alvidia, so we could cross the Indian Ocean and the Atlantic because his destination was Rio de Janeiro. He thought Helga would feel safer with him, on a bigger and slower boat, Michael sailed like Willie, our German philosopher, without radio and electronics instruments. And Des would help me sail Alvidia across the two oceans. What a generous offer from someone we just met. But how we would split, Helga and I?

While in Gove, Michael and I found out we had a thing in common we could not avoid to talk about. We both had been computer programmers of Jurassic languages such as Assembler, RPG II, COBOL, Fortran, Algol, and Basic. We both used computers with only 12K of memory and punched cards. And at seventy years of age he was a dreamer just like me, probably condemned to be a dreamer forever, thank God. Once back home, in Ireland, Michael would dedicate time to develop an idea he had while cruising. His idea was an artificial being which community would be arranged by a mathematical model based on the theory of "one and a half". Everything within the said system would respect the standard "one and a half" so any unit could not survive, or function, without the help or interaction of the other and while doing this there would never be one, nor even two, it would be three at least otherwise it would not work.

Speaking about numbers and completeness, while it was so good to be among such interesting people, I realized that my dream did not come true only once, it came true seven times, and a Bible passage came to my mind, "...You shall not forgive seven times, but seventy times seven." And if I was incomplete without Helga, I was not giving up my dream, actually I accomplished it in a much more excited and unexpected manner than I had dreamed in first place. I had been on many beaches with white sand, I had built my own boat; it was pretty and everyone liked it – a boat with personality, and I had crossed so many oceans inside myself while sailing all kinds of seas, bays, and creeks, and had met so many angels. Space and time sailor.

...August, yet another horizon.

Pangur Bán headed to Darwin, Fleur de Lys headed to Thailand. Gwenaskel would leave next day towing Alvidia through the Hole in the Wall.

The passage from Gove through the Wessel Island Group, a stretch of rocks perpendicular to the coast like a shredded wall, could be done around it or via Gugari Rip, also known as the Hole in the Wall, one of the many openings. This route cuts off about 50 miles, if traveling around Cape Wessel to the north and being only about 50 meters wide and one kilometer long it is quicker. However, it is really important to get the tide times right, because they can race through on a spring tide anything up to 12 knots. The turbulence of the water and the need of a precise calculation of the arrival time at the entrance makes it a challenge, kind of the reason why at the Gove Club you could give a Post Doctorate degree lecturing about how to sail through the "hole". A rum drinker in one of the tables of the club was telling us that once upon the time a single-handed sailor anchored at the entrance and fell asleep, the next morning he woke up at the other side, pulled by the tide stream.

Gwenaskel left first and Alvidia was right behind. Bernard had in his curriculum among many sailing experiences a dozen passages across the Atlantic, Cape Town, and Cape Horn. His 51' boat was made of iron. With that sort of towing, I was confident of being safe, adding to that being able to speak on the radio all the time in Portuguese with Bia.

The plan was to anchor at Elizabeth Bay and wait for the correct tide to cross the "hole." From Elizabeth Bay, we sailed ten miles and reached the Hole in the Wall in my calculation a bit earlier, but according to Bernard a little after. We never knew who was right but the passage was fun. Gwenaskel weighed twenty tons and was zigzagging in front of us and Alvidia was too fast, being hard to hold on, at one point

Gewnaskel almost went entirely sideways and I thought I would hit it right in the middle but Bernard steered his way back straight on and other than that the whole crossing was a breathtaking – the beauty of the place. It was similar to the Albany Passage but with no trees, all rocky. Unique.

At the other side in calm and transparent waters we anchored next to Gwenaskel. Bernard and Bia came aboard Alvidia and brought beers. We slept that night as we had not done in a long time, so in a peace of mind, in such calm and silent anchorage, and left early next morning refreshed. Destination: Darwin.

No wind as a rerun of the passage from T.I. to Gove. Bernard had good charts and chose a course next to the continent. Without charts, I preferred a course more into the Arafura Sea and soon we had no sight of land. I also decided not to make contact with Bernard and Bia over the radio so not to let them worry about us when the storm comes, because it would come according to the weather forecast.

Two days went by without a puff of wind. Once again I turned the engine for a couple of hours and kept waiting for the wind. We brought in a huge tuna – the first time we fished with a trick learned in Gove, instead of the hook and bite we used a can of beer shredded with scissors, like a wig, and spread ourselves out in the cockpit, eating, drinking natural juice, snacking, reading, not talking too much, surely thinking about our lives and sometimes it was like being anchored, not even a current was making us to move.

There is nothing more inviting for the monkeys we have living in our loft to make them excited than absolute silence. In my loft, my monkeys gathered in a board meeting. Their agenda was to verify the decision of my heart. My brain was the one anxious now, asking to see the whole thing to finish quick, that the wind invade and avoid any extra waiting so I would not suffer or start to regret the decision made. And it came. In the first night with the sails reefed to the third point Alvidia sailed like a lady and we could sleep almost together, Helga and I. Our watches were split in 30 minutes for each one who would go to the cockpit for five minutes and come back down below while the other would crash, so we were always more or less together. In my watches, I would have an eye on the navigation to make sure our course was correct. The many bangs of the waves against the hull of Alvidia would propagate in Helga´s exhausted small frame body and during the day she was seasick. She had been brave but I could see that if we continue across the Indian Ocean she would endure in the automatic mode and perhaps sight a horizon whatever it would be regardless of what she would actually see, she would not be there anymore only her weakened body.

We reached Cape Croker, near Cobourg Peninsula, and had a quick chat on the radio with Bernard and Bia. We had to calculate the right time to approach Dundas Strait, a passage to the Van Diemen Gulf. Notes from John Deegan with arrows reminded me of the strong current and the right moment to use them to our advantage, otherwise, it would be tough from that point up to Darwin. In this area, the tidal range is the largest in Australia exceeding ten meters. Not even thinking about getting in at the wrong time. But the wind was so good that even with those two days of calm we reached the entrance with British punctuality. Our problem was that the wind in our beam until then would now be on our nose, at night. We had been punished for thirty hours with strong gusts on our side, as soon as we turned the corner street it was right on our face. Bernard called us on the radio and said he was beating a wall, could not move forward. While I was talking to Bernard, Helga called me on the cockpit and what a view. A fleet of five warships passing by our side. Monsters silhouette in the dark. Interesting view for our log.

Early in the morning, we were right in the middle of the Gulf. Again Bernard chose a course more to the coast and we could see his sails small in the horizon. I remained on the warship route while the wind started to increase and being inside the Gulf I should change tack every hour and a half more or less to sail more comfortably, avoiding the gusts right on our maximum point of close haul. While once I was changing tack, that custom plane came to run that same questionnaire and even asked if I knew the yacht with the blue hull, two masts, and white sails nearby because Bernard did not reply to them.

"Yes, they are friends, a French flag and I have a question for you: why you did not come last night during the storm?"

"We don´t like to fly through a storm, Sir," the customs plane replied and flew away.

Right after that chat with customs I let the head-sail sheet out of my hand, a little inattention was enough, and the sail went out of control starting to bang lose with the wind. Alvidia was bouncing the bow in and out of the waves, like a crazy goat and I tried to roll in the head-sail but the sheet stuck inside the drum of the furler.

"We have got a situation!" I told Helga, but in a joking way. And I hooked my harness onto the U bolt of the companionway and crawled to the bow to fix the furler and the sail sheet to hold it down or put it back to work. It was a situation similar to the one I faced getting out of Coffs Harbour and again I had lashes from the sheets on my face, feeling the taste of my own blood. This time, however, inside myself I had confidence, sure I was going to fix the sail. Helga almost fainted, she told me later, watching me sit at the bow, both legs spread out on the boat and at times when Alvidia sunk the stem in the water I was going with it, almost disappearing in the middle of the waves. But it was one of the times I felt better on the deck of my Alvidia and eventually I fixed the sheet and the sail in place ready to anchor at Cape Hotham. This was a strategic point to wait for the right time for the tidal route to Darwin sixty miles ahead, a day of sailing.

Sometimes one needs to lose in order to win; it was a lesson I learned from Lloyd. I arrived in Darwin convinced that this was an opportunity to lose. It was going to be a big loss, but it was also an opportunity to save a bigger value, to win again and forever the most important thing of my life. Alvidia would be with me forever in my memory, and I had more than I dreamed of. From Darwin we would fly back home after many years we would learn again how it is like to live in Brazil, maybe it would be the time for me to learn the language of the Guarani Indians, another secret dream I had, a typical Brazilian tribe known by its search, the utopian idea of a land without madness and death. Helga and I would make a list of places we would like to live with as little as enough we need, where we could nourish the things we learned with the sea life. On such a pace we anchored at Darwin. Once anchored, Alvidia did not seem to have sailed five thousand miles. Very slowly, I organized the sheets on deck, made it very tidy as if I was putting a baby to sleep and went to sit where Helga was down below. It was my turn to cheer her up, she was sad because she knew how much Alvidia and sailing meant to me by then but I had to bring her smile back. I was fine, I was more than fine, I was light.

It was an intense moment. I had to do it without looking back otherwise it would not work. I was losing to win, win Helga and a whole life of dreams together.

"That´s it," I said to her, laughing with tears, more laughing than tears. "It might hurt me, I really don´t know but it is solid, don´t worry," I said to Helga and added, "All I want now is to see you relaxed, smiling again and I want to thank you for helping me build factories and dreams and to come all over up where we are."

We put the dinghy in the water, rowed to the beach among boats with flags from all over the world. Canadian, German, Turkish, French, American, Swedish, Irish... Willie was there, Michael and Des, Steve, the gay couple we never actually met and many others we saw along the coast. It was a true and perfect cruiser atmosphere. We also saw sailors from the opposite route who had just crossed the Med Sea and the Indian Ocean. Whoever arrives in Darwin is a winner somehow. The way ones leaves Darwin is not as important as arriving, I told myself. We went straight to the local Club´s reception to check in as a temporary member and to be granted a well-deserved shower of fresh water. I could feel Helga feeling like a feather – such was the lightness surrounding both of us. After the shower it was her turn to say things to me but she did not need to; it had been all said already. We went for a walk on the beach just to have a glance of the whole area and headed to the veranda of the local restaurant to find many known and unknown faces, with undone hairs, unshaven beard, suntans – they were all smiling or bursting out laughing, and I did as in the Los Angeles airport when I was invited to meet up with a potential investor, to pray for people without letting them know. I wished that they too would have their dreams come true and I guessed what would be each one´s dream, and especially that the sea was going to be generous with them and that they never lose their winner's smile, even if they lost. I went on wishing that we all kept respecting what we have learned from the sea life while on shore or in the so-called social environment in the cities. I was going to give them the news, that we ended our adventure right there. I was going to hear different reactions, suggestions, questions. My spiritual initiation back then was not ordered, I had picked up things here and there on my own, but now all the venues I took started to make sense as a natural avenue. It was true that the confusion I have made with the fears and dreams now was pointing to a clear horizon yet bigger. I was immersed in these thoughts when Helga next to me said, "Let´s start everything again, let´s build another boat in Brazil, I promise you I will help you again."

God does exist! It was real, it came to my mind hearing Helga. And she added:

"Let´s start to plan right now and together!"

Luís Peazê

Epilogue

Alvidia was sold to a local resident of Darwin in less than a week with a small hand note placed on the board of the yacht club, contrary to all the comments that Darwin is the last place to sell a boat. A Timorese Family, owner of the local restaurant inside the Darwin Yacht Club gave a special dinner to Luis and Helga, a surprise to Luis, a dinner for thirty people on the day of his anniversary. Adriano, one of the members of the Timorese Family was a fan of a gaucho folk singer and player called Teixerinha and asked Luis to translate the word "tchê", a typical form of saying "mate" in the gaucho way. Curious situations continued to happen to Luis and Helga. Willie cried trying to convince Luis to cross the Indian Ocean and, in the end, he lamented not being able to buy Alvidia. Steve, from the yacht Alien, took a picture of Luis and Helga sailing and made it a gift to them, a print picture. A German couple approached Luis saying they were impressed seeing Alvidia being anchored in Cape Bowling at night, that place where it was impossible to see a sandbank.

On the same week of the arrival in Darwin, Luís signed to race in a local twilight competition of the yacht club and Des was aboard amazed how sweet was the tiller of Alvidia and how easy it was to put her sails in groove, they were one of the last to start and were among the first to cross the arrival line. Before they handed over Alvidia to the new owners, Luís and Helga gave their stock of food to Willie, placed personal belongs on Gwenaskel who's destination was Rio de Janeiro, and went out for the last sail together. The wind was of fifteen knots, Alvidia sailed for one hour into the sunset and when they came back to the anchorage in the dark, slowly on sails with no engine on, they left Alvidia there, quiet...

While going back to Brazil, Luís and Helga flew to Malesia and then South Africa where the material for this book was compiled. Then, as the plane back home had an extra stop in Argentina, they stayed one month in the country going to the Misiones region, where Luis wanted to visit a true tribe of Guarani Indians to investigate aspect of their culture for a novel Luis had in mind, "*O Punhal de Pedra*" (Portuguese) / *The Stone Dagger*, another dream, eventually published.

The author

...after Alvidia´s experience, Luís Peazê became journalist, writer and translator, including among his works the acclaimed translation (into Portuguese) of *For Whom the Bell Tolls*, by Ernest Hemingway. Entrepreneur by heart, founded the Brazilian Coastal Institute (BRCostal – Instituto Brasil Costal), was awarded with the medal Friend of the Brazilian Navy and Brazilian Navy School. Granted the friendship title of Brazilian Consul of the Wooden Boat Foundation (Port Townsend, WA, USA). Yet related to boating, have been sailing and building woodenboats since 1994, when he built Alvidia, has built several true replicas of the Herreshoff Columbia 11´–1/2", two units of which are sailing in USA (Hawaii and Vermont), others scattered in Brazil.

Engaged with Oceanographers to help the recognition of the Ministry of Education at Federal level for the validation/accreditation of the discipline as a University course, until then not recognized and that all the marine studies had been commissioned to only marine biologists in Brazil.

Author of dozen of books on sports & law, medicine, chronicles and fiction, including *Santiago and the Sea* (novel).

Member of the Hemingway Society and Pen Club in USA, also member of the IGKT - International Guild of Knots Tyers (London), Luis Peazê maintain an online zine 1997 "Conversa no Píer" (Pier´s Chat) and own a California registered business, Capt Lui LLC.

www.luispeaze.com

Luís Peazê

www.ingramcontent.com/pod-product-compliance
Lightning Source LLC
Chambersburg PA
CBHW030342120726
47901CB00007B/1874